THE ROADS OF HOME

THE ROADS OF HOME

Lanes and Legends of New Jersey

HENRY CHARLTON BECK

Foreword by Carl Carmer

RUTGERS UNIVERSITY PRESS

New Brunswick   *New Jersey*

Ninth paperback printing, 1987

Library of Congress Cataloging in Publication Data

Beck, Henry Charlton, 1902–1965.
  The roads of home.

  Bibliography: p.
  Includes index.
  1. New Jersey—Description and travel. 2. New
Jersey—Social life and customs. 3. New Jersey—History,
Local. 4. City and town life—New Jersey—History.
5. Folklore—New Jersey. I. Title.
F134.B455 1984   974.9   83-9685
ISBN 0-8135-1018-X

To

William J. H. Abey, M.D.

Samuel E. Bullock

Alexander B. Garwood and

Charles A. Philhower

for reasons they best know

Contents

Foreword

The writings of Henry Beck are easily and genially communicative. The fact implies, at least to anyone who has composed sentences for publication, that he has worked hard and long to create his lucid conversational effects. He seems to take for granted his readers' interest yet he is never presumptuous. Once a few of his sentences have been sampled, the sampler finds himself eagerly sharing the experiences of the writer.

To many an American, the words "New Jersey" in sequence call into mind few and widely disassociated images—dank meadows blanketed by the odors of industry; that Gothic jewel, Princeton; the crowded peripheral cities, Newark and Jersey City; the docks of ocean-liners at Hoboken. But Henry Beck loves his state and has set about faithfully to introduce to all who would enjoy them—the glittering country lakes, the wooded mountains, the old houses. He adds, too, a diversified group of characters, living and dead, saintly and sinful, calculated to catch the fancy of readers in Americana though they reside in the Aleutians or the Virgin Islands.

Dip into Dr. Beck's first chapter, "Land of Waiting," as I did, and you will find that you have been transplanted into an area where the past speaks more plainly than the present. The men who lived in the ancient houses along the Old Mine Road and left them to trudge over to Sussex County Courthouse in 1775 and enlist in the Continental Army—the Deckers, the Van Campens, the McCartys, the Hasbroecks, the Rosencrans, the Carmers—seem more in command of the country now than do its living inhabitants. Even the casual visitor gets the impression that somewhere in this wild and lovely and sparsely settled region an effort at communication is being attempted by personalities out of a deep past.

Because, like all good historians, Henry Beck is a sympathetic and observant man, his chapters prove him a sensitive interpreter for those who are possessed by a yearning to speak and who are at the same time silenced by the years.

CARL CARMER

Preface

It would not be an exaggeration to say that the material from which *The Roads of Home* has been written has been piling up in notes, pamphlets, books, manuscripts, and other material through more than thirty years. Ever since the first journey to Ong's Hat provided contradictory variants of the legend of Jacob Ong, inspiring later sketches that were revised and expanded to become such books as *Forgotten Towns of Southern New Jersey*, *More Forgotten Towns*, and *Fare to Midlands*, I have traveled the State's byways, seeking out people and places and their stories.

When the three earlier books were published in the 1930's, I learned many things. One of these was that those most reluctant to talk say loudly afterward that they were overlooked when I came around. Another was that others with things to say knew little for certain, but this in no way prevented sieges of volubility. Still others who seemed shy and, from appearances, lacking in what I sought, were revealed as among my best sources. Above all, I learned in time to be not too credulous, but I cannot understand the point of view of those who refuse to believe *anything* in a given set of circumstances unless there is proof for this relatively unimportant detail or that.

History too often stops its ears while folklore accepts the best it can find and then sets out to obtain additions, alterations, and improvements.

This book is a sampling of the lore of the whole State, an honest attempt to present some of the outstanding stories as they have been remembered or tucked away in yellowing publications hard to come by. To this I have added as careful a revision as can be managed of what I consider the best of the contents in the *Forgotten Towns* books.

I hope, above all things, that *The Roads of Home* will begin the weaving of an adequate expression of my deep appreciation to those who have continued to write letters all through the years, criticizing, supplementing, and suggesting, as well as those who have volunteered to go with me on this journey or that. Naturally I am deeply indebted to the *Sunday Star-Ledger*, of Newark, New Jersey, for opening its pages to this sort of material and so allowing me to keep my writing in a kind of continuity that might not have been possible otherwise and without which the necessary research would have bogged down. After all, it was the *Star-Ledger* that revived a routine abandoned in Camden many years before. I have said and written my thank-yous with polite regularity but they have not been enough.

I have done my best with what is here, but there is much more where it came from, and I hope it is God's plan to allow me to do it justice. I do not know why I feel so strongly about New Jersey. I was not born here, although I was brought to Haddonfield from Philadelphia when I was nine. My father was a native of the Island of Jersey and my mother's mother was from Liverpool—perhaps the experts in such matters, recognizing New Jersey's namesake in the English Channel, will find some solution here.

HENRY CHARLTON BECK

Pennington, New Jersey
April, 1956

THE ROADS OF HOME

I

Land of Waiting

Tom Quick could begin it well enough. However, I have been warned that the legends that go into the story of the most celebrated Indian slayer in New Jersey would make far too gruesome a beginning. So Tom must wait and I shall take you first to some of the country Tom knew, a country which in many places even now would seem the same to either Tom Quick or the ninety-nine ghosts that haunt him.

We shall start off in the mountains of Sussex, and then reach down into Warren somewhere along the Old Mine Road, having dipped into New Jersey from Esopus (now Kingston), New York. One reason for this beginning is that I always have longed to do the story of the Delaware River in the words and memories of the people who live along its banks, last descendants of the first men and women of a last frontier, but have settled for the proposal that the upper reaches of the river be treated in such a way.

Here is a land which many who live in New Jersey have never seen and in which as many more do not believe. It is a land of brooding purple mountains or flowering hills, according to the season. It is a land of crags and crowding precipices of the Kittatinny Ridge, of winding roads that were the paths of the Indians, of quiet and seldom-seen mountain lakes, of noisy brooks and flashing waterfalls, of hundred-year and even older houses at every turn. Here the Appalachian Trail, first crossing from New York State into Sussex beside the shore of Greenwood Lake in Passaic, wanders down through High Point Park to the Stokes State Forest and through the vast wilderness lately purchased by New Jersey; then the trail leaps the river at Delaware Water Gap in Warren. Here a traveler who prefers riding to walking may move even closer to the river past an island called Mashipacong, meaning either "the Great River" or "a place where many moccasins are made"; then past Quick's Island and the site of a mid-eighteenth century inn which has been bulldozed away because it had grown shabby and a new traffic circle was wanted; finally through Peter's Valley and Wallpack Center and Flatbrookville. Peter's Valley has maintained the old family name of Bevans on its post office and Flatbrookville has dressed itself up, in summer more than winter, but these seem to be a series of motions for the motions' sake.

Whenever I have wandered up from Columbia or down from Port Jervis the picture has seemed to change with every moment, only the little lakes and ponds and brooks holding on to the old names of the people who, if they had not departed, were reluctant to speak. Now and then, in spite of the improvements that have come even to the Old Mine Road, there is no more than a shelf in the side of the mountain. And, however watchful one may be, a twist in the trail sends one wandering in needless circles, especially in and around the Wallpack Bend. It is a waiting country; it is a watchful country. Here, indeed, is a country that provides, like the Jersey Pines far off in another direction, a setting in which anything can happen.

Once when I was breaking through yesterday's doorway in terms of the last octagon school in service in New Jersey I came upon a man who had remained loyally in a profession to which I return, now and then, with misgivings. His name is Leslie Coss. Actually I had planned to talk with Mrs. Coss, the teacher in the one-room octagon, but she was indisposed. Leslie Coss revealed that he was the principal at the one-room school in Lafayette but he made by chance a much more important revelation as far as I was concerned. He had known the Old Mine Road well, he said, and he had known the surrounding country since he was a boy. He had been born in Bevans—he never called it Peter's Valley, and he often reverted to an even earlier name for it, "the Corners."

A day came when rumors began to bear down on the rocks of the upper Delaware, promising reservoirs and dams and watersheds that would bury homes and even whole villages. I went back hastily to invite Leslie Coss to travel the Old Mine Road with me, to introduce me to the houses that had been forts and to the people who might talk because they knew him. Leslie reminded me of a book which might do as much for me as he could—Amelia Stickney Decker's *That Ancient Trail*, published privately in 1942. All the houses I "met" are in the book, with almost a hundred more, but I wanted music to go with the libretto of homesteads, of gravestones, and of the other markers set up by the author, her husband Ralph, and the Daughters of the American Revolution. I wanted proof that a native's return in a purposeful journey would not to any great extent break the haunting quiet that had dulled the edges of so many memories, proof that, unless I or someone went to live upriver to *be* of the river people, it would remain.

Leslie took me to what is called the Tri-State Rock to which we walked through a Port Jervis graveyard. There we stood in Pennsylvania, New York, and New Jersey at practically the same time, looking down on what seems to be the whole world from a sort of devil's tempting place. We went to the little Minisink cemetery—below the village of Minisink itself—with many of its stones among the trees visible only in winter. We looked down toward the river from the old road as Westbrook Fort once did, long ago, and we saw the venerable but small dwelling of the Bells, who had made a home for nine generations there. And Leslie took me to the site of a blockhouse on what has become Blockhouse Hill, just across the way from the house of Captain Shimer, a house rich in stories of barricades against attacking savages but echoing and empty in the years I have known it. Although markers have been placed at these and other places, I found Leslie's knowledge of the Indian shelters startling, especially when he showed me one I would have walked past if I had been alone, now reconstructed as a background for an Indian exhibit in the State Museum in Trenton.

In view of all this, as well as the canvas Mrs. Decker has

filled with contrasting colors of the land in which she lives, I felt and still feel the tingle of urgency to see and to have you see and hear all that can be while the old road and the valley and the houses are still there. For this was home, known and loved by such sturdy pioneers as Leslie Coss recalled as we moved from house to hill and back again—especially "the woman" who, he insisted, was typical of the breed.

"The woman" was already the mother of thirteen and she lived, I think, near the Wallpack Bend. Never once, when the time was upon her, had she called for a doctor or a midwife. "Might have done no good to call," Leslie said. "She was on the reaper in the morning. The fourteenth child came around eleven o'clock and she made the house just in time. By late afternoon she was out in the fields again, taking up where she had been compelled to pause for a while."

Not far out of Newton I had asked Leslie Coss about the Gallows Hill. "What is now called Spring st.," says the record, "because it leads out from the village in the direction of the Big Spring, was formerly called the Gallows Road, on account of a number having been hung along that road." Leslie explained: "They're still uncertain about Gallows Hill. They're not sure it is Gallows Hill, where the official hangings took place, or Gallus Hill, where a despondent farmer hanged himself with his galluses."

I noticed a sheer rise of rock wall in the distance and Leslie told me that deer (called mountain veal in Sussex and, I suppose, elsewhere) are killed there each year when they lose their footing on the iced and mossy face of the precipice.

"How cold does it get up here? Sixteen or more below, like as not, but it's a dry cold and you can take it."

It was Mrs. Decker who wrote: "The Old Mine Road, first road of any great length in the United States, still arouses excited interest and enthusiasm after years of discussion, exploration, and research." This is a summary of the conclusions made in the earliest known records of the winding and widened black-top highway, maintained by Sussex County but lost altogether here and there unless the traveler is alert. "The wonderful thing

6

is," said Leslie Coss, "that you can be just as much of an explorer along the old road today as you could have been in the days of the Hollanders—or whoever they were!"

"Up to a point," I argued. "In the first place, a lot of more important people have tried their hands at explaining the mines away and they haven't come up with much. By now the good folk who live along the road either don't remember much of what their ancestors told them or they are afraid of the big water coming in. Maybe I've noticed it more because I come in from the outside. And you really can't explore very much when these new signs are everywhere: no hunting, no fishing, no swimming, no trespassing."

John Barber and Henry Howe, compilers of the *Historical Collections of the State of New Jersey*, have provided interesting and valuable information about the Old Mine Road and the mines, much of which they found in an earlier record called *Hazard's Register*. This old record has been quoted in one form or another by almost every writer who has been intrigued by the mystery of the mines, but I shall try to show you, without quoting its ponderous text, at least the way to where these pioneer miners left their marks in almost everything but books.

There was an interesting interview with the "amiable Nicholas Dupuis, Esq." in June, 1787, when M. Dupuis appeared to be about sixty. He was asked who built the Old Mine Road and when, what kind of ore was dug, and "from whence or how came the first settlers of Meenesink in such great numbers as to take up all the flats on both sides of the river for forty miles." M. Dupuis could only reply with what he had heard from older people, and the gist of his story went like this:

In some former age there came a company of miners from Holland, who built about one hundred miles of road and worked two mines. He understood that an abundance of ore had been hauled on that road, but did not know whether lead or silver. The settlers followed the mine road to the large flats on the Delaware, where the smooth cleared land and the many apple trees suited them. They bought the improvements of the native Indians, most of whom then removed to the Susquehanna.

7

With such as remained, there was peace and friendship until 1755.

The Old Mine Road was first "the Trade Path" and after that, in 1682, "the Path of the Great Valley." By 1737 it had become established as "the Old Mine Road" even if the mines were only holes in the ground, and, with the Revolution, it was proclaimed to be "the good Esopus Road."

The Old Mine Road is one hundred four miles long, reaching from Kingston (old Esopus) through Port Jervis (once Mackhackamack) and then on through forty miles of Sussex to the puzzle of the Pahaquarry copper mines. The mines were in an area that was part of Sussex until 1824, but now they are in Warren. "Even the earliest settlers could give only traditionary accounts of the Old Mine Road," reiterates Mrs. Decker.

Recurrent generations without much knowledge of dates maintained one thing above all: that the men who built and used the first road came from Holland, as names up and down the trail would seem to indicate, even today—Hasbroecks, Kuykendalls, Schoonovers, Schoonmakers, and a veritable army of Vans: Van Aukens, Van Campens, Van Ettens, and all the rest.

The Dutchmen of Kingston were mostly farmers but some of them had itchy feet and once they heard about the fabulous mine in the interior they took their chances with hardships and natives of the Minisink country. It is clear that they talked a lot about what they were looking for inasmuch as they seem to have been joined by others outside their congregations—Armstrongs, Courtrights, Drakes, Fullers, McCartys, Roes, and many more.

Where and when the story of fabulous wealth deep in the Kittatinny Ridge began, no one is quite sure. It is known that as early as 1641 the *Journal of the Netherlands* was telling tales of "high mountains exhibiting strong indications of minerals." By 1645 the agents of the Dutch West India Company were probing into the chatter with indications that the actual location of at least one mine was known. By 1658, Governor Stuyvesant had been told that investigators had come up with a piece of "good and pure copper from New Netherlands" and that there was a copper mine, sure enough, "in the Neversinks." It remains obscure, however, how such an enterprise, still impressive in what remains of it, could have been established in secret, just as it remains uncertain who was responsible

In 1735, Governor Cosby wrote the London Board of Trade that in the Jerseys there could be found an extraordinarily rich copper mine which, he explained, was difficult to reach. "Situated near the Delaware Water Gap," he said, "no attempts have been made to get at it from the south, but access is easiest from Esopus." The road remained in far better condition than the mine holes and remains so today, marked here and there with granite stones and bronze tablets, graced by the charm of old houses, and edged by the tombstones of men and women who knew more about it than any I have found.

Some of the houses were homes from the time of their completion. Others are by now in varied disguise. A surprising number were forts, manning an irregular line of defense up from the flats of the Delaware against Indians who were at the very least anxious, one may be sure, to have the strangers go home. There were murders and raids and kidnapings up and down the valley, from the beginning of the French and Indian War and through 1763.

As for copper from one of the eighteen mine holes that have been found, sometimes with almost disastrous cave-ins, no one ever has offered to show me any and the best I can do is suggest that the next time you are in Holland, pause long enough to visit the National Museum in Amsterdam. There they have on exhibit some copper said to have come from Minisink, dug along the Old Mine Road, the label says, by Claes de Ruyter, in 1657. Such souvenirs of the first invasion are what persuaded the Dutch to try another although there must have been a lapse of considerable time, for such a road took time to build or even to repair and all of it is said to have been in order fifty years before William Penn set foot on American soil in 1682.

Leslie Coss had said that there were a few people along the road who could remember the tales as they were handed down, perhaps reaching back to the days when the mines were closed or had begun to fill in. "You've read of Nicholas Dupuis and

9

the rest of the family," he went on. "The name is Depue by now. I know that the Depues are there, in the old house. Alonzo ought to be there and his sister, Laura, who was my teacher when I was in the second grade." The name became Depue mostly by mispronunciation, he said. "Like the tombstone man, you get to spell things the way they sound. . . ."

The stone Depue house, more than a century and a half old, is one of more than a hundred that Mrs. Decker has carefully catalogued, with pictures and a smattering of family history to match. Alonzo Depue quickly came from the farmyard across the road. He was eighty then but he looked no more than sixty-five. A lean, angular man, gracious but a little ill at ease, it became evident that he would not use two words where one would do. Yes, the Depues were descendants of the pioneer Dupuis family. Yes, the house was older than the change of spelling in the name. Yes, the mines were at the bottom and farther up the mountain, back of where the Boy Scouts had their camp. No, he hadn't been there in a long while. It was almost as if Alonzo was frightened of any talk about the land along the river.

Such a conclusion was strengthened in my mind when Alonzo Depue shifted his shapeless hat to the back of his head, brightening with a sudden changing of the subject. I don't think it was merely because Leslie did the talking, either. He said he had expected to see Lauren, Alonzo's brother, and he asked about Lauren's automobile, one of the first of its kind in the neighborhood. But Lauren was not at home. "That was an old International sidewinder," Alonzo said, "and it run long after anything of its kind was forgotten round here. We always said it had wagon-wheels, just like a spring-wagon with an engine in a box. . . ."

Leslie tried another tack, only to have one of his fanciest legends deflated. He told Alonzo that he was showing me some things along the Old Mine Road and that before we went home he was going to show me "that cave up the road where Tom Quick used to hide." "Guess you can find the cave all right," Alonzo replied. "It's just a big crack in the rock into which a man can go sideways. I been into it." This was no boast; Alonzo, if he were not so tall, could have gone through the crack in a door. "But we always figured it didn't have nothin' to do with Tom Quick. Got its name, probably, from somebody's old tomcat. Here's how it was: Somebody tossed a cat deep into the crack in the rocks to see if he would come up. He didn't. But he come out a hole down at the foot of the mountain along the river. Tom Quick? More like tomcat!"

The threat of the reservoirs was on Alonzo's mind, I know, and I wonder if it hasn't been on the minds of many who have never had and never wanted anything more than what the land along the Old Mine Road provides. "What I'm remembering most is," Alonzo Depue said, as I put my questions away, for keeps, "is if they're right when they say that only the peaks of the roof will be out of water over there at the old house once the dams are built."

Only a moment earlier Leslie and I had passed another old house, part of which had been built of stones used in the sturdy parsonage occupied by John Casperus Fryenmuth, a young Swiss. Educated for an itinerant ministry along the Old Mine Road, John eventually became the pastor of four churches in the neighborhood—Mackhackamack, Minisink, Wallpack, and Flatbrookville. With the Old Mine Road at its best, even the most agile of preachers would have had trouble keeping all the services of those churches on schedule. "Sometimes John Fryenmuth used to add another one—over in Smithfield, which wasn't too far from Shawnee, across the river," Leslie informed me. "But you've got to remember that church services were held in those days whenever the parson arrived. Services were often put in motion when the people responded to the blowing of a long tin horn. And the collection was taken up in a series of little black bags in which there were little bells—"

"What were the bells for?" I wanted to know. "To keep the congregation from helping itself to change?"

"Nothing like that. They were to let the churchgoer know that the man taking up the offering was coming close. Actually, I think the bells were to wake up people who had gone to sleep during the sermon."

What I wanted to be certain about, I told Leslie Coss when he and Bill Augustine and I were discussing the strange and sudden taciturnity of the people, was that New Jersey would never forget the lore of the Old Mine Road, houses that go back to raids of the French and Indian War, and mine holes that go deep into the past, even as some of them go into the depths of the earth.

"There was one raid up at Montague," Leslie said quickly, "in which twenty-one Indians crossed the Delaware and attacked a house then occupied by a family named Jobs. Wait a minute— the name of Shimer reminded me. After the raid in which three men were killed and two women taken prisoner momentarily, they crossed Shimer's Brook and surrounded Captain Abram Shimer's house. Come on, we'll go see it."

The house was empty that day, with no one to speak for it at all. It was the same not long ago when I went back along the Old Mine Road to make sure. "You know," said Leslie, on our first visit, "this is where the captain was with five or six slaves when the Indians turned up. He was sleeping but he was aroused as the Negroes chased the first intruders out of the house. Then the place was barricaded downstairs, the slaves were armed with axes, and the captain, covering all but one pane in one of the windows upstairs, hid behind a feather bed with the only gun available. Captain Shimer shot at the Indians and they shot back at him; his cheek was grazed by a ball and one of his shots broke the thigh of one of the Indians. The shooting aroused the militia down at the fort, just across the hill there, and they came on the double. The Indians, trying to make time across the river, left their women prisoners behind. You'd certainly never think anything like that had happened right here at that house. And unless people stop their cars to read what's on the marker and then go away to fill in what had to be left off, they still wouldn't know—

"Let me look at the book a minute," Leslie suddenly interrupted himself. Hurriedly he checked Mrs. Decker's text and then my worn copy of the old directory. "Just as I figured. Even Joe Brandt, the half-breed Indian raider, was here. And what is more, they say this is the first house in Montague Township with more than one story—"

"If you mean that one way, it certainly is an anticlimax," I told him "If you mean it another way, then it seems to me that all the houses along here have more than one story. The only thing they lack is people to tell them or, when there *are* people, some who don't act as if the world is coming to an end."

But Leslie had remembered other things and was trying to cram them in. "Speaking of corn, I've noted that they shock corn differently than they used to up in this country. There used to be seven hills of corn square, making forty-nine in all, and you were able to cut all forty-nine without changing your position. And, I meant to tell you, they used to grow tobacco along the Old Mine Road, too; the soil's just right for it even now. And you might make a note that the Bell house I showed you, where the nine generations had lived, is known to have been a part of the ancient village of Minisink where Indians and white men got along all right, no matter what was going on around them."

I let him talk, content to make a note as a kind of index to later discussion. My eyes were on the hills and my thoughts on the back of Kittatinny Ridge, I'm afraid. Traveling down the ancient trail, as Mrs. Decker preferred to call it, we came to a stretch under repair not far from the Van Campen inn of long ago, site of an earlier cabin that was built by Harmon Rosencrans in 1742. Leslie said: "This is where John Adams stayed overnight as he rode his horse from Massachusetts to attend sessions of the Continental Congress in Philadelphia. Count Pulaski was here and so was General Gates. Somebody named Captain Samuel Bowers wrote in 1763 that he found better than one hundred and fifty men, women, and children lodging there in refuge from marauding Indians. Old place is pretty much as it was— Say, what's the matter with you?"

There was nothing the matter with me and I said so: "I was thinking. I was listening but I was thinking, too."

"What were you thinking about?"

"About those mine holes up the mountain. About Sunfish Pond and Catfish Pond and all we could see if we could only get up there."

"We'd never make it," the schoolteacher from Newton assured me. "Haven't got the feet for it—or the wind, either. Beyond that, neither you nor I can take the time. Even if we had permission we'd probably have to have one of the rangers or a guide—they'd both come from the same place but we'd have to have them. And even with a guide it would take all of a day to get to the top of the Ridge and see things on the way. And what would we do about coming down? You just couldn't come down right away. You wouldn't do it anyway, for it would be dark before you'd get half started."

I nodded agreement. What Leslie Coss said made sense. But for a moment I had known the same sentiments that engulfed me years ago and made me want to drop everything and hurry away to the sedges along the Mullica River. There must be something wrong with me, I said, for there was nothing that I could see or feel, there in the shadow of the Kittatinny Ridge and Blue Mountain, that had anything at all in common with the tall grasses of the lowlands and the scent of cedar water far away. "You're right," I said; then again, "You're right and you're sensible. It's just that what's up there still bothers me, that's all."

"It bothers lots of people. It has bothered *me*. It has bothered all kinds of people for a long, long time," Leslie admitted, and he surely knows more about the Mine Road country than I. "Tell you something," he added, with an emphasis that had been put together in schoolrooms through the years and yet with a tone that implied that he thought perhaps he had been too frank, "the only way to get up there in a hurry is up one of the improved woodcutters' trails in a jeep!"

And that, I may as well tell you now, is how we made it—not then but later in the summer when the mud had hardened on the dirt roads and when water, oozing from depths that must know all about the old mines, no longer draped the frozen crags in spurious stalactites along the way.

£ake of the Mountain

When Bill Augustine and I returned to the Old Mine Road the adventure moved toward its climax and its summit, our steps retracing the way the wanderer had come from the Water Gap in the 1840's, except that the ferry was left out. There had been a ferry at Shawnee—one of the last, we knew. We began searching the road again, not for forts or tombstones this time but for a lane, a farmstead, and, perhaps, a flat-bottomed boat of the past. Almost without warning the brakes squealed, and we went down a steep grade to the edge of the river. The barns, the farmhouse, and all the proprieties were ignored and, in a moment, I knew why. With amazement we were gazing on what turned out to be the last flatboat ferry of the upper Delaware River.

It didn't look much like a ferry. As far as I could see, walking around it as it lay drawn back for safety on the frozen bank, it was very much like the hay barges I had seen at Clark's Landing. But this was a ferryboat, *the* ferry, sure enough. There could be no doubt about it. A lean and raw-boned youth who walked like an Indian came sauntering from the house, quietly amused at my amazement. He told us, when it came time to mention names, that this was the Van Campen farm and that he was Walter Van Campen, Jr.

"Boat hasn't been used as a ferry in a long time," he said. "She's sittin' here now, waitin' for the next hayin' time over on the other side of the river. You know how they used it? Sure, you do. Poled it across, with an overhead cable to keep it on course Some fliers were up here during the war. The ferry was further up, then. One of the boys got to seein' how close ne could fly to the river. Nobody told him about the ferry cable and in the half-dark the plane hit and pancaked into the water. The pilot got out of it all right but the Army put the ferry out of commission."

It was Walter, whose hair had a trick of getting in the way of his eyes in those days, who called Sunfish Pond, as it appears on modern maps, the "Lake of the Mountain." "Some people like to see the Lake of the Mountain," he said quietly. "It's more than a walk. Doubt if you could make it anyway without knowing the way. We can use the jeep if you want. Too late today, though. Dark before we could get there. . . ." Walter added that one of us was to call him up a day or so before if we really wanted to go. My mind suddenly flashed back to what Leslie Coss had said, that the only way you could get up to where the Dutchmen worked at the top of the mountain now was in a jeep. Having told us about the ferry and having made as generous an offer as any I have had, Walter turned and went into the dark house without looking back.

That telephone call was in itself an experience but, looking back, it was the kind of neighborly experience that might have been part of the days when earlier Van Campens knew something of the lure of the Old Mine Road. Strangely enough, the operator at the Gap knew her country well and so was ringing the party on the line, three-rings, almost as quickly as a local call. Three-rings didn't answer. At length, two-rings broke in with apologies and said that three-rings wasn't at home, that there was sickness in the family but that he, two-rings, knew where three-rings was. He would take a message. I gave him the message about going to the top of the mountain. Two-rings volunteered that he thought everything would be all right, that Walter's father was with a relative who was sick, but that he would find out. "Call me tomorrow," he said. "If Walter's not around, I'll have his message for you. The name is Decker."

The call went through next day and two-rings had a favorable message. I never knew why I didn't go back to calling three-rings and talking to Walter himself.

Next morning early, with only the deer, the squirrels and chipmunks, the groundhogs and a few hikers, we rolled once again into the dark dooryard of the Van Campen farm. It was summer. The flatboat ferry was gone, pressed into service at Fred Waring's club across the way at Shawnee. Three days of rain had washed away a bridge golfers used to get to one of the greens. Walter and his brother, Harold, had been up since dawn, looking after fifty head of cattle and finishing up the chores so that the ascent could be made.

"What's the book?" Walter asked me. I said I had brought the Brodhead so that I could tell him what Hidden Lake, or the Lake of the Mountain, looked like in 1870.

"Not much sense in that," Walter said, as if no time should be wasted. "Looks the same as it did then." Temporarily, I put the book away.

Now I know that he was right. The journey remains sheer poetry. But it was really something more than that, for I tried to imagine those others who had come there, the men who knew what the mine holes were all about and the men who had journeyed up the Pennsylvania shore, crossing by ferry to make this very climb. "The lake is reached by a carriage-ride to the ferry at Shawnee," Mr. Brodhead had said, "and then by a rugged mountain path, accessible to all who have stout limbs and good lungs."

Leslie Coss had said something about "having the legs" for the climb. Legs were limbs in 1870. I was grateful, now, for Walter Van Campen's strong and skillful hands and arms that ruled out the requisite of stout limbs and good lungs. I was grateful for the jeep and its four-wheel drive, for we needed it all the way. Groaning up and up, it took us among tall trees seldom seen, through long stretches carpeted with cinnamon fern, at the edge of depths of leaves hemmed in only by towering rocky formations, and the unbroken quiet of the forest. Time and time again any trace of the road along the ledge seemed to be lost. That we were on our way was shown, now and then, by a ditch painstakingly dug long ago to bring water down the mountain.

"What about those Indian graves?" I asked, wondering what direction they might be from the lake. Walter admitted to knowing nothing at all about them, so I flipped open my book to approximate what Mr. Brodhead had said.

In the year 1811, John Arndt, of Easton, wrote to the Rev. Mr. Hackwelder concerning an Indian grave "found at this solitary spot, near the shore of the lake. He was buried in a stone vault, the rock having been split apart so that it was made wide enough to admit the body, and covered with large flat stones. With the skeleton were found a small brass kettle, some beads, and bits of ivory which weren't ivory at all."

"What were they?" asked Walter Van Campen.

"Wampum," I said. "Here's the book. It says 'a parcel of ivory tubes, resembling pipe-stems' and 'circular bones of ivory of the size of a silver dollar, pierced with two holes through the diameter.' That's wampum. Then Mr. Brodhead says, 'Nearly opposite, down the mountain from this grave, on the flats or lowland, there was a large Indian burial ground. Could this have been the choice of this solitary inhabitant? Here was a lake with plenty of fish, abundance of large whortleberries, excellent hunting-grounds, etc. Can it be presumed that he was a noted chief or warrior to whom such distinguished respect was paid, as to deposit him so much nearer Heaven and the Great Spirit?' Brodhead leaves it there. I wonder who he was."

"I wonder what became of the grave up there or those down on the flatlands," Walter said, more to the point. I urged him to be on the lookout for family journals that might make some reference to it. After all, Van Campens had been on the same land from the first. "Brodhead was here several years before he wrote his book," I suggested, "and that was long before people came in such droves that they crowded each other on the sidewalks of Delaware Water Gap. All that's hard to realize now. I would guess that Mr. Brodhead was here at least eighty years ago. Colored beads, clay ornaments, fragments of blankets, rusted wrecks of guns, and brass tobacco boxes—what became of them, nobody knows."

Brodhead quotes a letter dated 1865, showing that some curious travelers opened other graves without qualm, pointing out that skeletons were found two or more feet down and that they had been carried up the mountain from the riverbank. Respect for the dead that would not permit burial where floods might disturb the graves was hardly shared by those who came after. I said as much as we crossed a path of sunlit fern called Broadway.

Moments later—the whole ascent required unrelenting climbing of more than forty minutes—we came to a little clearing beside the lake, a stretch of gleaming water screened by trees that grew straight up from a scramble of rocks.

Walter matched his knowledge of the seemingly limitless sea of blues and greens with that of Leonard Lee Rue, youthful caretaker of Camp Pahaquarry, who was also secretary and ranger for the Coventry Hunting Club's four thousand acres next door. It was Leonard, I remember, who took me deep into the cavern behind the Boy Scout camp, one of the principal mine holes of the Old Mine Road. That winter Leonard was also the unofficial keeper of twenty-eight brown bats who spent the winter in the mine and moved out, overnight, when spring broke through.

Straining our way up and easing down from the slope of Kittatinny moments later, Walter spoke lovingly and familiarly of Dunnfield Hollow, Dunnfield Gorge, and the old Rosencrans ferry. He said he had once been a pupil in the Calno school, only one-room outpost of its kind in Pahaquarry Township. "They're cleaning it up for something," I told Walter. "All the desks were outside as I came by. Obviously somebody's not afraid of the reservoirs." Walter said nothing at all nor did he suggest anything when I pointed out that the population of the township, 205 in 1910, was down to 67 in 1950. Much farther down the trail, as if he had been thinking, he said, "That doesn't count the deer and the squirrels."

Once, when I went back, I found an old man living in a tiny house just out of Millbrook. Squinting in the sun and rubbing the back of a big hand against a grizzled chin, he said that he was Lester Spangenburg, that he was seventy-five, and that he had lived on the Old Mine Road all his life. "From here to Flat-brookville ain't paved," he said. "You come out down there across a little bridge. Lots of people gets lost that way." It was Lester who sent me back to the little cemetery, well cared for in spite of its isolation on the flats of the river's edge. This, Lester said, was where the church that was moved to Flatbrookville used to be. I moved among the stones and read the names of those who could have told many a tall tale—there were Garrisses, Paddocks, Hulls, Howells, Labars, Deckers, Dimons, Cressmans, Depues, Shups, Hornbecks, Shafers, Swartwoods, Loseys, and Smiths. The Smiths, as might be expected, outnumbered all the rest. Many fieldstones, without names or initials, were scattered here and there. Some stones, I was told, have disappeared.

Not long ago, when I was up that way, Lester Spangenburg had disappeared, too. His house was empty.

So, then, we move down from the country from which "the water is gone" and to which, men say, they must flood it back again. What is to be, ultimately, I don't know, and perhaps it is just as well. All I do know is that the jagged trail up which we climbed to a far-off lake is now barred by a new gate, hand-somely lettered. On one end there has been tacked one of the little signs that are all about. "This land," the signs begin, list-ing an array of detailed regulations, "belongs to the people of New Jersey . . ." And the letters on the bars of the new gate spell out: "Fire Lane. No Motor Traffic. No Fires. No Camp-ing."

There is but one ghost story that I can connect with Beattystown, the quiet Warren village once ex-pected to overshadow both Washington and Hack-ettstown in industrial importance. It might well be called the legend of the marching feet. When the wind is right and the night is starry-clear comes the sound of shuffling footsteps, making a painful effort to keep to the swing of marching. Suddenly in the dark someone will say, "Listen, here they come!" And most of those on hand will stare and nod and quickly move off toward home.

3

New Jersey's Sodoms

Sodom, one of the most ancient of Syrian cities, ranks high among the unmentionables of all time. Commonly associated with Gomorrah and, less frequently, with Admah, Zeboim, Bela, and Zoar, it was evidently the chief town of the settlement, although its location may never be known with any exactness.

Some authorities maintain that Syrian Sodom lies at the bottom of the Dead Sea. Others declare that all these little cities were in the Arabah, north or northwest of the Dead Sea, or that Abraham saw the smoke of burning cities from the height of Hebron. Whatever the solution of the age-old mystery, it would appear safe to conclude that both Sodom and Gomorrah, singled out for punishment on those who practiced an abominable vice as a religious rite, vanished in a storm of meteoric stones which set fire to the bitumen or pitch with which their soil had been saturated.

With Sodom, New Jersey—or with the Sodoms of New Jersey, for indeed there were two—there must be some other background of rise and fall. Why any village should be called Sodom in the light of the fate meted out to a Syrian predecessor remains a mystery to me even after years of talking with old men and old women who knew where the Sodoms of New Jersey were and what they had become. Neither houses of crumbled asphalt nor a lake of sufficient proportions to provide a watery grave can be found in Hunterdon's Sodom, by contrast buried under a layer of innocent names like Spruce Run, Clarksville, and Glen Gardner, or in Warren's Hainesburg. Perhaps there is some connection with a strange evangelist called "the White Pilgrim" or with some other wandering preacher quoted by an early surveyor not too fond of work.

The names accorded these two settlements of an earlier frontier plagued me for years. Tom Gordon's *Gazetteer* half concealed the first Sodom with two lines: "Sodom, Lebanon t-ship, Hunterdon county. (See Clarkesville)." Turning to Clarkesville, I found this: "(formerly called Sodom) p-t. of Lebanon t-ship, Hunterdon co., on Spruce run, and on the Musconetcong mountain, on the western line of the t-ship, 14 miles N. of Flemington, 31 from Trenton; contains 1 tavern and store, 2 saw mills, 2 grist mills, and 6 or 8 dwellings; the surface is very rough and stony, but parts are productive; iron abounds in the mountain, and plumbago is also found in places upon it, near the village."

And here let me assure you that plumbago is graphite, even though there are no such diggings in Hunterdon's Sodom of today.

Tom Gordon recorded the second Sodom as a place still existing under that name in his day, a "p-t. of Knowlton t-ship, Warren co., on Paulinskill, 12 miles N. of Belvidere, 4 E. from Columbia; contains a grist and saw mill, tavern, store, and some half-dozen dwellings. Some smelting works have lately been erected here, said to be for precious metals, discovered in the Jenny Jump mountain." Listing the towns and post offices of Warren County, however, Gordon placed Sodom beside New Village, Broadway, Knowlton Mills, and Gravel Hill, even though in his chronicle of 1834 he seems to have preferred to hide Sodom, in Hunterdon, between Centreville and Clinton with its then newer name, Clarksville.

A handsome hand-colored map for the same book, provided by a Mr. A. Finley, preferred to ignore Warren County's Sodom, to which Gordon had given greater distinction. Brooding on these and other aspects of the puzzle one evening, I turned from the main road down from Washington to Clinton—as you must in these days if you wish to travel along Glen Gardner's Main Street—and put a cautious question to a bearded man. I asked him if Glen Gardner's former name was Clarksville, or Clarkesville before the "e" had been dropped.

"Yup," he answered quickly, and then added, almost in the same breath, "and before that it was Sodom! But if you want to know about such matters you'd best see Bill Banghart. Lives atop the railroad station, he does. Used to be the station agent. Retired now."

Bill Banghart, who then was seventy-six, got about almost as well as the Jersey Central trains he had once signaled across the mountain. A baldish and grizzled man, more at home with the stump of a well-chewed cigar in the corner of his mouth, he "went to work for the road"—the Central—in 1890. He served as agent at Spruce Run and Glen Gardner from 1907 to 1937. "My wife didn't like the idea of staying on and living in the station, with trains passing our apartment windows upstairs all day and all night. But she sort of got used to it. As for me, nothing else would have been natural."

I confess that at first I shared the shudders of Mrs. Banghart at the thought of living almost on top of the trains which have had their own troubles, through the years, in climbing Musconetcong Mountain. Perhaps there is comfort in the thought that a husband, going off to work, only had to go downstairs.

"Sodom was the name, sure enough," Bill assured me. I sat across his breakfast table from which he offered to share his fruit, cereal, and coffee. "There never was a Sodom post office, as far as I can make out. There was a little road down by the schoolhouse that was called Sodom Lane, but I never knew why. The name stuck to the hotel, the blacksmith shop, the mill, and the store where Russell Gordon lives now—well, that was the name up to 1850, maybe." I wanted to point out that Tom Gordon and his mapmaker were hiding Sodom in Clarkesville as early as 1834 but I was afraid to interrupt the train of easy thought, suddenly interrupted by a noisy train beyond the hall.

"Railroad came here in 1852," Bill went on, announcing that we would move into the living room and away from the trains as soon as the second cup of coffee had been stowed away. "Railroad people were the ones who called the place Spruce

Run. There's a Spruce Run Church still up the hill, you know, so that name's still around, anyway. It came from the stream just below here—you'll see how it's marked, plainly enough. Then, all of a sudden, the name of Clarkesville, with and without the middle 'e,' moved in. Glen Gardner came along only after the Gardners arrived, setting up little factories for making chairs and picture frames—that was in 1860, maybe, because somewhere in the 1870's the chair-and-picture-frame business went up the spout."

We moved into the living room. The Bangharts had all the comforts of home. Looking up at the second floor of a railroad station from the outside rarely provides an invitation to travel beyond or to imagine delights of cozy family living. The apartment—living room, bedrooms, kitchen, dining room, and a sun deck out back—had curtained windows brightened with flowering plants. There were family pictures, of course, but more prominently displayed were some authentic Godey prints. Back of the station was a sheer climb up the ridge with a narrow road demanding low gear of cars and trucks. Out front, the Bangharts looked down on the lower end of the village, even as Abraham looked down upon another Sodom from a greater distance.

Bill Banghart told me that he had grown up in Sodom-Spruce Run-Clarksville-Glen Gardner. His father, William Shipman Banghart, was born on a farm that became part of the Glen Gardner Sanitarium on Mount Kipp. "I helped my father haul some of the stone used by the railroad in building the arches and culverts and bridges—they came from up on the mountain, you see. We worked from sunrise to sunset in those days. I often 'made' a load of stone before I had my breakfast. Then I ate and the team got fed at the same time.

"The picture-frame factories? Guess the ruins are covered with leaves although one of them was right across the valley from here, opposite Drake's bungalow. One factory was Dr. Hunt's and I can remember it well. The lumber used for chairs and frames came in here by the carload—one-by-threes in four-foot crates or bundles. It was rough wood, not planed off. Yes, come to think of it, the place was still called Sodom when Tom Hunt was doctoring here. Sodom Lane's the road that comes out near Sickle Corner. There's another name—goes back to Joe Van Sickle, president of the Clinton bank till he died. Worth $150,000, he was, and they always said he didn't have a penny out that wasn't good.

"Those were days when a lot of tradin' went on. I remember a story of how Joe Van Sickle wasn't sure how many peaches he'd take for how much wheat. Those were days, too, when lots of mustangs were shipped through here on their way from Texas. Some people around here bought mustangs but not many—they were always hard to break and not much good when they were broke. Wish I could have talked to Doc Hunt about Sodom but he died just a little too soon for me—at least, before I could get around to it."

Bill, with a little coaxing, pulled out a box of old photographs and soon was lost in the recollections that went with each exhibit. I began to read from the *Historical Collections* of John W. Barber and Henry Howe. "They skipped a lot," I told Bill. "Here's what they say about Clarksville in the 1840's, with no mention of Sodom at all. 'Clarksville, on the road from New Hampton to Clinton, five miles from the latter, is in a romantic and picturesque dell among the mountains, and contains a store, tavern, a few mechanics' shops, a saw and grist mill, and several dwellings.' There must have been more to it than that. As for those writers of the guidebook that came out in 1939, they wrapped the whole matter up in a bit of fun and a few paragraphs, remember? They quoted the Clinton *Democrat* of sixty years ago to say that snakes lurked under the footwalks of Main Street and then pointed the way to the tuberculosis sanitarium."

"What can you expect?" Bill retorted. "Some of those fellows were just passing through. They never lived here—like these people in the pictures." The photographs were spread out by now. "These people used to watch stagecoaches and remember the days when the stage lines signed up an extra man to keep the wolves away. They remembered how the horses were changed at the Brick Tavern, on the Easton road out of Clinton. It's still there, occupied as a house. The Bethlehem Township Committee used to meet at the inn there. Glen Gardner's in Lebanon Township, you see. Spruce Run's the dividing line. . . ."

Time and again I tugged on the line with a query related to Sodom, almost as if I were playing a trout in Spruce Run itself. However, I had to be content to let Bill tell it his way, bringing in many things that rarely get into books. With all the pictures strewn about, Bill began talking of his continuing ability to work a telegraph key, his Bible that had belonged to his grandfather, and his memory of a man named Fritz who had met his death after a "battle" with a will-o'-the-wisp. "He'd been down to the tavern and got himself a little loaded up," Bill told me. "Lived near Woodglen, he did, and he had to go by what we call the Sand Flat in order to get home. That was where he said he saw a ball of fire rise out of the ground near the woods. He swore at it a little and then threw a stone to hit it. Next morning he was dead. Don't know what there was to the story but I remember that the youngsters around here never wanted to go by the place. May be that this was the way their mothers kept them close to home."

"Perhaps," I suggested, "that ball of fire was a little bit of Sodom coming through."

Bill saw no solution in that nor did I find any in the town, at the post office or at that hotel. Up the mountain roads the answers were pretty much the same. Up the Spruce Run Road, beyond the mill with the bridge with the wooden railings, from where I could see the killies swimming below, one of the friendliest men I ever have met came riding along—Joe Lomerson, caretaker of the church, gravedigger, and even a carpenter when a carpenter was wanted. "Heard the name, of course," Joe said, when I mentioned Sodom. "But not here. This was always Spruce Run."

"I can remember a lot," Joe said, smiling and hitching up his pants. "I remember moving those horse sheds at the back all by myself for $100, for instance. But Sodom? Well, that stays in the Bible where I'm concerned, I guess."

I continued to puzzle over the matter for a considerable time—the stories of the Old Testament Sodom, all that Bill Banghart had told me and all that he might have kept at the wet end of that mangled cigar—when suddenly I was in the midst of it once again. Wondering why Mr. Finley had failed to show a precise location for what Tom Gordon said was a post town "of Knowlton township, on Paulinskill, twelve miles north of Belvidere" and "four east from Columbia," I began plotting distances and with my own crude map invaded the hills once again.

At the same time I wanted to learn all that I could concerning the first Sodom in the hope, I suppose, that there might have been something that would quickly explain New Jersey's use of the name. I discovered that in 1924 Albright and Kyle directed a joint expedition of the American School and Xenia Seminary. They found five oases at the southeast corner of the Dead Sea, and evidence, they said, that a considerable population there had ended abruptly about 2000 B.C. All evidence, however, was now under water bordered by the "slime" which, actually, was bitumen, asphalt, pitch, or a lustrous solidified product of petroleum.

For a time my search for pitch, or even a village with a changed name, resulted only in more misleading adventures. A man in Washington, Warren County, sent me first to a place called "the Hensfoot" and later to one called "the Fiddler's Elbow," where it was revealed that these names came only from a formation of the old roads. The first clue of any consequence came from a fine old lady who, insisting that she had acceptable reasons for wanting her name withheld, suggested that I might have forgotten the White Pilgrim and that this rustic prophet may have been the one who had left a curse upon New Jersey's second Sodom.

The White Pilgrim was Joseph Tomas, sometimes spelled Thomas, whose grave is marked by a white obelisk in Johnsonburg's Christian Church Cemetery. Joseph, described as "a minister of the gospel in the Christian Church, known as the White Pilgrim by reason of wearing white raiment," rode a white horse into the area back in 1835. His saddle, his boots, and all his trappings were whitened by either chalk or some mixture confected of lime, none of which protected him when

27

a smallpox epidemic struck the region. Joseph, after one sermon, died at the age of forty-four.

The story goes that leaders of the little church demurred at burying the prophet in their cemetery, digging his grave instead in the forsaken burial ground of the Dark-of-the-Moon Inn so that their late lamented, even in death, might not be contaminated. Not until eleven years later did leaders of the church, at a formal synod meeting, decide that the White Pilgrim was safe for reassociation with the bones of his fellows. That is when Joseph Tomas was dug up and reburied where you will find his stone now.

I listened to several variants of the tale and then began to wonder. If the White Pilgrim had preached but one sermon, it must have been exceedingly powerful to blacklist a town and, afterward, to achieve an extinction equal to that of the original. What was more, it seemed evident that Sodom, no matter what its name before and after, had continued to exist subsequently to Joseph's inhaling of some of the fire adjacent to his own brimstone.

The second clue came from Hilton L. Butler, then clerk of the Board of Chosen Freeholders of Warren County. Hilton said he had found something in a history written by A. Van Doren Honeyman, from which he quoted:

"Hainesburg, on the Paulins Kill, four miles from the Delaware River, is a station on the New York, Susquehanna, and Western Railroad, and the main line of the Delaware, Lackawanna and Western Railroad passes through it. As a town it dates back to 1843, when the Beck brothers acquired the site which Andrew Smith had owned for thirty years, and cut it up in lots. Hainesburg was early known as Sodom, but the first post-office was given its present name in honor of Joseph Haines, who made a liberal donation to the school." Hilton Butler made it clear that he, himself, could add nothing to this surprising revelation which matched the location on the crude chart I had worked out. "Hainesburg unquestionably is the Sodom of long ago," he said, "but no one I know remembers the earlier name or what its meaning might be, there in Warren County."

The name Sodom was being used as recently as 1842. In Barber and Howe's *Historical Collections* such villages as Knowlton Mills, Centreville, Walnut Valley, and Sodom were strung out like beads for equal distinction. Columbia, said those twin explorers of more than a century ago, had a large sawmill and several mechanic shops; Blairestown, which had given up a more significant name, Gravel Hill, had a store, a gristmill, several mechanics, and a tannery, all part of a picture that included Presbyterian and Methodist churches as well as about twenty houses.

It was at this point that a legend or at least the rumor of a legend, recorded in 1939, tumbled out once again. In that year it was written that "Hainesburg was known more than a century ago as Sodom, for what specific sins the historians do not relate." The WPA writers could have said that the sins were as unspecified as the location or even that, unless one was especially interested in Hainesburg, one might miss the slight reference altogether. They preferred to write with tongue in cheek and let the rest go. Be that as it may, with an added sentence they seem to have supplied a missing piece of the puzzle, perhaps for Glen Gardner as well as Hainesburg.

"It was customary," they pointed out, "for traveling evangelists to confer that name on any settlement characterized by hardness of heart." Well, then, was the traveling evangelist here the White Pilgrim, that long-haired wanderer with the whitewashed boots? Or was it some other frenzied preacher, like Lorenzo Dow, who, having found only stony hearts in the village, did more than shake the dust from his feet and lingered, actually, to throw the sticky mud of a name like Sodom?

Time and time again it has happened, and not so long ago it occurred all over again, this business of walking directly to a half-hidden place, perhaps led by an unseen force, and there coming upon the outstanding folksay authority of a whole neighborhood. As in other experiences, this authority revealed a name to go with all he said. He said he was Will Mericle, that he was seventy-four, and that the fishing wasn't as good, there at Hainesburg, as it used to be. He made a few more artful but unsuccessful casts, the gentle swing of his arm belying a stooped shoulder over which he tossed his words.

"I'm looking for Sodom," I told him bluntly.

"This is Sodom," he said quietly. "Of course it's Hainesburg now but Sodom's what it used to be."

I asked him who had named the place Sodom and why, but Will Mericle pretended not to hear. "Born here, I was," he said. "Why, I've been here so long that I can remember George Adams, who built the sawmill that used to be here—just over there where those bushes are. This here's the sluiceway that used to feed the mill. Just over there used to be the Hainesburg station—this was the line of the New York, Susquehanny and Western. Just about abandoned down here at the bottom now, except for use in tucking a few cars away. Tracks beyond here are all torn up. Couldn't use that turntable beyond the station if they wanted to—"

"About Sodom, Mr. Mericle. Who was it—?"

"Up there's the big bridge of the Lackawanny," he said, looking directly at me as if to say that he had heard me the first time. "I worked on the building of that bridge, I did. What they needed in the way of ricks for the concrete mix came from that quarry you can see across the Paulins Kill. New York, Susquehanny and Western came through first. Guess I was just a chit when that was put through here and on across the Delaware into Pennsylvany. Big bridge of the Lackawanny didn't come till later, maybe thirty, forty years ago. It's just a hundred and twenty-two feet high—"

"They say that a surveyor who didn't want to work took the name from a wandering preacher who'd been given the brush-off in the village. Sodom, I mean. You see, I've been trying, ever since I can remember, to—"

"See the big house over there? That goes back to George Adams's time, sure enough. That was built for the men who worked in George's mill. Right here, where you see only the stone foundations, were some of the stables. And there was quite a creamery, too. There was a tannery, run by a man named Kaiser, but lots of the mills went down when the dam was washed out. That thing in the middle of the stream is what's called a fish basket. Fellow who's built a new house over there put it up but I don't think he's caught anything much. Ain't much to catch here any more. I've been mooching along the Kill, sort of looking for places to put out some traps a little later. Get a pension, you know, so at last I can do a little of what I want to do when I feel like it. But—"

"But Sodom," I persisted in one last forlorn try, "how on earth did anyone give a town a name like that?"

Will Mericle looked at me searchingly. Then he said, "Wouldn't know. But Sodom it was, you can be sure of that. And there ain't nobody here who can give me an argument over it!" With the agility of a far younger man he reeled in and pushed off upstream.

There are some historians who will say that Sodom was no mere label applied by a thwarted preacher on horseback but that it was the derivation of a name imported by early Hollanders, men who took the secrets of the Minisink mine holes to their graves with them. However, my examination of various atlases has so far failed to bring out any testimony in support of such a conclusion. Similarly, I think, any attribution of such a name to the Indians can be neatly dismissed.

Will Mericle had left me there beside the Hainesburg station, abandoned at least since 1946 according to yellowed calendars on its dismal walls. On a bulletin board was perhaps the last official notice to employees, suggesting that World War II was just about over and that this was a time, above all, to safeguard schedules and railroad property.

"All that seems so long ago," I said aloud, there beside an empty station and a singing stream that was older than the first name the town had known. "No wonder people have forgotten about Sodom!"

4 ~~~

Switchback Canal

One day while waiting for a friend to emerge from a meeting of the Council of New Jersey's Department of Conservation, I was informed that this session had come to an end but that members had solemnly assembled in another, the meeting of the Morris Canal and Banking Company.

"There is no canal," I said. "It was abandoned long ago." It had become little more than a memory and the banking company must be presumed to be dead. How could managers or directors or whatever they were hold a meeting? What could their decisions concern? I conjured up a picture of ghosts seated around a phantom table, making believe that today was yesterday.

The explanation was simple and it went like this: An act was passed December 31, 1824, incorporating a company "to form an artificial navigation between the Passaic and Delaware Rivers." The company was to be called "The Morris Canal and Banking Company." Jacob S. Thompson, of Sussex; Silas Cook, of Morris; John Dow, of Essex, and Charles Board, of Bergen, were named as the original incorporators. George P. McCulloch, John Scott, Israel Crane, Joseph G. Swift, Henry Eckford, and David B. Ogden were appointed commissioners, to receive subscriptions for $1,000,000 in stock at $100 per share. An additional $1,000,000 capital was authorized for banking purposes. The right to condemn lands and waters necessary for canal purposes was conferred, the State of New Jersey retaining the right to take over the canal at the end of ninety-nine years, at a fair evaluation. If the State did not desire to take over, the charter would remain in effect for fifty years longer, at the end of which time the canal was to become the property of New Jersey without cost. Banking privileges were to remain in effect thirty-one years, presumably with or without the benefits of the canal's own paper money.

The original charter, granted in 1824, was given a life of one hundred fifty years by subsequent developments. So, although the Morris Canal itself has been in its grave, officially, at least since the last land along its banks was sold by 1928, a live charter of a dead Morris Canal and Banking Company demands live administrators—and these, at least until the State Constitution was revised, were members of the Council of the Department of Conservation. These members merely adjourned a meeting of the department and then called to order a meeting of the Morris Canal and Banking Company for whatever matters might rightly come before the corporation.

There are some who will tell you that the Morris Canal was a failure from the very beginning, and that the whole venture was a mere matter of pouring money into a gully where other money already had disappeared. But this is not true. Promoters of the canal had visions of relating and developing various industrial enterprises of the area with an official waterway just as, Down Jersey, backers of railroads hoped to link together the faltering bog ore furnaces and glass plants. Actually, the canal materialized where it was proposed, with many good years to its credit.

George P. McCulloch, a Morristown businessman, first proposed a water highway that would carry Pennsylvania coal to New York and at the same time provide a new avenue of transportation through northern New Jersey. McCulloch arranged, back in 1822, a meeting of all interested citizens in Morristown. This meeting was attended by many notables, including the governor. The immediate result was the passage of an act, dated November 15 of the same year, naming McCulloch, with Charles Kinsey, of Essex, and Tom Capner as commissioners with authority to employ technical aid and conduct an investigation into

33

the whole plan as it was outlined by McCulloch. Ephraim Beach, an engineer with experience in the building of the Schuylkill and Erie Canals, was signed up and Professor James Renwick, then teaching natural and experimental philosophy at Columbia University, was retained as a consultant.

The summer of 1823 was a busy one for McCulloch, who lived in the country, talked with farmers, and put together an array of topographical information.

"The plain good sense and local information of our farmers," wrote McCulloch in this connection, "stake out the most difficult passes of the boldest canal in existence, and in every important point the actual navigation merely pursues the trace this indicated." This statement, it seems, was not entirely accurate because some of the best minds in the engineering field were consulted before preliminary plans for the canal were pronounced complete.

The extraordinary thing is that a canal so daring, so extensive, and so expensive to put into existence across the State could have vanished as completely as it has, with good people, as in Stewartsville, living almost beside it and denying any existence of so vital a ribbon of transportation. I remember becoming involved in something of a heated argument with a storekeeper who said that the gully that cut across the fields within sight of his establishment had been left behind by an old river which had gone dry "before the war."

In July, 1823, Ephraim Beach started taking levels and making surveys. Governor Clinton, of New York, came into the picture, along with Judge Wright, once chief engineer of the Erie, coming over into New Jersey at frequent intervals to see how things were going. The commission reported favorably on the project when all the surveys were in. Although it was recommended that the State build the canal, the Federal government belatedly joined the parade, Secretary of War Calhoun ordering General Barnard and Major Totten, Army engineers, to file their own report.

Oddly enough, there was a communion of opinion, with the Army men, Governor Clinton, and the commission urging state ownership that would rule out private enterprise. The big fly in the ointment was that the difference between the summit level at Lake Hopatcong and the elevations at Easton and the Passaic River were much greater than had been supposed, but this obstacle was declared to have been overcome by the inclined plane developed by the professorial Renwick. The inclined plane was a kind of switchback up which canal boats were hauled by rope and cable to where, beyond a ridge, they were "dropped" into the next lock, usually down at the end of a chute. Old Number Five Plane at Port Murray was, as the folk in the village still point out, "three stories high."

The plan was presented in detail with the varying levels shown from the Delaware River end, rising gradually in Warren County, moving toward a peak in Sussex and Morris and then Sussex again, and then leveling off through Morris until the big drop, almost due north and south, from Essex through Hudson. For all the care with which the plans and findings were presented, however, the Legislature turned down the proposal that New Jersey build the canal. This setback gave birth to the act of 1824 whereby a company was to be incorporated. By the spring of 1824 stock subscription books were opened and at first there was a ready sale. By July enough funds were on hand to start construction. Before the end of September, thirty miles of digging were under contract and seven hundred men were at work. Excavation came first and the building of the planes was left until later.

By the latter part of 1828 only fourteen miles of excavation remained unfinished between Newark and Phillipsburg. Attention was quickly switched to the building of planes but in the meantime, from 1829 on, small sections of the canal were opened for local use. In the autumn of 1830 the planes on the Eastern Division, as it was called, were tested. Five boats loaded with iron were sent from Dover and these used the planes without incident. This was indeed encouraging, as the mechanical difficulties in the construction of the planes had proved greater than expected, due to difficulty in obtaining mechanics familiar with that type of work.

35

These men were more than mechanics, they were pioneers. Nothing quite like the Morris Canal had been built before. For every man who said the venture would pay off there were two or perhaps three who stood off and declared that such devices as the planes that carried boats across mountains were tempting the fates. Be that as it may, the canal was in operation from Dover to Newark in 1831, and Byram Pruden, a veteran of the War of 1812, was the first pilot to conduct his boat, *Dover of Dover*, through. This called for a Dover holiday with one of Dover's storekeepers riding supercargo.

In November the first trip was completed from Newark to Easton. By then it was evident, however, that the company was in its first financial difficulties. The estimated cost of the canal had been $817,000 but the final cost was computed at $2,104,413. In order to meet this cost, a loan, known for a long time as "the Dutch Loan" because it was floated through the canal-familiar banking house of Wilhelm Willink, Jr., of Amsterdam, was obtained, with the entire Morris Canal as the mortgage. Then came other troubles.

Not long after the canal was opened, the *Electa*, a boat owned by Joseph Jackson, of Rockaway, went into a nose dive with a load of iron from the summit of the Boonton plane. As the boat passed the summit the sprocket chain broke, releasing the cradle with the boat inside it. Down went cradle and boat, plummeting along the plane like a crude and noisy freight car on a rampage, hitting the water with crashing impact. The boat is said to have behaved something like a flat stone hitting the surface of the water, leaping up and over an embankment twenty feet high and landing in the lower limbs of trees. The incredible thing is that the captain's wife and two children were on board, that none was hurt, and that the good woman, on being interviewed after her rescue, proved her gifts for understatement:

"I'll allow that the boat went down right fast," she said, "but this was my first trip—and I thought that was the way the thing worked."

Other accidents had more serious endings and the company was compelled to spend large sums of money repairing equip-

36

ment, making new parts because there were no duplicates anywhere, and settling all kinds of suits. Exaggerated reports of these events brought discouragement to balance the boasts of a five-day schedule along a 91-mile route with a carrying charge of $2.25 per ton on coal shipped through to tidewater.

Completion of the canal did not immediately bring the high revenues that had been predicted, and an additional grant of $1,000,000 capital scheme by the Legislature, plus another loan of $150,000, served only to stay the inflationary days of 1836 when the canal company made every possible use of its banking privileges.

In 1844, when a new Morris Canal and Banking Company was formed, there was an immediate flurry of activity and interest. The new operators widened and deepened the canal. After due proclamation headlines in the newspapers, they built one hundred new and larger boats, promising all kinds of things, only to discover that the brand-new boats, built in two sections and hinged in the middle, could not pass the planes except in one section at a time. This slowed down such old favorites as the veterans of the first canal company's fleet—the *Socrates*, *Lady Clinton*, *Othello*, *Henry Clay*, *Constitution* and *Independence*, as well as the later and more informally named *Vulture*, *Never Sink*, *Bridge Smasher*, *Wild Irishman*, and *Lager Bier*. Actually, the prosperous decade for the Morris Canal was between 1860 and 1870.

"Couldn't blame the failure on any one thing," said Casper J. Sutton, at Port Colden. Down at the village Trading Post they told me that Casper, then in his eighties and happily married fifty-seven years, was still living within sight of where, for many years, he was in charge of the Number Six Port Colden Plane. When I saw Casper I knew that I would have to go on and on, searching along the towpath and the birn and in the little towns adjacent to them, until I had tracked down every possible fragment of recollection. Casper told me that even as the canal was enjoying its best year, the Morris and Essex Railroad began carrying coal in competition. "That was in 1866, a little before my time," he said, "but not much."

In 1868 this railroad was leased to the Delaware, Lackawanna and Western and competition really became serious. The best time a canalboat could make was five days from the Delaware River to New York Bay unless, as Casper explained it, "the captains was pushin' real hard. Sometimes they made the distance in three days, but that wasn't often. The railroad, you see, made the trip in eight hours." Even with the 70-ton sectionboats in use on the canal, three cars on the railroad could haul as much as a boat. "And you got to remember that the railroad could run all year," Casper said, "while the canal had to suspend operation for the winter."

Casper Sutton, grizzled and white-haired, didn't move about with any great agility. However, his humor was keen although he admitted to me that he had grown a little tired of remembering a canal he had once thought might come back. For thirty-four years he was in charge of the Number Five Plane at Port Murray in days when three hundred six boats were negotiating the waterway. "Those were days," he said. "Mules and horses were everywhere. There were stables all along the canal and new faces to look on every hour of the day and night. Don't know why the railroads couldn't have stayed in their own backyard.

"I'll never forget the time one of the captains was skeered the boat back of him would try to pass. He pushed his boat all the way, that night. Then, all of a sudden, he found out that the light behind him wasn't on a boat but on a train. You see, the railroads wasn't content with breaking up the canal. They had to run tracks right alongside and rub it in.

"Yes," Casper admitted, as his memories traveled back along the whole length of the canal, refreshed by some of the forty-year-old pictures I showed him, "there was lots of pictures and books, too. I'll give you a picture of how I ran my wife's washing machine with a belt from a wheel that was turned by the waste water in the canal. See? And here's the only one I ever saw of Plane Number Five at Port Murray—three stories high, she was. Books? Oh, yes. All us plane tenders had 'em, especially when we weighed the boats. We kept the names of the boats in line, along with the names of the captains and anything else that might be of interest. Like a diary, some of 'em was." Casper's son admitted that he used to play with his father's canal journal in an old barn. But both barn and book have disappeared.

In earlier canal days, when Casper Sutton was a "braker" on canalboats as they came along, planes broke down more than once. He remembered the time when Number Six broke and the hinged boats went crashing back into the canal. He was aboard but managed to survive and rescue the captain's wife and family as well. Casper spoke of Number Six as "the plane I broke in on."

After he "broke" as a braker on the plane, he turned to "boating." The old canalmen, such as Peter Lingstring, Pompey Pierce, Decker Petron, Dan Winter, Johnson Mahoney, Danny Blizzard, and other colorful characters whom Casper quickly recalled, had a way of talking all their own. "Own brand of humor, too." he added. "You ought to look 'em up—but not many's here any more, I guess. The history's important but what some of those fellows could tell you . . ."

Old Casper threw down a challenge without knowing—or perhaps he did know, for his eyes were twinkling when he told me one story as a kind of sample At Port Murray, those long years after, he said, they still told the tale of a man who fell from the bridge of the lock when the ice in the canal was frozen solid. "Boy, did he hit that ice with his head!" Sutton laughed as if witnessing the tumble all over again. "You know, he hit the ice so hard that when spring came and the ice was all melted, you could still see the dent in the water!"

Belatedly it began to dawn on me that, although there were places in which history merged with folklore, even as Casper Sutton had suggested, they were separate aspects and the folk-say was frequently the more reliable of the two. So I have tried to make a digest, with the essential history in outline on one side of the fence and some of the folklore on the other. I shall give you, then, something of the saga of the little black book and of the notes penned painstakingly upon its pages through more than twenty years. Here are the legends of ghosts and the lore of men who knew them, as well as the story of a boy who, now grown to manhood, was fascinated from the first by the buried wonders of "the Ditch" and "the boats that climbed the mountains."

"The old canal has fascinated me ever since I was eight," Douglas Williams wrote me from Upper Montclair. "That's how old I was when I was taken for a walk along the canal's banks by a friend of the family—and that was a good deal more than twenty years ago."

Williams said that he knew many stories of the canal. "There was one, for instance, to the effect that its boats were used by the Underground Railroad, transporting runaway slaves in pre-Civil War days. Old-timers of the region through which the canal passed assure me that no 'canaler' ever had to lead a 'single' life. Indeed, several of the boatmen had a different 'wife' on every trip. . . .

"The canal also had its ghosts and men of mystery. There was the boatman who was reputed to be forever wandering up and down the towpath in search of his lost wife. He had committed suicide, you see, on her running off with another boatman. And I could tell you something of the 'millionaire boatman' who liked the life of the canal because he wanted to get away from it all.

"A character known as 'Old Man Crane' was a part of the canal for many years, striding along its banks, a long scythe over his shoulder and a long white beard flapping in the breeze like some Biblical prophet. Rumor had it that his job was to keep the weeds and rank grass down along the banks, but those 'in the know' always insisted that he was searching for treasure which other boatmen were said to have buried along the banks. It would seem that these boatmen had come by their treasure, if there was any, by giving a lift to a mysterious man who died on their hands. This is rather an involved story."

This was my introduction to a man who, by now in his forties, has the happy faculty of appreciating yesterday in the light of today and, in the process of his researches, making friends of and talking easily with those whose memories reach back into the Morris Canal's gayest years. The correspondence, begun in a chilling March, extended into a May that waxed cold and hot.

Then, suddenly, a meeting was arranged at the corner of West Passaic Avenue and Broad Street, in the Brookdale section of Bloomfield.

"Here in Brookdale," Williams told me, "the farmers always planted two or three rows of corn and vegetables that they never harvested. These were the rows nearest the Morris Canal. The canalers, you see, always pre-empted these rows and it was better to plant three rows for their use than to try to keep them from stealing crops. Canalers were too clever, anyway—they could steal a whole row of tomatoes and the ears from a row of corn even as a vengeful farmer mounted guard nearby. Jacob Reis used to recall that canalers could 'snake' a bagful of prime roasting ears right under the noses of landowners and their hired hands, some of whom were posted to watch the fields all night. In the morning whatever had been growing along the canal the night before was stripped clean, time and again."

What about the ghost tree? I inquired. Actually, it was but a few steps away, not far from a new housing development for veterans. "I can tell that it's the tree," Douglas Williams assured me, with authority, "because it's the oldest along the canal and, for some reason or other, somebody has considered it important enough to erect a protective fence around it. Men who knew the canal, which, as you can see, is only a few feet away, say that there was an earlier stone wall . . ."

Let me take the Bloomfield ghost story from the little black book, just as Douglas Williams took it down, word for word, from an itinerant laborer in 1937:

"This is a true story, I'm sure, as I knew the Bloomfield lock-keeper well back in the nineties and used to smoke a pipe with him outside his house on many a summer's evening. There were not too many boats in those days—that is, not near as many as in earlier days of the canal, and sitting with the Lock you'd get to know most of them in no time at all.

"There was a coal dock right near the lock and two fellows, the captain and his helper—I forget their names but I remember the name of the boat because it was such an odd one: *Lager Bier*—not beer as in the beer you drink but bier as in that which is your last bed to sleep on in this world—it was a most peculiar and appropriate name, you'll soon agree.

"Now about this time a gambler fellow in Paterson won a deal of money—all in gold it was—and being as how he was afraid of the losers in the card game wanting their money back he took off from Paterson by way of the canal. He must have figured they wanted it back bad enough to watch the trains and livery stables. . . .

"Now this was all in the papers at the time and if Webb Mitchell was here he'd show you the paper, as he saved it. There was a big ruckus about it as the gambler disappeared right off the face of the earth. Now, above the Bloomfield plane— and I knew the keeper there, too—there was a bridge over the canal and above the bridge there was a big oak tree. A farmer there had a slip of a girl for a servant and, being Irish, like myself, I'd got a bit friendly with her. 'Twas she who tole me about the *Lager Bier* tying up near the bridge one night. It was a Saturday night and, believe me, no beer to be had for miles.

" 'Why would they be tying up there?' she thought. Well, as she was on her way back from Confession she gave it no thought then although she did tell me later. Now, then, what does my friend the Lock tell me two nights later but that the captain and crew of the *Lager Bier* has quit canaling and taken to hanging about Pat Farrell's saloon. And the next thing a body knew they had a falling-out and one stabbed the other but the other shot him in the head as he fell.

"Now I put two and two together and I think: 'Them two gave the gambler a passage and done him in for the money.' But they must have hid him and the money, being too smart to be spending it right off. Then I thought: 'Where could they have hid the body? Why, near a landmark, of course. Why not the old oak?' Well, I could have gone off and I might have found it but the Spanish-American War came along and in the excitement I forgot all about it until lately. But Old Man Crane, the towpath walker, knew about it and spent his life looking for the money. Yes, and his old ghost comes out of the graveyard back of the church on Stonehouse Plains still looking.

"I've seen him on a foggy night plain as anything with his long white beard."

Legend, Douglas Williams had written further in his notebook, has persisted in saying that a man was killed for his gold by two canalers. "On dark and stormy nights the murdered man's ghost seeks out his killers. But he cannot leave the tree because the gold is buried nearby and he loved it so much that he must always remain near it. So he climbs high in the old tree and wails for his slayers to come to him so that he may exact vengeance on them."

The ghost tree is a little past Watchung Avenue, behind the school whose supervisor, it is said, was responsible for placing a formidable fence where the stone wall had been. As for "Old Man Crane"—

"He was actually one of the many towpath walkers employed by the canal company to watch for leaks on the canal's embankments and destroy muskrats which were a major source of trouble as they burrowed into the banks of the canal, fairly honeycombing them. Old Man Crane had a long beard which fell to his waist. On windy days it would flap out behind him, over his shoulder, or even straight out in front of him like a pennant. He carried a scythe and was a veritable picture of Old Father Time. He was known to at least three generations of boys and there are men in Newark today who remember him quite well. Two of the men I talked to always insisted that he was hunting for the treasure they were sure was buried somewhere along his 'beat,' which ran from the bridge at Second River to the Peterson Lock."

All the old men to whom Williams has talked about Old Man Crane told him the same story. "Craziest thing was," insisted an old farmer who was ninety-one in 1939, "that they found him dead by the big oak tree. I think the boatman's ghost scared him to death. There was one as used to howl up in the tree at nights 'cause I've heard him."

In Montclair a few may remember a character whose name, he claimed, was Prince Stokes. He insisted that he had been brought as a child from the South via the Underground Railroad, with his mother "on a canalboat." Not long ago a friend wrote Douglas Williams that he had discovered a court record as well as a portion of an address made by an abolitionist on a North Carolina plantation substantiating such a story. The abolitionist was convicted on the statement that "boats that climb mountains shall be used so that we may spirit you away to freedom."

Let me weave together some of the disjointed entries in the little black notebook; all are direct quotations from men who knew the Easton-Jersey City "ditch."

"The men who drove the boats were a fierce lot, generally. I used to watch them crossing the Peckman River where the lock was. I'll be darned if I ever saw many of them with the same woman twice. Why, it was common knowledge around Paterson that if some woman wanted to go to Newark or Jersey City, all she had to do was go up and wait at the stable by the bend. That's where fresh mules were kept for hauling the boats.

"I'll never forget the day one of them gave me a lift over to Paterson I was about fifteen and was going over on business for my father. Well, we reached the relay house, or stable, and the captain and his helpers started to change the team when along came two of them women. Both wanted a lift but the captain said he could only take one. The helper asked, 'How about me?' The captain told him to shut his mouth, and like all canal skippers, he could really cuss. When those women heard that, they started squabbling as to which would go and which would stay. Then the hair-pulling and screeching started and out came the stable boss, and giving the pair of them a shove, he allowed that it was a warm day and both had best cool off in the canal. At that the boat pulled away, leaving them floundering around in the water, all over mud and pretty sadly bedraggled."

Ed Courter, one of the last to remember the canal in operation in the vicinity, is a dignified old gentleman, proud of his great-grandchildren and his great-great-grandchildren. He is edging on ninety with a mind as clear as a bell and a gift for colorful talking when he's in the mood.

"Any old woman who had no place to stay"—this entry was

made in Williams's notebook after several interrupted visits—
"could get in with a canaler and be sure of her food and drink.
Why, I mind the time I was out in Paterson and see three of
them standing by the bend near the canal stable, waiting for a
boat to come along. They wanted to go to Jersey—that was the
way they always referred to Jersey City. Well, a boat did come
along and the captain couldn't make up his mind, without the
benefit of privacy, which one he wanted as supercargo.

"So he invited all three into the cabin. What Ed Courter, the
helper, and the stable boss saw through the cabin window had
best be described hurriedly, but it is enough to suggest, I think,
that what transpired was in the nature of a beauty pageant or
fashion show without the benefit of either bathing suits or dressmaker's skill. Do you think those women cared? No, sir, they
did not. Two of them was quite put out, of course.

"There was one canaler who used to pick up a different girl
every trip, putting the old one off at the Market House in
Newark.

"Another time I was out early one morning on my way to
work. I was apprenticed to a mason. I worked over in Paterson
and I used to walk over along the canal every morning. Along
about the Hill Road Bridge there was a boat tied up for the
night and I heard someone splashing in the canal. The captain
was on deck, smoking, while the helper was hitching up the
mules. It was a woman in swimming, and just as I got by the
boat she climbed out, up by the bow, and run back aft, naked
as a jay bird and as pretty a girl as I ever seen. She stood by
the cabin, drying herself off before getting dressed. I was nearly
an hour late for work that day."

Another man, formerly a butcher in Mountain View, was responsible for this entry: "The canalers were a tough old lot—
they used to even drink canal water and live. Some were quite
respectable and had wives and families. My shop was near the
canal and they used to trade with me a lot. A canaler's wife
could never be beaten in a trade, that I do know. One time a
boat captain's wife came in with a loaf of sugar—must have
weighed four pounds, all done up in a purple wrapper. She

offered the sugar in trade for a ham. When I went to take the sugar she made me wait a minute so she could take the paper off. She had some things she wanted to 'wash with it,' she said. 'The paper makes good bluing,' she informed me.

"As you know, butchers are a hard-drinking lot. But those canalers could outdrink any of us any day. Those fellows thought nothing of downing a pint of whisky in a gulp and a quart between two of them was but a drop. . . ."

The skipper who was often called "the Millionaire" left behind him an air of mystery that has never been fully explained. "He had a refined manner, never swore, and never took women on his boat." He had two helpers, one a colored man called Zodiac, who did the cooking, the other an Irishman called Jonah, who drove the mules. The Millionaire wore fine clothes and gave his pay as a canalboat captain to Zodiac and Jonah. There were all kinds of stories about him. He always smoked long cigars in contrast to most canalers, who were content with their pipes. "Nobody ever found out who he was or what became of him in the end."

There were, as might be supposed, "canaler medicines." One "receipt" reads: "For sinus and hard colds take a horse chestnut at least two years old, peel it, and grate it up fine. Then sniff it up the nose like snuff." Another: "For lung fever, take the inner bark of a wild cherry tree, preferably a young tree, and let it soak in clear rain water for thirty days. Strain through four layers of good cheese-cloth and store in an airtight bottle. Take a goodly swig as needed." Still another: "For gangrene: Take a two-month-old chicken, split it alive, and lay it hot on the afflicted member. Also good for proud flesh."

Douglas Williams, with his carefully indexed book, and John Carey, with his photographs, and many of the canalers themselves have helped me know these people better.

Harry Swayze, an old canaler, always wanted us to come up to Phillipsburg again but there never was enough time. Then one day the news came that he had chosen his own way to join the companions of the canal who had left the towpath already. I realized for the first time that Harry, burly and sharp-eyed and gabby, was essentially a lonely man and that a special kind of loneliness broods upon the canalers whose canal has been taken away. I remember his chart of canal stopping places, not only because of place names like Port Washington, Guard Lock 5 West (Saxton's Falls), and Pompton Feeder Junction, but because of names he had written in the margin: A. H. Vough, who was the super of the Western Division; James Powers, the super of the Middle Division; Thomas Heaton, at Boonton and Montville; John Mallon, of the Paterson Section.

I must tell Harry Swayze someday that I made the most of all he told and showed me, and together we must try to identify some of the ghosts, especially the phantom with the falsetto voice who, on dark and wintry nights not far from Lake Hopatcong, sings:

> Old Davey Miller, ridin' on the tiller,
> Comin' 'round the Browertown Bend . . .
> Old Davey Ross, with a ten-dollar hoss,
> Comin' down the Pompton Plane . . .
> Old Reddy Wright and his old naggin' wife,
> Waitin' for the Bloomfield Lock . . .

It was an experience to have the Misses Susan and Eleanor Weart conduct me through the Hopewell museum. The two rooms that I always looked forward to were those in which the Misses Weart had gathered together the wearing apparel of all the women who had been active in the community's past. Gowns and dresses dating from the 1700's on were draped on dressmakers' forms or makeshift dummies. The "ladies" were headless, but Miss Susan would go about calling each by name. "Now here, Aunt Mollie," she would say, "you deserve more prominence than that. Now, Mrs. Osie Whitlock, you stand here. Which of the tall girls will I put beside you? This, you see, is Mrs. Abraham Stout." Now that Miss Susan and Miss Eleanor are gone, I wonder if their dresses have been added to the exhibit.

5 ᴀᴄ

Schooley's Mountain Springs

So well remembered, as the saying goes, but in another sense all but forgotten, one of America's earliest summer resorts lies half buried atop a New Jersey mountain. Although some of its bones lie bare or in the shallow graves that time has provided, and although some of its former glories can be summoned to life from hotel registers and German-made postcards in quiet houses of the neighborhood, the mecca of health and magic water that was Schooley's Mountain has vanished forever.

Two stone gateposts and some leaf-buried steps of one of the last hotels, a long barnlike building in which you will find dusty shuffleboards and the mahogany of old bowling alleys, stone-filled and jagged cellar holes and water that goes plunging down the rocks mostly out of sight in a new course created by men blasting for a new road—these are among the sad remembrances of Schooley's Mountain now.

I became interested in Schooley's Mountain many years ago in remote New Jersey spots rarely associated with a region so far to the north. First there was an entry in the yellowing journal of old Martha Furnace, deep down in Burlington County, revealing that the proprietors and their relatives journeyed, at least at the end of every summer, to Schooley's Mountain Springs. Then came the revelation that Joseph Bonaparte, who later set himself up in splendor in Bordentown, had considered settling in the vicinity of "the Springs" or at least beside Budd's Pond, as they sometimes called it then. Later still, while rummaging around Long Branch, I learned that General Grant and his daughter, when they felt in need of a change, rode off inland to Schooley's Mountain and its celebrated Belmont Hall.

I may have scratched the surface of the story without knowing it at still another time when I was not too far away, talking with people who were upset because recurrent rumors of the Bunnvale water project were in the air, lending credence to a lingering threat to inundate such places as Califon, Long Valley, and Naughright along the south branch of the Raritan River.

I asked about Schooley's Mountain in Califon. Some loiterers told me that the name had been California until some "volunteers," offering their services to repaint the station sign to an agent who did not suspect that too much of another kind of paint had been imbibed already, made the place C-A-L-I-F-O-N before their bold strokes ran out of space. I asked more questions in and around the ruins of the old German church at Long Valley, which used to be German Valley, and pressing my search for a copy of a book I have long esteemed, *The Early Germans in New Jersey*, I made new friends, among them Charlie Messler, proprietor of the Long Valley Inn where I customarily pause if it is mealtime.

Charlie, lean and casual and a little tired, was usually willing to talk, especially if the bar and dining room were not too crowded, and so he told me many things at one time or another: how the old church around the corner operated without a stove and with only the heat of old-time religion supplemented by a bonfire in the middle of the floor under a hole in the roof; how people by the thousand were attracted by the "life-giving" powers of the mineral springs; how the nearby village of Chester, once called Black River, was settled during the reign of Queen Anne by "immigrants" from Long Island, and many other things. Old tombstones in German script attested to how a fire got out of control at the old church, tumbling its charred beams among the faithful, long before the Revolution; and anchors included in the design of grave markers proved that there were sailormen buried at Chester, but Charlie kept his own secret buried best of all. Charlie was a bellhop at the Dorincourt, once the Belmont Hotel, when the gay days of Schooley's Mountain Springs were drawing to a close.

"There were three big hotels, you might say," Charlie told me long after I thought I had drawn out all there was. "There was the Heath House, which they tore down and carted off to Brooklyn where, I always heard, it became Sagamon Hall. There was Belmont Hall, that burned down. And there was the Dorincourt, that grew up out of what was left—it had four hundred and twenty-five rooms, you know. Some say it had four hundred and fifty but I ought to know—I worked there. And all the rooms were carpeted."

Although there are probably more mineral springs in New Jersey which, in their day, were celebrated as water cures, I have visited but three. Colestown, down near Haddonfield, had one in the early 1800's but Colestown, oddly enough, was mostly a cemetery until recent sprawling suburbia came that way. Paint Island Spring, on the old Court House Road between Mount Holly and Freehold, was another. Of them all, Schooley's was surely the most celebrated.

The next time I climbed the mountain I doubt if Charlie Messler or his son recognized me as the curious intruder of far earlier days, for Charlie began in the familiar groove concerning his own celebrated hotel. He used to say that his establishment was built in 1778 and that it had served hard liquor longer than any tavern in New Jersey north of Trenton. "I'm only the third proprietor in over one hundred and sixty years," he said. Once a guidebook quoted Charlie as saying that no less than George Washington had enjoyed a glass or two at the inn, but he never mentioned the matter to me.

The German Valley Hotel has had its face lifted several times, but underneath it is the same old inn that it was when Matthias T. Welsh was there. Matthias married Mary Hager, daughter of Captain John Hager—"of Revolutionary fame," as they put it in the Valley—who was known as the wealthiest man around. "Never's been anything but a hotel," Charlie told all comers, "although it served during the Revolution as a headquarters for the soldiers—and I don't mean only the barroom. Never a blemish has marred its reputation and, if you're counting those members of the same family, it's been run by only six different men.

"After Matthias Welsh there was Sylvester Hann and he gave it up to take the Puddle Hotel up Chester way. Sylvester was a well-known heavyweight—he tipped the scales at better than five hundred pounds. No, sir, this hotel's been the hub of everything in Washington Township since anybody can remember. . . ."

I kept breaking in with questions about the hotels on Schooley's Mountain and what had happened to the magical cure-all water. At last Charlie said that he had known the times when there were between six and seven hundred guests stopping at "the Springs." "There was a fourth hotel, too, I've always heard," he said. "The Annex, I think they called it." I have wondered if this was not the Alpha of other accounts but I dared not interrupt. "The water's deep down in the mountain and it comes out, pretty much as it always did, down at the bottom of the hill off the road to Hackettstown. When they fixed the road, they shot off a lot of powder and the water changed its course. You'll find a little spring at the foot of a tree where the water boils out a little. The springhouse was taken away by the road men—they said it was falling down and in the way, anyhow. Concerning anything magic in the water . . ."

As for that, it is much better to tell what Gordon's *Gazetteer* and others had to say and then pick up the pieces of what there is now. After explaining that the top of the mountain was six hundred feet from the bottom, "a calculation, made by approximation, on the falls of water, on the different mill dams along the rapid channel of the Musconetcong river" and then adding, hastily, that Schooley's attained a height of eleven hundred feet above sea level, Gordon struck out boldly:

"From the top of the mountain a turnpike road runs northward to Sussex, another westward to Easton, a third eastward to New York, and a fourth southward towards Trenton. The mineral spring near the top has given much celebrity to the region. . . ." As far as I have been able to ascertain, the spring, according to those familiar with it, is close by the bottom, rather

51

than the top, of the elevation. "It is said to have been known to the aborigines, and to have been employed by them as a remedy, which, with characteristic selfishness, they would have concealed from the whites. The latter, however, have resorted to it, since the settlement of the country. Remarkable cures have been ascribed to it, season after season, on account of the benefit they have received from the use of its waters. . . .

"The spring is, in strictness, a rill which issues from a perpendicular rock, having an eastern exposure, between 40 and 50 feet above the level of the brook, which gurgles over the stones, and foams down the rocks in the channels beneath. A small wooden trough is adapted to the fissures so as to convey the water to the platform where the visitors assemble, and to the structure containing the baths. The temperature of the water is 56 degrees Fahrenheit, being 6 degrees warmer than the spring water near the summit. . . ." This is the first mention of baths, something forgotten in most accounts and recollections of Schooley's Mountain Springs. "The fountain emits about 30 gallons per hour; which quantity does not vary with any change of season or weather. The water, like any other chalybeates, leaves a deposit of oxidized iron, as it flows, which discolors the troughs, baths, and even the drinking vessels. The bare taste and appearance shows that it is chalybeate; and it is strongly characterized by the peculiar astringency and savour of ferruginous impregnations. Though remarkably clear when first taken, the water becomes turbin upon standing for some time in the open air, and after a long interval, an iridescent pellicle forms on its surface. Ochre and other indications of iron are dispersed extensively through the surrounding rocks and soil. Iron ore is so plentiful in the vicinity that furnaces are worked, both in the eastern and western district of the chain, and much of the ore is magnetic. . . .

"The analysis of the water, by Dr. M'Nevin, of New York, has given the following result: 'Vegetable extract, 92; muriate of soda, 43; muriate of magnesia, 50; carbonate of lime, 65; carbonate of magnesia, 40; silex, 80; carbonate oxide of iron, 2; loss, 41, total 16.50.' The iron from the mineral water is very easily separated. Exposure to the atmosphere induces metallic precipitation; and transportation to a distance, even in corked bottles, produces a like effect; and when thus freed from its iron, the water may be used in making tea. The heat of ebullition, also, seems to separate the ferruginous ingredient, and to prevent any dusky or black tint; for if an infusion of green tea be mixed with water fresh from the spring, a dark and traceable hue is immediately produced. The carbonic acid which this water contains, is altogether in a state of combination, and hence it never occasions flatulence or spasm in the weakest stomach, whilst it gradually strengthens the digestive powers. . . . This chalybeate is considered by medical men as one of the purest of this or any other country, and as beneficial, in most cases of chronic disease, and general debility, and especially in cases of calculus in the bladder or kidneys. . . .

"To those in pursuit of health or pleasure, this region presents equal attraction. A short journey brings the patient from the level of tide water to a very desirable elevation, which tempers the summer's heat, and braces the relaxed frame. The plain on the top of the mountain affords very pleasant rides amid ever changing and delightful scenery, in which cheering views of improved and profitable agriculture are blended with the velvet plain, the craggy hill, and shadowy vale. Thus the invalid has every incentive to exercise, by the highest gratification from his exertions. To him who seeks relaxation from the cares of business, or to change sedentary occupation and feebleness for activity and vigour, the excellent society which assembles here during the summer months, the abundant sport of fowling and fishing, and the delightful scenery, hold forth strong inducements; to which, we would be unjust not to add the excellent fare, cheerful attention, and comfortable accommodation given to visitors at the three hotels, and several farm houses in the vicinity of the spring. . . .

"Belmont Hall, kept by Mr. G. Bowne, situate on the highest part of the mountain, shadowed and embowered by various fruit, forest, and ornamental trees, is a fine building 50 feet square and three stories high, with very extensive wings; and the Heath House of Mr. E. Marsh, less showy, but not less commodious or pleasant, afford the visitor all the means of enjoyment usual at watering places; whilst their distance from the fountain, (about ¾ of a mile) by adding the benefits of exercise, does not diminish the salubrious effects of the water. There is, however, a third house, immediately at the spring, where such visitors as desire to be near it, can be accommodated. The season commences here on the 1st of June, and continues during the hot weather.   . .

"For the man of science, the mineral region, and geological formation of the country, possesses much interest. It abounds with iron and other minerals. The first, in a mine opened within gunshot of the Heath House, is highly magnetic; so much so, indeed, as to render the use of iron tools around it very inconvenient. The following extraordinary circumstances we give on the authority of Mr. Marsh. The tools, by continued use, become so strongly magnetized, that in boring the rock, the workman is unable, after striking the auger with his hammer, to separate them in the usual mode of wielding the hammer, and is compelled to resort to a lateral or rotatory motion for this purpose; and the crowbar has been known to sustain, in suspension, all the other tools of the mine, in weight equal to a hundred pounds. These facts are supported by the assurance of General Dickenson, that the magnetic attraction of the tools, used in his mine, adds much to the fatigue of the workmen; and that it is of ordinary occurrence for the hammer to lift the auger from the hole during the process of boring. . . .

"Besides the houses for public entertainment, at and near the springs, there are several others, which, with a church and school house built by Mr. Marsh, with the aid of the visitors, and a post-office, give the neighborhood a village-like appearance. And, among the attractions of the mountain, we must not forbear to mention the fishing and boating on Budd's Pond, a beautiful sheet of water, two miles in length by one in breadth, at seven miles distance from the spring. This little mountain lake of great depth and clear as crystal, abounds with perch, sun, pike, and other fish."

54

This is the earliest description I have found, although Gustav Kobbé quotes from an account of a French scientist, Milbert, and his *Itinéraire Pittoresque du Fleuve Hudson et des Parties Latérales*, written after the author had "made his trip in 1815." Declaring that "the road across Schooley's became a regular turnpike in 1809" and that the mountain "was one of the most famous summer resorts in the United States," Kobbé says that Milbert's description is "embellished with two engravings, one of the rock from which the spring flowed (there was then no spring-house or basin), the other of the cataract, still a natural feature of great beauty."

I have seen pictures of the springhouse on some of the postcards printed in Germany, but the one shown on these was obviously a successor of that included in the lavish but concentrated description of John Barber and Henry Howe. In their *Historical Collections* of 1844 it is pointed out that "there are two splendid hotels, pleasantly embowed by trees, usually thronged in summer months with strangers, drawn thither by various attractions, not the least of which is the fine bracing mountain air, and the delightful landscape scenery in the vicinity." This came after the declaration that Schooley's Mountain Springs had "been a place of fashionable resort for about forty years" in the estimates of these authors, who, by the way, added that "previously, visitors erected tents and shanties, for temporary accommodation."

The spring they described as "a small rill, not larger in diameter than anyone's little finger, issuing from a rock by the roadside, covered by a small, neat, wooden structure, with seats for visitors." Whereupon another authority, "the learned Dr. Mitchill," was permitted to give his own analysis, with the following statement which, in many ways, has a familiar ring—repeated here only because Barber or Howe or both offer a personal commentary: "Notwithstanding its ferruginous impregnation, the metal [in the water] is so precipitated and modified by boiling, that the infusion of tea-leaves is not blackened or discolored at all; but is as good as that made with spring-water. . . . When the hostess at the inn told me this," comes the hasty addition, "I was so incredulous that I offered to bet her a bonnet and a shawl that it would not turn out so.

"She declined the wager but said she would make the experiment. Water from the spring was boiled, and employed for making an infusion of Chinese tea. There was no discoloration whatever: whence I found that, if she had had the courage to lay, I should have lost the stake. In like manner, when one of my friends requested me, a few years ago, to make some experiments on a bottle of water he had bought from the spring, I told him I would do so, and authorized him to bring as many persons as he pleased to witness the proceedings. The company assembled, and the tests for iron gave not the least indications of its presence. We were all puzzled and disappointed."

Gustav Kobbé has argued that there was a hotel on Schooley's Mountain as early as 1795 and contends that the old building was the start of the Heath House. "In it," he wrote, were "several old mirrors and pieces of furniture, relics of the hotel accommodations of an American summer resort of the last century." To me it is evident, here and elsewhere in Kobbé's little books, that the author made a point of seeing and sampling the things and places he wrote about, subsidized, as he undoubtedly was, by the early railroads and hotels. He adds another analysis of the water—seemingly someone was always coming along to fortify the claims of the springs—this time by Dr. T. M. Coan, in 1889 or 1890. He puts the spring itself half a mile from the hotels and his statement is proved by such things as people say, as well as my old topographical map. The map shows the spring far down the road to Hackettstown, where, in those days in a country filled with little mines, it was the neighbor of one called Young's. Those who know anything of Schooley's at all may say that the spring's outlet remains elusively out of sight and that even the cataract pictured in *Jersey Central* must be sought up a wood road at the base of the elevation.

If you were passing and wanted a drink of the celebrated water in Kobbé's day, "glasses can be obtained for a small fee in a neighboring house but visitors are advised to take them from their hotel or cottage. The water can also be ordered at the hotels. It is especially recommended for calculus, kidney complaints, torpor of the liver, and as a tonic."

The Alpha, Kobbé says, was "probably a road-house, flourishing on the patronage bestowed upon it by the passengers of stages which followed the post-route across the mountain. It is even said to have been a jug-tavern, similar to those which in olden times flourished among the Jersey Pines, and which owed their peculiar name to the fact that their whole stock in trade consisted of a jug of apple-jack, from which, however, any liquor called for by a customer was poured." Then: "As the Schooley's Mountain Spring became more famous, the jug-tavern and road-house improved in character. Additions were made until some three hundred and fifty guests could be accommodated, and the original little building seemed so remote an object of history, that it was dubbed the 'Alpha' pretty much as if it were the beginning of creation. It is thought to be, and probably is, the oldest summer resort building in the United States."

If it is true that the Alpha was part of the Heath House and if the Heath House, as Charlie Messler says, was dismantled for reassembling somewhere in Brooklyn, that is where someone should have looked for the oldest summer resort stopover in the country. When the Heath House was still there, Kobbé found it comfortably furnished and said that its table was "plain but plentiful. It makes no pretense of furnishing fashionable amusement, but seeks rather to attract those who find recreation in restful quiet, and are satisfied with homelike accommodations. Among its guests are several who have made it their summer retreat for over thirty years."

Single rooms at the Heath House were available at $14 per week, with double rooms from $24 to $28. Nurses and children who would have their meals at the children's table paid $7 but children under twelve who insisted on eating with the grownups had to pay $10. Transients were accommodated at $2.50 per day, all found. The Heath House provided a stage for amateur theatricals and a darkroom for amateur photographers. Carriages pulled by horses used to climbing roads far less impressive than those crossing the mountain now were available at $6 for drives to Budd Lake, half that to Hackettstown, and at $1.50 per hour if the added safety of a double team was preferred. Stage fare between railroad connections at Hackettstown or Long Valley was fifty cents.

Kobbé, writing in 1888–1889, declined to "rate" old Belmont Hall because it had just changed hands and was about to attain new fame as the Dorincourt. "It is a fine building, however," he said, "and its proprietors purpose to cater more to the fashionable element." Of all that the Dorincourt was, there remain only some jagged holes in the ground, the steps, the sentinel gateposts, a deserted and dusty bowling alley, and some famous names in a book.

When I was again on the mountain with Alden Cottrell, Spencer Smith, and Bill Augustine, I saw what appeared to have been a barn, and yet it could not have been just that. Beyond the tufts of Indian grass and the locust trees on the rise was a long and narrow building, obviously a leftover of the Dorincourt. The door was fastened but not adequately. In spite of a hole in the ceiling and a huge window at the back which, without glass, had allowed a filtering of the last snow, the old atmosphere held on—this was clearly the old bowling alley. Two alleys were evident in the gloom, beyond furniture heaped up in storage. The posts at the end of the troughs down which the bowling balls had been returned had been rudely hacked but the very hacking revealed solid mahogany. Upstairs there had been billiard tables.

That was when Mrs. Kurt Meyer appeared, gracious but anxious. News travels quickly, even on Schooley's Mountain in winter, and someone had telephoned from a house down the road to say that "some strange men" had just invaded the place. Pleased that any could show such an interest in the past of "the Springs," Mrs. Meyer explained that she and her husband, a nurseryman, had bought the site of old Belmont Hall, later the Dorincourt, that they were living in what they had been told was the principal quarters for the hotel help, and that they had great plans for the revival of the mountain's popularity. Mrs. Meyer produced a colonial lantern, a coachman's plug hat, and a piece of china bearing the Dorincourt's name.

"That stone ruin out back was the icehouse," she said. A heavy snow had buckled the roof only that winter. "And here are some postcards of old Schooley's Mountain. Here's the springhouse, shown as it used to be. And here's the stately Dorincourt with its tall pillars and style of the last wonderful years. Do you know, you should go across the way where Louise Blake lives. Just over there. Tell her I sent you. She has some registers of the place when it was Belmont Hall."

Miss Louise Blake put the registers of Belmont Hall at our disposal. It wasn't long before the bold strokes of a pen wielded by General Ulysses S. Grant leaped up from one of the pages. "U. S. Grant and daughter," the entry read, "Long Branch."

Much later a note from Mrs. Grover C. Apgar led me to Pleasant Grove on the plains beyond the mountaintop. The Apgars were in the cellar, making and bottling quantities of the cider for which they were celebrated throughout the neighborhood. Mrs. Apgar was even more celebrated for her interest in history and folklore, and in spite of cataracts that clouded her sight she had made a point of writing down odd scraps of information in a gallery of little notebooks. These and scrapbooks and books of reference were all of a tumble in the warm and friendly room in which she remembered what she could of Schooley's Mountain Springs. At that moment I was trying to learn more of Ephraim T. Marsh because of his connections with Belmont Hall. Mrs. Apgar showed me a likeness of them both.

It seems that Judge Marsh, who perhaps has been more celebrated for his management of the Morris Canal, was born at Mendham in 1796, went to Schooley's Mountain in 1816, and took over the Heath House in 1820. Whatever its past had been, the judge completely revised the inn, even to naming it in honor of his wife. Judge Marsh was at the Heath House until 1850, and the mountain largely owes its fame and success as a summer resort to his enterprise and business energy.

Mrs. Apgar's notes takes the discovery of the magical springs back to 1734 and the Culverites. Her notes, however, have mainly to do with the last days of the old hotels, once she has called the roll of some of those who knew the mountain retreats in their palmiest days: John Sargeant, once a candidate for the Vice-Presidency; Vice-President George M. Dallas, Governor Edward Coles, Dr. George B. Wood, Richard Vaux, General John Cadwalader, Garret D. Wall, Peter D. Vroom, Philemon Dickinson, William L. Dayton, Governor William Pennington, Samuel L. Southard, the Hon. Theodore Frelinghuysen, and the Hon. Frederick T. Frelinghuysen, all from New Jersey. New Yorkers in Mrs. Apgar's lists of guests included Jacob LeRoy, C. V. S. Roosevelt, ex-Governor E. D. Morgan, the Rev. Dr. Spencer D. Cone, the Rev. Dr. George B. Cheever, and others.

"In 1852," runs one of Mrs. Apgar's notes, "two physicians, Dr. William Taylor and Dr. Moore, both of High Bridge, came to Schooley's Mountain and looked the situation over, deciding to build a sanitarium there. This soon became known" once again "as a rest cure and water cure resort and the enterprise turned into a highly profitable venture. They had a large patronage but there was a quarrel" involving the alleged misappropriation of funds. "This resulted in the closing of the sanitarium and the sale of the property to David A. Noe, of Elizabeth, who ran it as a summer hotel for a time. . . .

"Patrick Matthews, of Newark, then bought the place and ran it as a hotel which had to close because the officials decided that he was conducting a common gin mill. In 1867 or 1868 Matthews sold out to Rev. Luke I. Stoutenburg who overhauled the building and opened it as a preparatory school. He conducted it for a number of years and it made an enviable record as an institution of learning. It was officially known as the Schooley's Mountain Seminary. There came a time when Mr. Stoutenburg was obliged to relinquish the business and after it had remained tenantless for some time the school was purchased by a man named Sonneborn. It was conducted as the Forest House Hotel for some time and later burned down."

Leslie V. Clawson, who lived in Hackettstown when he last wrote me, said that he was at the old springhouse on the mountain when he was a boy. "The spring was almost at the foot of the mountain on the Hackettstown side. When I was there the water that ran over the rocks was all rusty and that's what amazes me when I hear the spring itself is so hard to find. Everybody I knew called it the iron spring. When they widened the road, the spring, I guess, went with it. . . .

"I could tell you something more about the old Dorincourt, too. Where the kitchen was there was a big oak tree that stood and grew along where one of the cook ranges were. And as the tree grew, the roof above was cut so the tree could go through. In the early 1900's it was still there because I'm the one that cut the hole bigger when they remodeled the kitchen. You speak of stage-coaches. There were three, as I remember them back in the 1890's. They ran to Schooley's Mountain, Pleasant Run (now Pleasant Grove), and German Valley. They all started from the arrival of the 10 a.m. train from New York. These coaches all carried mail as well as passengers. As a boy I rode the stage from Hackettstown to German Valley. It took some time to get there. Today it is a matter of minutes."

Many mysteries still haunt Schooley's Mountain, in spite of the piecing together of records tucked away in old books hard to find and the homespun research and fond recollections of those I have come upon in years of wandering. What, in truth, happened to the trumpeted medicinal qualities of the water from the spring, or the springs, inasmuch as the Dorincourt claimed to have seven on its property alone? What happened to the springhouse and the water that gurgled up from beneath it— was it so disreputable in appearance that removal with dynamite by the roadbuilders caused no flurry of excitement, no tears at all? Was it actually the habit of people like the Grants as well as natives who lived along the coast to hurry inland for their holidays when those who lived in the cities sought recreation on the beaches? Where did the name for the Heath House come from and where did the Heath House go? To only one of these questions have I an answer that satisfies me and that came from the tombstone of Judge Marsh, whose wife, the stone revealed, was the former Lavinia Heath. To the resolving of the other riddles drinking of the kind of water that still runs down the mountain has been no help at all.

George DeHart of Washington's Crossing, at eighty-four, was wrinkled though bright-eyed, careful though agile. I found him in the middle of a well-groomed truck patch, loudly crediting his good health to the herbal remedies handed down in his family. "Never bother with doctors," he said. "Take sciatic trouble, now—never had any in my life and you know why? I make my own boneset tea, I do. Make it just the way my mother always did. Brew it just like any other tea, a small quantity at a time. Then I drink a peanut butter glass of it before going to bed. Why, when I was a boy they made me drink boneset every time I had a cold and they gave me tansy tonic whenever they figured there was something wrong with my kidneys. Usually used dandelions for toning up the blood—but plantain has lots of uses, too. People dig it up as burdock but they shouldn't. They ought to add some vinegar, salt, and hot water for a rheumatism cure." A taste of tansy tonic cured me of almost everything. George DeHart told me afterwards that tansy tonic is gin turned green by crushed tansy leaves.

6

Methodist Medicine

I am grateful to Mrs. Marsh of Mountainville for knowledge of the volume called *The Family Adviser*, by John Wesley, who went in for treatment of the body as well as the soul. Actually, *The Family Adviser* turned out to be two books in one, with evidence that William Wright, of Burlington, who called it his "doctor book" according to an inscription in the late 1700's, thumbed through the pages of the second quite as much as he did the first. It was the second, bravely titled *Primitive Physic, or An Easy and Natural Method of Curing Most Diseases*, by John Wesley, M.A., that came as a surprise because it all but escaped my attention. And it is that book, as well as the wandering adventures into which it has led me, everywhere from Hunterdon's Cokesbury to Bridgeton and Port Norris, much nearer the Delaware Bay shore, whose story I must tell you now.

However, it must be in the company of those two devout Wesleyan disciples, the Bishops Coke and Asbury, for whom many a town in New Jersey has been named, and who traveled the land restlessly as an example to the circuit riders of both provinces. The naming of Cokesbury is a little triumph in itself in that it combines the names of both. The name of Asbury, by itself, turns up in almost every direction.

To begin with, I think you will be interested in the sly implication that the cures delineated in these yellowing pages, effective as they well might be for all, would be especially effective among the supporters of Methodism. They were frankly urged, under pontifical imprimatur, to increase and perhaps confine their reading to books so recommended. The good bishops themselves make this suggestion in a remarkable addition to the preface directed to "the members of the Methodist Episcopal Church":

"The grand interests of your souls will ever lie near our hearts but we cannot be unmindful of your bodies. In several parts of this extensive country, the climate, and in others, the food, is unwholesome; and frequently, the physicians are few, some of them unskilled, and all of them beyond the reach of your temporal abilities. . . .

"Simple remedies are in general the most safe for simple disorders, and sometimes do wonders under the blessing of God. In this view we present to you now the primitive physic published by our much honored friend, John Wesley. But the difference being in many respects great beyond this country and England [this was the American edition] in regard to climate, the constitution of patients, and even the qualities of the same simples, we saw it necessary for you, to have it revised by physicians in this country, who at our request have added cautionary and explanatory notes where they were necessary, with some additional receipts suitable to the climate. In this state we lay the publication before you and earnestly recommend it to you.

"As we apply all the profits of our books to charitable causes, and the promoting of the work of God, we think we have some right to entreat you (except in particular cases), to buy only our books, which are recommended by the conference, and signed with our signature: and as we intend to print our books in future within the States, and on a much larger scale than we have hitherto done, we trust we shall be able soon to supply you with as many of the choicest of our publications, as the time and temporal abilities of those of you, who do not live a life of study, will require. We remain, dear brethren, as ever . . ."

There you have the preamble and there are several aspects which should be underscored, apart from the discoveries made later in many parts of New Jersey, that men and women are still quietly selecting the old herbs, or simples, and using them in much the same way as Dr. Wesley suggested. First, the

64

Bishops Coke and Asbury give every indication that they themselves kept fit for rigorous journeys with folk cures ready like pills in their saddlebags, in either book or natural form. Second, they altered the text as it appeared in England in at least twenty-three earlier editions to suit the herbs readily available on this country's frontiers. Third, they frequently recommended the judicious use of wines as part of their exhaustive prescriptions.

Here, then, are a few clues to the varied ways in which cookery and cures became closely allied, for Dr. Wesley's book, covering more than one hundred pages apart from an index and listed contents at the back of *The Family Adviser*, is called *A Collection of Receipts*. This was in 1793. In time recipes and receipts became one and the same, with the kitchen next door to the bedroom.

Dr. Wesley's own preface, inserted before that of his followers, Coke and Asbury, is at once a gastronomic history and a sermon. "As to the manner of using the medicines here set down," he wrote, after a generous bit of prying into trials and errors of the past, "I should advise: As soon as you know your distemper (which is very easy, unless in a complication of disorders, and then you would do well to apply to a physician that fears God) First, use the first of the remedies for that disease, which occurs in the ensuing collection; Secondly, after a competent time, if it takes no effect, use the second, the third, and so on; Thirdly, observe all the time the greatest exactness in your regimen and manner of living; abstain from all mixed, all high-seasoned food; use plain diet, easy of digestion, and this as sparingly as you can; drink only water, if it agrees with your stomach—if not, good, clear small beer. Use as much exercise daily in the open air as you can without weariness. Sup at six or seven on the lightest food, go to bed early, and arise betimes. Above all, add to the rest (for it is not labor lost) that old unfashionable medicine, prayer."

Thereafter came a warning against "all pickled, or smoked, or salted food, and all high-seasoned confections as well." Eight ounces "of animal food and twelve of vegetable in twenty-four hours" were adjudged sufficient for anybody. "Water, the wholesomest of all drinks," declared Dr. Wesley, "if used largely in time of digestion, is injurious. Strong and more especially spirit- ous liquors are a certain though slow poison, unless well diluted and cautiously used. . . . Coffee and tea are extremely hurtful to persons who have weak nerves. Walking, frequent cold baths and washing of the feet, and writing or reading while standing" were recommended. "The fewer clothes anyone uses, by day or night, the hardier he will be; but the habit must be begun in youth."

Thereafter came two hundred fifty-seven numbered ailments and ways of treating them, everything from agues to the making of Stoughton's Drops and Dr. James' Powders—these were as celebrated in their day as were Daffy's Elixir and Turlington's Balsam, the empty bottles of which have revealed the site of many a forgotten town in New Jersey. As a matter of fact, little villages of the Pines seem to have used Turlington's Balsam for almost every complaint, judging from the number of bottles that have come to light in forsaken cellar holes.

There must have been more agues in John Wesley's day and in the days of his earliest followers than there are now. The point is that Dr. Wesley's *Primitive Physic* devoted two whole pages to "an ague" which "is an intermitting fever, each fit of which is preceded by a cold shivering, and goes off in a sweat." "Nothing," wrote one of the medical revisers of the early text, "tends more to prolong an ague, than indulging a lazy, indolent disposition. The patient ought therefore between fits to take as much exercise as he can bear; and to use a light diet, and for common drink, port wine and water is most proper." A wide choice of treatments is given from the boiling of yarrow in new milk, salt of tartar in spring water, and powdered camomile flowers to the eating of "a small lemon, rind and all."

Agues of children have been cured, the revered authority hastens on, "by wearing a waistcoat in which bark has been quilted."

I mentioned that once to a man near Pennington who, much to the surprise of many of his neighbors, "grew" his own medi- cines and treated himself and some of his best friends with startling success. He never had seen the Wesley book. When I told him about the vest he asked me what kind of bark was prescribed. "Peruvian bark, it says here," I told him, "used otherwise as a purgative with jalap or rhubarb."

"I don't know the kind of bark or whether jalap or rhubarb was used or not," he said, "but that would account for what made my father's vest smell so funny."

"Where is it now?" I inquired.

"We got rid of it fast. If we hadn't, it would have walked up Main Street all by itself. Funny, I never figured the Old Man went in for any of that—or this!"

The discussion moved to St. Anthony's Fire, defined as a fever "attended with a red and painful swelling, full of pimples, which afterward turn into small blisters." "Let your diet," advised Dr. Wesley in this case, "be only water-gruel, or barley-broth, with roasted apples." Already prescribed, with an increasing feeling that in many cases the cures are as violent as the complaints, are: tar-water; a decoction of elder leaves "mixed with a little camphorated spirits of wine" or lime-water made with a pound of quicklime and six quarts of spring water. But I must hasten on to "canine appetite," cured, oddly enough, "by a small bit of bread dipt in wine and applied to the nostrils."

One day I ran into trouble when I showed the Wesley book to an old man who lived down beside Clark's Pond, near Fairton. He said he knew all about folk cures.

" '. . . Dipt in wine and applied to the nostrils,' " my friend repeated, after he had taken the book from my hands and scanned the page until he found the passage. Then he handed it back and stomped off into the house. "No such thing!" he called back over his shoulder. "No Wesley ever asked a man to do anything like that!"

Asthma comes next, with stick licorice steeped in water as one of the suggested treatments, heading up such proposals as a half pint of tar-water twice a day or living a fortnight on boiled carrots.

There was a fear even then of falling hair, inasmuch as a cure for baldness is sandwiched between colorful items running the whole gamut of ailments. "Rub the part, morning and night, with onions till it is red," says Dr. Wesley. "And rub it afterward with honey. Or wash it with a decoction of boxwood."

There is a continuing theme of the use of herbs and wildflowers. In the bleeding of a wound, for instance, Wesleyans and their friends were urged to apply the tops of bruised nettles or the powder of ripe puffballs. For consumption, two handfuls of sorrel—sheep sorrel which I saw in bloom as I wandered the hills, book in hand—were to be boiled in a pint of whey.

"Or, take a cow-heel from the tripe-house ready dressed," suggests the alternative, "two quarts of milk, two ounces of hartshorn-shavings, two ounces of isinglass, a quarter of a pound of sugar-candy, and a race of ginger. Put all these in a pot and set them in an oven after the bread is drawn. Let it continue there till the oven is near cold and let the patient live on this. . . . I have known this to cure a deep consumption more than once. Or, every morning, cut up a little turf or fresh earth, and, lying down, breathe into the hole for a quarter of an hour." Who knows but that this was a forerunner of the so-called miracle molds of the earth.

For children's convulsions freshly scraped peony roots were urged as applications on the soles of the feet. Again the old, familiar plantain leaf was proposed for dropsy—"apply green dock-leaves to the joints and soles of the feet, changing them once a day," directed the medico-cleric. For earache from cold, sufferers were urged to boil rue, or rosemary, or even garlic, allowing the steam to rise into the ears. Wormwood tops with the yolk of an egg were prescribed for inflamed eyelids. Juice of ground ivy, burned mussel shells mixed with hog's lard, a "strong infusion of elder-buds," and boiled white and red sage mixed with wine are among the many ingredients of curatives listed for everything from "the green sickness," known as "depraved appetite," to "the King's Evil," which is defined as a case of swollen glands demanding "a strong decoction of devil's bit."

Armed with new ways to eliminate warts—"rub them daily with a radish"—and methods of treating the bite of a rattlesnake—"apply bruised garlic"—I took to the hills and valleys

68

and, beyond, the flatlands to the south. I usually had my little brown book in the car as I wandered the byways. Soon, especially up from Cokesbury itself, I came upon people at almost every turn to whom the ancient herbs and the cures derived from them were commonplace, at least by family hearsay. Few wanted to say much about it, whether they believed or didn't believe, whether they used the cures and cookery of their fathers or no, and many insisted that anything they might say in a modern era would make them appear foolish.

Inspired by the De Harts of Washington Crossing, who grew herbs in their dooryard as if they had been a part of everything else that happened more than a century ago, I wandered farther afield, over the Hunterdon line once again to Asbury, down below Schooley's Mountain, where Indians had first imputed magic to the waters, to a Mount Airy other than the village up from Lambertville, and finally to Wood Glen and off to Newport, once Nantuxet, in faraway Cumberland. All along the way and through the years I had met friendly people who had talked of herbs and cures, and now I went back to find out if they would be more communicative than they had been where the trail of John Wesley's *Primitive Physic* had set me off.

Although there were ardent Methodists among those I saw, I found none who knew of John Wesley's medical side or of the book-selling talents of the Bishops Coke and Asbury. It is possible that many are not presently "churched," as the modern classifiers use the term.

When I saw the name Red Mill, it was only natural that I look for the mill itself. I found it in the possession of Mr. and Mrs. John Felks, who had come there from Vienna many years before. Mr. Felks was seventy-three, he said, and his wife, who buzzed around like a bee, sixty-nine. In the beginning he had worked in Newark, and when hard times came he went back to his old trade in one of the big breweries. At Red Mill they grew herbs and made teas and other liquors for cures, the way they had in the old country. Perhaps that was why the government agents came, to see what the "liquors" really were.

"When John put electricity in the mill and when lights appeared where they never had been before so that I could help with some of the work," Mrs. Felks told me, "that's all the neighbors needed. We had talked about our home-made herb cures as liquors. One of the ministers told government men that the old red mill was doing something wrong. They came here and they soon found out."

Up the slope I heard of what used to be called "Great Spirit Tea," a mixture that demands boneset leaves, juniper berries, elder flowers, wild ginger, and "flag root"—all for the home-spun treatment of fevers. Martin Rippel, who lived on the table-top that is Hunterdon's other Mount Airy, was not at all reluctant to admit that snakeroot, nightshade, boneset, and all the other ingredients grew in profusion "all over the mountain."

Rippel, who retired from the Army in 1935, walked the mountain like a drill sergeant on parade. I used to see him marching along in the middle of the dirt roads, as if to the accompaniment of a military band. Tall and gaunt, and swinging his arms as do the regiments of England, he seemed to be in uniform no matter what he wore. Although he said that he was a native of Pittsburgh, it seemed evident that he had picked up some of the speech habits of the people around him.

"Plantain?" he repeated, musing. "Sure, lots of it. Use it for cholery and pleurisy, too—that's what the old people up here say." Then he told me guardedly of finding a rare herb which he dared not mention for fear of an Oriental invasion. And he added quickly, in case I might have new questions ready, that never had he associated any kind of cures with "the Methodist brethren." "The Methodists," he said, looking down from a great height with professorial dignity, "had a difficult time up here. Why, there was a time when the Dutch Reformed Church 'read out' its members around here for listening to what the Methodists had to say."

I left Martin Rippel to his chores on the mountainside, digging deeper into the uses of such necessaries as might be required in a liver tonic originally calling for liverleaf, mayapple root, and something he referred to as "sacred bark." I went beyond the hills that once were in isolated possession of the Lances and

Cassners. Still beside the waters of Spruce Run, I was told of Isaiah Bryant, principal landowner in days when the name of the village was changing to Slabtown. It was Bryant, they said, whose house was on the corner, and there was his millpond. But his mill disappeared long ago and even a successor, the Apgar mill, was out of action when I was there. But the neighborhood talk was not of Bryant or the Apgars or even the mills that had been and were no more—it concerned the best "receipt" that "everybody knew all about."

This, I discovered with a little prying, was "kidney leaf compound," a "cure" that combined a leaf of that name with sassafras, raspberry leaves, elecampane, bull nettle, and gravel plant, with something I never had seen—the "cheese plant."

Everywhere new friends and old want to know what is happening to a book I had once thought of writing when I found that in New Jersey, at least, kitchen cookery went with country cures. Based on discoveries from homemade little books that began listing the cures at one end and the cookery recipes at the other (or are they truly more properly in the reverse of such a sequence?), I had always wanted to call it, quite simply, *Cures and Cookery*. When they heard what was afoot, men and women began looting their attics for the family secrets scrawled in the backs of other books or painstakingly inscribed in home-stitched pocket manuals.

One day there must be woven into the pattern of people and places the remedies they brewed and powdered, leaving behind them on adjoining pages such questionable delicacies as "bream pie" and ways to make varnish at home.

7 ✑

Purses of the Dead

Here and now I must tell the story of a Frenchman who died at the end of a rope in the square at Morristown, on a gibbet that used to be just about where the flagpole is now, a gallows which remained intact but forgotten in the loft of the courthouse nearby. The ghost of this villain is said to come back over the ground of his last earthly journey every now and then, looking for a gruesome pocketbook. This purse, they told me at the beginning, could not have been his as long as he lived, and that was enough of a riddle to set me wandering.

In the 1830's there lived in Morristown an elderly and respected couple named Sayre. Their home remains today—concealed by new lines of Winchester's Inn—"on the west side of South Street, a short distance north of the corner of Madison avenue." The house itself goes back to 1749. When Ambrose E. Vanderpoel, who edited the personal memoirs of his uncle, Edwin Ely, referred to the place it was in the possession of the Lidgerwood family. Behind it was a stable which is now a mere hole in the ground, or less, bordered by foundation stones. This building is vital to the story—as vital as the house turned inn.

In the days of the Sayres a Frenchman whose name seems to have been John P. Fusier maintained a boarding house at 75 Fulton Street, New York, a place that had become what now would be a kind of international employment agency subject to an anti-Communist inquisition. At the very least it was a resort of M. Fusier's countrymen and to it was directed the attention of men and women who wanted servants fresh from France. On

72

or about April 29, 1833, Samuel Sayre journeyed to Fusier's, stating that he wished to employ a gardener.

The man who claimed to meet the specifications was Antoine LeBlanc, who had come from France but three days earlier and whose plans, although he took care to say nothing about them, were to accomplish his purpose and take ship home as soon as he could. There he would join the girl who, he said later, was waiting for him. "Although the stranger's knowledge of English was very meager," says the Ely-Vanderpoel record, "Mr. Sayre seemed pleased with his personality and chose him in preference to a number of other applicants."

There is no certainty that LeBlanc knew anything about gardening but the memoirs say bluntly that he was a moral degenerate who, within a week, planned to murder the family of his employer, rob the house, and return with his plunder to his native land. The writer of the memoirs has said that LeBlanc chose a Saturday for his crimes so that the absence of the Sayres might not be noted until Monday, when, if he was lucky, he would be on the high seas. There is a contradiction here, for Antoine LeBlanc, although planning so well, threw caution to the winds once his foul deed had been begun. His greed overcame his first intention to take nothing but money and a horse, and frustrated his hope of easy escape. The Saturday night he chose was May 11, 1833. On that night he induced his employer to accompany him to the barn where he "terminated the old gentleman's existence."

In his confession, a part of a brochure which bears the title of *Murder of the Sayre Family at Morristown, New Jersey, by Antoine LeBlanc, May 11, 1833*, the culprit says that he went to the house and found Mr. Sayre shaving.

"I pretended to be frightened," he wrote, "and indicated that something was wrong in the stable." All of this was written, it is explained, from the notes of an interpreter. "I ran out and waited inside the stable door. There I hit him with the back of a spade, on the left side of the head. I aimed another blow at his forehead just to make sure. Then I dug a hole in a heap of manure" and quickly concealed the body.

Mrs. Sayre was decoyed from the house in the same way and by a similar understatement, that something was wrong in the stable. "She came out in a hurry without any light. I hit her the same way," said LeBlanc. The blow was not as well aimed and the aged woman began to scream. "I gave her another blow but with like effect; she screamed again and again, clinging hold of me, and begging for her life, and it was not until I gave her several blows that I brought her to the ground. I got tired of striking her with the spade and then I kicked her on the head with my heavy-shod boots. She died a terrible death and I see her every time I close my eyes to sleep.

"When I found she was dead," he went on, "I covered her up in the same manure."

LeBlanc then described his third murder, for it is evident that he planned all three from the start. "I then went to the kitchen," he said, "with a club in my hand. I took a light, went softly up the stairs to the garret where Phoebe, the colored woman, was sleeping, and with a single blow she passed into eternal sleep. . . . She did not stir after I had first struck her. I then took the chissels [sic] where I had seen the carpenter put them into the cornstalks, and opened all the drawers and trunks in the house. My object only was money. The silver money found around me" —presumably when he was caught—"belonged to Mr. Sayre, as also the change the sheriff took from my pocket, except for a few shillings left from the five-franc piece which Mr. Sayre gave me. I would not take the paper money, as I did not know the value of it, and I was afraid it would lead to my detection; nor would I take the silver spoons, etc., for the same reason."

There were obvious changes in plan, for an array of loot dropped from the horse's back and blazed a trail to LeBlanc's hiding place next day. Furthermore, why did the carpenter conceal his tools among the cornstalks? Had he planned to join LeBlanc in his dreadful deed and then withdrawn? At any rate, LeBlanc describes how he changed his bloodstained clothes for one of Mr. Sayre's suits and then saddled a horse.

"The beast would not go very well," he declared. The memoirs state that LeBlanc stowed too much loot into pillow cases which he suspended from the saddle, some of which fell to the ground between Morristown and the Newark flats which, after losing his way, the fiend eventually reached.

The horse "wanted to go in at a white house in the first village I came to," perhaps because this was a house visited by the Sayres. Later, after the culprit found the horse repeatedly unmanageable, he decided "to cut the horse's throat, but she ran away while I was resting." The Frenchman wound up his version by saying that he did it all for Marie, whose name appears in the record in just that fleeting declaration.

LeBlanc was caught by the sheriff and his Sunday morning sermon-deserting posse and brought back to Morristown. The gallows still in storage at the Morris County courthouse was used to dispatch him and his mortal remains were even more roughly disposed of than were those of the Sayres and poor Phoebe. The record tells that "the execution was witnessed by a great multitude assembled from all parts of the surrounding country. The gibbet was erected on or near the present site of the liberty pole and was guarded by a strong body of militia. The body of the murderer was delivered to Doctor Isaac Canfield, a local surgeon, for the purpose of dissection."

The skeleton was articulated, we are told, and "the skin was tanned and certain portions of it used in the manufacture of pocketbooks and similar mementos of the occasion, one of these gruesome souvenirs being now in the possession of the New Jersey Historical Society."

Officials of the society had lost track of the pocketbook when last I inquired and so LeBlanc's ghost can be safely imagined seeking his skin.

In the Rutgers University Library copy of the Sayre brochure I found a three-cornered bit of something that looked like parchment or even leather, and proved to be neither. Under it, written in a careful hand, were these words, serving as a kind of caption:

"A piece of the tanned skin of LeBlanc, taken from his right arm, given to me by Davis Vail, late of Iowa, but now of Boston, Massachusetts. Montrose, New Jersey, October 26, 1881."

I tried to interest Commissioner Sanford Bates in the story when we shared a television program not long ago, seeking to prove that in penal methods we have left behind much of the brutality that was New Jersey's own. I don't know if he believed the story of New Jersey executions at which confessions were sold in the crowd, to which special trains were run by enterprising railroads, and where, as it is now obvious, a man's skin was cut into portions suitable for more unpleasant souvenirs.

Donald Sinclair of the Rutgers University Library agreed with me, however, that we have come a long way, and he produced many brochures in addition to the Sayre booklet. Here are some of the titles:

The Life and Confession of Bridget Dergan, which reveals details of the murder of "Mrs. Ellen Cariell, the lovely wife of Doctor Cariell, of New Market, New Jersey, to which is added her full confession and an account of her execution at New Brunswick."

The Great Trunk Mystery, in which the murder of Alice A. Bowlby of Paterson is recounted in detail. Title pages themselves are works of art, for little is left to the imagination and we know at once that Miss Bowlby's body was "placed in a trunk and labelled for Chicago." The illustrations are line drawings made in 1872, indices to a case in which there were many strange incidents and a sinister unlicensed medico who, as far as I could find out, was never found guilty.

Trial of Peter B. Davis for the Murder of Baltus Roll is surely a story by itself. Peter Davis lived in Camptown, Essex County, and was directly accused, with Lycidius Baldwin named as an accomplice. A neat subtitle on the false title page is just this: "He was found a corpse in his bed."

I must look into *The Highlands Mystery* one of these days, for the brochure about it recounts details of the trial and execution of one James P. Donnelly, accused of dispatching Albert S. Moses at the Sea View House, Highlands, in 1887. This little book was prepared by A. H. Morris, a member of the jury that found Donnelly guilty. "Perhaps no crime has ever been committed and tried before any tribunal that created a deeper and more widespread interest," the front page maintains.

A different note is sounded in *The Protest of Peter W. Parke, Who Was Executed on Friday, August 22, 1834*, in which "he declares his innocence to the last minute of his life, also his opinion concerning the Changewater Murder with a brief examination of the character of the testimony of some of the principal witnesses for the State." This item was frankly published for the benefit of Peter's widow and three orphaned children and, issued in New York, was sold "at all periodical stores."

And there are other titles, such as *The History of the Woodward Trial at Newton*, in 1876, and *The Trial of Peter Robinson*, in 1841, involving the murder of Abraham Suydam, Esquire, president of the Farmers' and Mechanics' National Bank of New Brunswick.

This kind of literature sired the penny dreadfuls of the day and was based on actual cases. In many instances the sales served to pay funeral expenses of those who were executed or to give a few extra dollars to the family thus bereaved. In others, public demand for excitement went the full gamut.

Eayrestown is one of the oldest towns in all New Jersey. Not far from Lumberton, it was once a busy shipping point on the Rancocas, the old Northampton River. Eayrestown told me its story in sporadic chapters, the first coming from Mary Moore, an old lady who was making the most of a home in the closed grocery store, a makeshift curtain draped across its sagging window. Some of the weather-black workmen's houses, going back to the time when the sawmill and the gristmill were established—a sawmill was there in 1712—were empty even then, but George Stricker had built a new mill on the foundations of the old. Then the town began to die. Or is it dead?

8

The Old York Road

A lot of people firmly believe that the Old York Road sets out, wanders off, and comes to an end on the western side of the Delaware River. And that is why I must tell you as much as I can about this road which, by its very name in both New Jersey and Pennsylvania, gives a clue to the fact that from the very beginning it led a bumpy but fairly direct way from Philadelphia to York State and what now is New York City. By this time most of the mud is gone and some of the tarred or macadam curves have been left to their own pleasant devices by more efficient but less picturesque ribbons of concrete but, even so, many of the old houses and, more to the point, the old legends hold on.

Quite easily I could have been among those who thought that the Old York Road, as the signs proclaim it even today in Philadelphia, remained on that side of the river. My fond parents led the family with almost weekly regularity to picnic in Willow Grove Park, which in those days was as well known for symphonic music as it was to become for attractions of the midway. The way to Willow Grove was out the Old York Road, by trolley car. In late summer, if we were lucky, we had the added thrill of at least part of the ride in "open cars," protected when it rained by pull-down curtains that flapped in the wind as the trolleys lurched and rolled.

I soon discovered, however, that I had known only a small section of a celebrated and historic highway that crossed at New Hope into Lambertville, pushing on through Mount Airy,

Ringoes, Larison's Corner, Reaville, Three Bridges and Raritan, and then through Plainfield, Scotch Plains, Westfield, Elizabeth, and Elizabeth Port. Travel only a part of this ancient highway and you will soon pick up the skeins and clues of something vital—descendants of some of the earliest pioneers of the old road still live beside it. If you make a business of being casual you will hear stories of grandfathers and grandmothers who came home with bruises, chilblains, minor lacerations, and tall tales of wonderful journeys in the "Swift-Sure" stagecoaches "far away."

I have traveled the length of the Old York Road many times and often have had my dog-eared copy of Emogene Van Sickle's *The Old York Road and Its Stage Coach Days* beside me. It is a source book of information as commendable in its scope as it is lacking in organization. I would urge you to begin at Lambertville, the old Coryell's Ferry, and then go out the Naraticong Trail through Mount Airy, where the old road has been deserted by the state highway; through Ringoes, where John Ringo set up a tavern in spite of himself; and then from Larison's Corner to a point beyond Centerville where you will become engulfed in neighborhood arguments as to where the road was and wasn't.

We shall pause briefly at Coryell's Ferry in order to spend a little more time in the shadow of the old Amwell Academy, home of the Tenting School, and close by the mammoth stone marking the grave of Johann Peter Rockefeller, antecedent of all the Rockefellers. We must go back to days when enterprising citizens provided rude ferryboats and gave their names to the fords and crossovers, picturesque names that remained until bridges replaced ferries, mostly after the War of 1812. Coryell's Ferry was long the memorial of George Coryell, a public-spirited citizen who gave land for the Union Presbyterian Church and cemetery in 1817.

The old bridge between New Hope and Lambertville was far different from the one there today, repaired and repaired again after damage by floodwaters that have sometimes isolated whole areas of the town. It was a covered crossing, one of the few that remained to recall a time when crossing the river was still a romantic adventure, one of the first to replace the little boats known to George Washington's time and not the larger craft from Durham Forge that made the crossing for the Battle of Trenton possible. Benjamin Parry joined with Samuel Ingram and others to complete what they called a wooden tunnel over waters that were frequently very turbulent. By that time Captain John Lambert had come into prominence as a United States senator, combining the establishment of a post office, the completion of the bridge, and the building of some of the older houses in 1814.

Then it was that John Coryell, son of George and an officer in the Revolutionary War, had built a house at the corner of Church and Main Streets. And it was only natural that Captain John Lambert, nephew of Senator John, should find the operation of the first post office in what had been the old ferryhouse an enjoyable task. Captain John, however, had other ideas and so, with the coming of the bridge, he built the Stage House which now is operated as a hotel under a newer name. Here the stage horses were changed until the Belvidere and Delaware Railroad, the old "Bel-Del," pushed through its tracks along the river in 1853.

If you pass through Lambertville intent on a destination farther along, you may conclude that what remained of the Old York Road, in spite of the transition from ferry to bridge to stagecoaches to trains and buses, was buried long ago. That isn't quite true. Linger long enough to seek out York Street and you will discover that a segment of the old trail is much the same as it used to be, with some of the older houses standing guard beside it. The same is true of Mount Airy, where the old road insists on climbing up through the old village with imperishable fidelity.

Such a realization came suddenly one day when, looking on the old signposts that had been left unharmed within sight of the Mount Airy Presbyterian Church, I came upon an old friend, Paul Holcombe, and his brother, Harold. They pointed out that deeds to property in the vicinity refer to the road down to forgotten Bowne Station as "the Queen's Road." This is curious because Mrs. Van Sickle says early in her book that, although no record had been found of any decision having been made by which ferry the stagecoaches should go, a deed at Ringoes, dated in August, 1726, described the York Road itself as "the King's Highway." The Holcombes made no reference to family trees but I can tell you that it was John Holcombe who, as early as 1705, "took up" several thousand acres of land opposite Wells's Ferry, now New Hope, on a part of which Lambertville was to become a small city.

The Ohio Company, formed by veterans of the Revolution, had bought more than a million acres of land from the government in 1787, and once the War of 1812 was out of the way the "National Road" was completed, continuing the Cumberland Road from Baltimore to Cumberland and on across the Alleghenies. The Old York Road was supposed to be a feeder to this new and, for those times, elegant highway, so that carts, covered wagons, and other vehicles chiefly associated with the western migration rolled down to Lambertville to cross the Delaware in an almost unending procession.

The Historic Sites Commission's roadside markers tell something here and there about the celebrated "Swift-Sure Line"; but these stagecoaches are said to have borne little resemblance to the old "stagewagon" of 1765, a rolling egg-shaped vehicle in which almost anything could happen and often did. The Swift-Sure was equipped with Troy post coaches, built broad and high and mounted on leather straps that made many riders landsick. What is more, many a passenger was almost crippled by a ride merely to Philadelphia and back, no matter what comforts were boasted of on the old posters.

This fact was revealed firsthand one day by a chatty and ragged old gentleman—Walter Fisher, of Ringoes. At that time he was seventy-six, but as chipper as ever and more energetic than many men of fewer years. "A lot of people," he told me, "have come to think that the road didn't go anywhere. I remember my grandfather going to Philadelphia on one of the stages. Cornelius Chew Fisher, his name was, and he told us all about the trip he made when he was sixteen. The coach must have been crowded because he had to lie on the bottom to get any comfort at all on the way home.

"Trip sort of crippled him, it did. His left hand was always bent a little after that, as if by arthritis or something. But the trip didn't do him any permanent harm, for he lived to be over ninety." Walter Fisher took time out to enjoy his tobacco more thoroughly and then, apropos of nothing, indulged in a moment of philosophy on the subject of man's eternal pursuit of money. "Money," he said, evolving a simile that is new to these records of Jerseyana, "is like leaves. You get a lot of it and suddenly it blows away. It don't mean anything, really."

I cannot tell you whether Cornelius Fisher traveled "all the way" to Philadelphia by the Swift-Sure or by a coach operated by its rival, the New York and Philadelphia Mail Stage, which left Philadelphia every Monday, Wednesday, and Friday at 8:00 A.M., arriving in New York the following day. The stopover was in Centerville, and the second day's journey came to an end, if all went well, at 2:00 P.M. Leaving New York, usually at 10:00 A.M.—apparently New York departures required a little more time—the horses were fed along with the passengers in Centerville, and arrival in Philadelphia was billed for 4:00 P.M. the day after. An advertisement in the New York *Post* in the summer of 1832 had this to say about the ride:

"The Swift-Sure Line is the pleasantest line now running between New York and Philadelphia. Fare reduced to $2.75. Passengers by this line start from New York every Monday, Wednesday and Friday morning at ten o'clock from Pier Number One, Washington Street, corner of the Battery, in the splendid new steamboat 'Cinderella' for Elizabethtown Point, Westfield, Scotch Plains, Plainfield, Bound Brook, Somerville, Centerville and lodge at Flemington." Presumably the Flemington stop was a later development because facilities at Centerville proved limited when some coaches sought sleeping quarters for riders traveling in both directions. "Start next morning via Ringoes, Lambertville, New Hope, Buckingham, Willow Grove and Jenkintown and arrive in Philadelphia to dine. This line travels thru a pleasant part of the country on a good road, and traveling by daylight will afford a pleasant mode of conveyance for ladies and gentlemen wishing to avoid night traveling between New York and Philadelphia."

A similar advertisement issued in January, 1832, refers to the steamboat *John Marshall* as a means of crossing the river and quotes a price of $4.25. Applications for seats were directed to the United States Mail Coach Office, then located at "Old Number One Cortlandt Street . . . second office from Broadway, in New York." Facilities were offered for extra baggage, boxes, and packages, although everything was taken aboard at the passengers' risk. The increased fare may also have included lodging at one of the three inns then in Flemington, operated by Mahlon Hart, Nathan Price, and Stephen Pharo. The biggest and best was Mahlon Hart's and its counterpart, the Union House or Union Hotel, still on the same site, was known to every correspondent and legal luminary of the Lindbergh kidnap trial.

However, I had no intention of leaving you stranded at either Mount Airy or Ringoes as no doubt the coaches did on many occasions in spite of the skill of drivers who knew how to handle from four to six horses on rutted and twisting roads. The saying goes in at least the Hunterdon countryside that a man who couldn't knock a fly from the hip of a lead horse with a casual flick of the whip was seldom permitted to hurry the Swift-Sure coaches through, but, even so, many riders had to walk their way to the Stage House at Mount Airy, now a private dwelling, or John Ringo's tavern, farther on, when wheels came off or horses went lame. John Ringo's inn, replaced after a fire that destroyed the old tavern in the spring of 1840, was probably a rather comfortable place in which to take time out.

"To make no mention of the first wilderness tavern, built along this ancient highway, would be an injustice to the name of Ringoes," wrote Mrs. Van Sickle. "From a trading post for both Indians and whites, and the first public shelter between Elizabethtown and the Delaware River, like the little village it founded, the tavern at Ringoes grew, keeping pace with the needs of the traveling public, being among the most popular hostelries east of the Delaware River." John Ringo, its first proprietor, had no intention of establishing a tavern and stopping place at all, but his frequent sieges by visiting relatives and other company forced him into the business.

"He had a pretty good house and, first thing you know, a lot of people find it convenient to stay there overnight," one old man told me long ago. "First it was John's relatives and then a whole army of relatives and friends. Rather than have them eat him out of business he started a tavern."

John Ringo as an innkeeper "was a staunch patriot," wrote Mrs. Van Sickle. "Long before the Declaration of Independence was signed, 'protest meetings' were held here, some of which are on record; while General Washington's portrait hung above the tavern door for half a century. John Ringo lived to be a very old man. He, like Henry Landis the saddle-tree maker, who was in his ninety-third year when he died, saw Ringoes grow from a few log cabins in a clearing to a thriving manufacturing village." The tavern stood where the Holcombe house later became well known—another of the Holcombes, for they are truly everywhere in this neighborhood—but it remained in the possession of the Ringo family more than seventy-five years.

You will have to search for the shaft that marks John Ringo's grave, almost in a backyard of the town. The name truly was Ringo at the beginning. It had become Ringoe's as in "Ringoe's Old Tavern" in an advertisement announcing its availability for rent or for sale in 1830 and, finally, the Ringoes of today. A not too dissimilar monument recalling George Coryell may be found near the Presbyterian church in Lambertville, reminding us that George was "the last survivor of the six men who laid the Father of Our Country in His Tomb."

Not long before John Ringo's inn was closed, there was the threat of fire. Later, after it was closed so that none but tramps could find a night's lodging there, fire became more than a threat and the historic tavern burned to the ground on April 22, 1840. The "New Tavern" was erected on the same site in time to serve the best years of the Swift-Sure stages and this building remains at the corner, distinguished by a firehouse, a Grange hall, and several garages. However, business as a tavern moved up the road to what used to be the Amwell Academy.

Here I want to tell you about my search for Pickle's Mountain. Where was it? Some historians, and others who should know, insisted there had never been such a place, but my own feeling was that it existed and that New Jersey's earliest Germans were a part of its story. I couldn't be certain of the spelling—Pickle or Pickell—but I was sure it had a German background.

The conclusion that most of the first settlers in Ringoes were German was supported by a 1721 survey which called it "the palatin's land." Johann Adam Boellisfeldt, one of thirty members of the German Reformed Church, had simplified his name at Copper Hill to John Bellis. And over at Sand Brook, William Rittinghuysen, formerly one of the Pennsylvania Dunkers, had become William Rittenhouse about 1719. Herr Pickle was somewhere here, I felt sure.

John Wanamaker and John D. Rockefeller were, it is now well known, descendants of this early congregation. Almost as impressive as the United Presbyterian Church of Amwell, just across the road at Larison's Corner is the massive granite stone in the ancient cemetery commemorating Johann Peter Rockefeller. But Hiram Edmund Deats, of Flemington Junction, who knows his Hunterdon County history and genealogy thoroughly, has insisted that Johann Peter isn't buried at the Corner at all but in a family graveyard not far out of Rocktown, all of five miles away.

Mr. Deats never has been wrong in any of his assertions, so far as I know, and the great pity of it is that he never has written down much about people and places in the county that once covered far more territory. He has reiterated his assertion about the big tombstone, large enough to hold down a whole army of Rockefellers. Almost within a pebble's toss of that memorial and overlooking the rolling charm of the valley to the east, there are stones recalling Henry Rockafellow, Jacob Rockefellar, and Elizabeth Rockafellar.

Farther along, among the field stones that bear only initials, are others defying the years as well as the weather with deliberate German script. Here, again, are Fishers—John, who married Cornelia Skillman and lived in the fine old house beyond Ringoes which, in its first century, proudly owned up to its name, "Queen of the Valley."

Across the road from the Larison's Corner burial place are the ruins of what once was another celebrated inn, as distinguished as the old storehouse in Mount Airy. Mrs. Van Sickle has said that Larison's Corner should have gone down in history as Sporting Corner, for it seems that George Thompson, an Englishman, built it in 1798 with money borrowed from Tunis Quick. A year later the tavern and the 55-acre tract adjoining it was sold at public vendue, and the record shows that it went to Quick for £302. A newcomer calling himself Edmond Burke took over in 1800, and he was succeeded rather quickly by a long line of owners until John W. Larison arrived, giving the corner at least its most permanent name. It was under Larison's direction that the tavern became perhaps the most celebrated on the whole length of the Old York Road.

This was where sleighing parties in winter and coaching parties in summer came from as far away as Easton, Pennsylvania, meeting here with the first families of Hunterdon County. "On these festive occasions," wrote one chronicler, "the four large double-doors that divided the several rooms were opened, as well as the board partition at the west end of the room" and the whole first floor was converted into a great ballroom. "While the brilliant scenes of the ballroom give us a charming picture of youth and gaiety," wrote the author of *The Old York Road*, with an unmistakable frown, "the old tavern had its dark and sinister side. This was a room on the second floor . . ."

We are told that this room had no windows and only a single door in which was a small shuttered opening. "Heated in winter by a Franklin stove, its only light was provided by candles placed in crude sconces fastened to the wall" and casting "thin fantastic shadows over the tense and set features of the men who sat around the gaming tables where, it is said, fortunes were lost and won in a single night." This room with all the rest has

86

gone and the drovers who traveled the York Road from Pennsylvania and Ohio for the New Jersey markets are in their graves, unaware of the changes that have come to Larison's Corner, especially one which has substituted the adjective "Pleasant" for the name of an innkeeper so beloved.

Legends of the Corner are many. There is one, however, that stands above the rest. There were signs at the tavern held in readiness for hasty use in the bedrooms when the company appeared to be unusually rough: "Please remove boots before getting into bed."

But I was still looking for Pickle's Mountain. Then, suddenly, when Hubert Schmidt's *Rural Hunterdon* introduced me to Balthazar Pickel, I was home free—I knew where Pickle's Mountain was! Back of Whitehouse there is a family graveyard which, I was told, was "full of Pickles." Pickle's Mountain is only another name for Cushetunk and, I was soon to learn, Cushetunk was first Mount Ployden—the first land observed by mariners approaching New York Bay.

In a schoolhouse in New Egypt, Elder Benjamin Winchester preached the first Mormon sermon in Ocean County to all who would listen. Winchester came down from New York and, as one of the early disciples of Joseph Smith, he visited several other villages, notably Hornerstown. Joseph Smith himself went to New Egypt, called Timmons's Mill before the miller revealed that he had a store of corn in contrast to the famine around him. There Joseph Smith told a wealthy man to go to a designated tree in the middle of the woods at midnight and the voice of an angel would tell him what to do with his money. The would-be convert went to the tree as directed, but he held onto his money. He said afterwards that the angel's voice that came down from the foliage of the tree was that of Joseph Smith himself.

9

The Tenting School and Mount Ployden

I returned to the site of John Ringo's little log tavern and came upon the Amwell Academy, which I had seen first when it was empty, with an owner living in Europe. Then suddenly I remembered "the book." I always have called it "the book" because I never have seen any quite like it anywhere. I also have the *Geografy: A Text Buk in Fonic Orthografy* by the same professor, Dr. C. W. Larison, principal of "the Academy of Science and Art at Ringoes, N. J.; formerly professor of Natural Science in the University at Lewisburg, Pa.," and author of *Elements of Orthoepy* and the *Biography of Silvia DuBois*. But "the book" remains outstanding: *The Tenting School: A Description of the Tours Taken and the Work Done by the Class in Geography* at the Academy.

I do not know whether *The Tenting School* was published in Ringoes. However, the *Geografy* was issued at the Fonic Publishin Hous, Ringos, in 1885. It is quite likely that *The Tenting School*, published two years earlier, was a product of the same "Hous," now a dwelling of stone that is almost black, with a later frame addition, around the corner from the Academy, which is now a tavern.

Turning to page 93 of Dr. Larison's highly original and decidedly complete publication, there is the title: *Trip to Pickle's Mountain.* Just beyond, there is a map, nicely drawn, showing related distances to Barkey Sheaf, Stanton, Scrabbletown, White House Station, Pleasant Run, and White House. Dr. Larison's

"Tenting School" flourished in the 1870's and early 1880's. Surely this was one of the first groups of New Jersey students studying geography and allied subjects in the field.

It was Titus Quick and Hannah, his wife, who on June 1, 1811, deeded to Colonel Bishop, George Dilts, John Lequear, David Manners, and John Schenck, as trustees of the Amwell Academy, the land on which the Academy was eventually built, the consideration being $90 "with all timber excepted." The description reads: "Beginning from a corner in the center of the Old York Road in a line of the Episcopal Parsonage lot . . ." and so on. The cornerstones for this gracious old building, as proud in its mien in spite of changes as it was in the old days, were brought from a field near Quakertown. The rest of the building stone came from Sandy Ridge and the Sourland, or Sorrel-land, Mountains. The Academy was erected with subscribed funds, with additional subscriptions of time, labor teams, and volunteer masons—a procedure to which many modern churches have turned with good result. With the Academy's completion, Ringos—or Ringoes, as they have made it now—became celebrated as a place of education, students enrolling from as far away as Baltimore.

The Academy closed in 1830 and its doors remained locked until it was purchased by Dr. C. W. Larison, author of "the book," in 1868. Dr. Larison, with his brother, the Rev. Andrew B. Larison, opened the school once again on January 1, 1860, to twenty-nine pupils of both sexes. The Rev. Andrew taught Latin and Greek, his wife English and French, and C.W. the natural sciences.

Dr. Larison, whose ideas of down-to-earth teaching died, or at best suffered a serious setback, in 1881 when the school was closed following the death of his brother, leaves little to the imagination in *The Tenting School*. I have referred to it many times as the most complete guide for camping out that I have seen anywhere, discussing everything from the dimensions of the wagon to team utensils, tents, "victualing apparatus," fire irons, lanterns, and candles. "For a school of small size," wrote Dr. Larison, "the equipment for tenting need not be cumbersome or expensive. The necessaries are in a carry-all, a team, and team utensils, blankets, and implements to facilitate study and the preservation of specimens." Then he outlines what he considered indispensable for "a party of 18 persons" and, using line drawings to supplement detailed text in the same favorite phonetic spelling, he listed saws, sledge hammers, monkey wrenches, ground pins, or stakes, tableware, pans, dessert dishes, tripods for cooking kettles, drawing tools, and what appear to have been the most uncomfortable chairs ever devised.

To give you some idea as to the detail in which the good professor all but lost himself, I quote what he said under the elementary heading *Lanterns and Candles:* "To illuminate, we usually use lanterns and candles. One or more lanterns are always needed to illuminate, in case for any cause, we should be benighted, or should need to attend the team, in the night. These lanterns act equally well to illuminate the tents. Altho we retire early, yet oftentimes, someone or ones wish to write at night. Then the lantern serves well. Candles are useful. But, unless the air is calm, they flicker and go out. As a rule they are very unsatisfactory. Two good lanterns usually suffice for all purposes."

I wish I could have seen the Larisons and their charges on the move, or, for that matter, bedded down for the night. When the students set out for Pickle's Mountain, they secreted away in the special compartments of the carryall such equipment as drawing tools, drawing cards for the making of maps, telescopes, compasses, barometers, plant boxes, microscopes, dissecting tools, jars of alcohol for "the preservation of anatomic and zoological specimens," steel chisels "for dressing or boring rocks," and small magnets "to determine the condition of iron ore." Multiply this and more by eighteen and you have something to pull for four horses on the back roads years ago.

Dr. Larison drew pictures, or had them drawn, so that the engravings in the book left no problems at all even for the flighty mind. When he talked about a water net, one suddenly appeared between paragraphs; when he spoke of dissecting tools, scalpels, scissors, and even ordinary hammers, he tossed in reproductions without extra charge. However, in demonstrating the individualistic traits of the wagon, or carryall, he outdid himself but at the same time left one or two matters dangling in the air. The vehicle was so constructed that two tents would easily extend from each side, presumably one for the boys, the other for the girls. "For a party of eighteen, two tents are required. For our purpose the 'A' tent answers very well," he says, referring to an engraving so labeled. "For this tent, when separate from the vehicle, five poles are needed. . . . But our method of pitching the tent is such as to obviate the necessity for two of the end poles"—this end was attached to the wagon.

Returning to his description of the journey up Pickle's Mountain, Dr. Larison has something more to say. "Where the meridian of 74-47 west of Greenwich crosses the parallel of 40-70 north latitude rises up that bold eminence known as Pickle's Mountain. Altho an eminence of modest proportions and tame outlines, it makes a bold and attractive figure in the landscape of Central New Jersey. Viewed from any part of the Redshale Valley, it is the loftiest and the most graceful eminence in prospect. It is that part of the American Continent first seen by the mariner as he nears that inbreaking of the Atlantic known as Lower Bay. In Hunterdon County it is the eminence first lighted up by the red of the morning and the last to shed the rays of the setting sun."

Long after that I made a supporting discovery that will be best included here—not my discovery, certainly, but a reiteration of the importance of Pickle's Mountain, or Cushetunk, in the words of Dr. Charles A. Philhower, retired supervisor of schools in Westfield:

"Cushetunk Mountain is the Mount Ployden of Beauchamp Plantagenet in the Province of New Albion, 1648—of this I am certain. John Bodine Thompson has pointed this out. A map with Sir Francis Drake's picture on it, entitled *The Sea of China and the Indies*, covers 'Ould Virginia' and Maryland and the country between the Delaware and Hudson Rivers. The date on this map is 1635 and the same conclusion is borne out."

"The King of the Raritans is said to have had his fortress home on the Kushetunk Mountain," wrote John Thompson in a pamphlet that is now very rare, "where he could look out over his people dwelling on the plains below. I have seen a book printed in Holland, more than 250 years ago, in which the seat of the Raritan king is described as 'two-mile compasse, 150-foot high, a wall-like precipice, a strait entrance easily made invincible, where he keeps 200 for his bodyguard, and under it a flat valley all plain to plant and grow. . . .

"This is a very good description of the place where the road from Drea-Hook crosses the mountain into Round Valley. In that valley large numbers of Indian arrow heads have been found; and the descendants of James Alexander tell us that when he was surveying on the mountain he found the graves of seven of these Indian kings or chiefs, all buried in their Indian regalia." Presumably, the graves must have been opened. Recent wanderings and inquiries have brought forth no trace of these burials. "Beauchamp Plantagenet who wrote the book says that he 'marched, lodged, and cabined among the Indians for seven years' together with Sir Edmund Ployden, to whom the King of England had granted all these lands between the Delaware and the ocean."

We must leave the Academy now and move on toward Reaville, Centerville, and Somerville, but not before I share with you Mrs. Larison's accounting of how the students fared, stomach-wise. Lambert Reed furnished fifteen pounds of sugar. Mary Rudebock provided seven pounds of sausage, two loaves of bread, thirty-six eggs, eight pounds of cheese, two tumblers of jelly and one cake, for a total value estimated in those days at $3.49. Bennie L. Johnson brought twelve pounds of cheese, two dozen eggs, two loaves of bread, and another cake. Orville Dilts turned in five pounds of coffee, thirty light cakes, two loaves of bread, fourteen pounds of ham, and another cake, presumably larger, all valued at $4.01. Other gifts of food were made by Sarah, Mary, and George Prall; Jennie Dilts, Lizzie LaRue, and Dr. Larison, himself, who seems to have departed from the routine with a liking for strawberries and fish, perhaps picked up on the way. The whole tour of what was described as "central New Jersey" called for a total investment of $28.09 in food, with an additional expenditure of $17.61 for such items as oats and hay for the horses, kerosene for the lanterns, and tools which, incredibly enough, had been forgotten. Amwell Academy on the move must have been a sight to behold.

Beyond Larison's Corner, Reaville had its own tavern. The names Greenville and Neshanic Ford, not to be confused with either Neshanic or Neshanic Station, disappeared quickly enough when Runkle Rea came to open the store and run the post office. There's an old haunt in this neighborhood because, no one seems to know how many years ago, a well was quickly filled up after a Negro boy had fallen into it, far beyond reach, drowning amid dreadful cries from the depths of the earth that many say they still hear.

The church which used to be a mile or more down the Old York Road, where only the cemetery remains now, is the first English Presbyterian church in Amwell, built in 1738 and moved to where you can see at least its exterior—the moving blocked the road for a time just a century later. The church was built again in 1883 and it still serves the town and the rural, rolling country around it.

One other legend still clings like the frequent ground fog to this winding segment of the road to York State. Its main character is an old slave who, given sufficient inducement, used to break things with his head. Then one night some smart aleck wrapped a millstone in cheesecloth and the performer was bidden to take a running start the way he had the previous night when the target was a wheel of cheese. To the amazement of all concerned, particularly the perpetrator of the trick, according to one variant, the Negro was hardly hurt at all. He stood still for a moment and remarked that this was "the hardest cheese I ever tried to bust."

The other variant is that the victim carried a head injury to his grave. Mrs. Van Sickle has recorded a meeting with a man from Ringoes whose father, a doctor, knew the man on whom the almost fatal trick had been played. The slave's name was Prime Hoagland, and for several days after his collision with the concealed millstone he remained unconscious. Then, following a remarkable recovery from a concussion, he took up a precarious living in a hut near Mount Airy where, lonely except when someone would call him out for a firsthand account of his encounter with the substitute cheese, he lived to an even hundred.

There were new people at the old store in Centerville when I first went there, but they failed to maintain or revive the business in a village chiefly celebrated for the fact that, as far as the twisting, winding, dipping, climbing Old York Road is concerned, it remains exactly halfway between Philadelphia and New York. There was a period of idleness in which even some of the old store's fixtures disappeared—and they made up a truly surprising collection—and then an unusually thoughtful purveyor of antiques took over, buying the counter and many of the other fittings wherever she could find them. Not all the adz marks of the old construction were retained, nor were the old ledgers or the smoky woodwork. However, some of the half-forgotten patent medicine advertisements and a notice printed for members of a local society organized to apprehend horse thieves do their best to recapture some of the old atmosphere.

Across the road that goes to Neshanic and Neshanic Station, behind a house that once was an inn, there is a large barn, something Centerville has been trying to save, year in and year out—as a community house, a meeting hall, or perhaps the headquarters of a historical society. However, some who were going about its refurbishing clearly had no plan in mind. Perhaps when you go that way you will find the stagecoach barn in which horses were changed or bedded down for the night still part of the village.

Beyond Centerville the Old York Road crosses the concrete of a state highway teeming with traffic. With this roadway, coming over from Flemington, the York Road has been quietly flirting through many a year and over many a mile. Once Larison's Corner had been attained, it clung persistently to its old ways, twisting with ease as the Indians who followed it always had. Beyond Centerville there is so much winding and so much uncertainty and so much argument as to where the old road truly ran its timeless course that many have gone back to roam the old trails with me to Somerville. There you can make the most of what is supposed to have happened when Quibble-town and Scotch Plains and Westfield grew up.

By this time, however, you may have wandered off to the pious atmosphere of the Old Dutch parsonage where Dominie Theodorus J. Frelinghuysen, the missionary from Holland, still dominates the scene, in spirit, with his five clerical sons and his two daughters who married ministers. To be sure, you may be even more interested in the attic smokehouse of the parsonage, kept going in the old days by smoke from the mammoth fireplace downstairs. As for me. I shall leave you here, either at the fringe of the noises made by the world outside closing in from the traffic circle or among the folds of quiet in the hills. I like the Old York Road best when Pickle's Mountain, or the Cushe-tunk of Tish-co-han, is watchful and still in sight.

To many the memory of Jersey Planked Shad all but restores to life the "King of Gloucester," Billy Thompson, who made the dish and all its extras a specialty at his hotel. To me the thought of planked shad brings to mind Walt Whitman. Old men along the waterfront in Gloucester told me they remembered both the "King" and "The Good Gray Poet." Whitman, they said, used to sit on the porch of Thompson's hotel facing the Delaware River. At just the proper moment, when the diners who customarily crowded the hotel in shad season were in good humor, Billy was remembered as having said something like this: "And now, if you would like some verses by Walt Whitman, I'll call him in. Walt is always ready for a good planked shad dinner."

10 ᴄᴄ⌐

The Butcher Who Was a Spy

I never have been able to make up my mind about Miss Anna Sutphen of Lamington. When she was seventy-eight and in the days that followed, she told me many things about the places and people of the countryside, things that were questioned afterwards by some of her neighbors. In many instances, however, what bothered some of the neighbors was that they hadn't told me first.

I wonder how much Miss Anna knew about John Honeyman, the spy. If she knew as much about him as I had been able to dig up in the flat and gently rolling country between Griggstown, on the abandoned Delaware and Raritan Canal, and Lamington, why did she do so much listening as I sat on the steps of her little vine-shrouded house, content to remain there because there seemed to be no room inside? There were many questions I could have asked but it is too late now.

It always has been my feeling that in spite of the telling and retelling of the Honeyman story there was still much to be discovered about George Washington's celebrated agent. Moreover, I had a hunch that when all the reminiscences were revealed, from the marginal notes in an old journal or the forgotten pages of a family diary, they would come from the neighborhood of Lamington, where John Honeyman spent the last years of his life, rather than from Griggstown where, until probably long after the Revolution people kept on saying he was a Tory.

For instance, I have no doubt whatever that John Honeyman knew Vliettown well, probably as Vliet's Mills or Vleet Mills.

96

But today that name, Vliettown, will be found only on three bridges spanning the stream—the Black, or Lamington, River—that divides Hunterdon from Somerset County. "Vliettown?" a man replied in the Lamington store, pronouncing it as if it were Fleatown. "Never heard of it." Others told me that there had been a celebrated mill at Vliettown but that more recent owners of the property had removed it, retaining the name only for a road.

The peculiar thing is that Miss Anna, quiet-voiced and genial in contradiction of the warnings that I would find her a strange recluse, proved to be one of the best audiences I ever have had. For reasons of her own she allowed me to tell the Honeyman story in my own clumsy way, all the while knowing so much of the Lamington story but especially the whereabouts of the Honeyman grave.

John Honeyman, most celebrated of Washington's spies, lies buried in a grave that was bedraggled and neglected until a few years ago, in the Lamington churchyard, the cemetery from which the church had been moved. Representatives of the Daughters of the American Revolution have searched out the marker in order to place a flag beside it once a year but, beyond that, this Revolutionary hero and most of his story remain unknown.

"Of course," Miss Anna told me, a little upset that she had overlooked the matter until I asked her about it, "I knew that John Honeyman's grave was there. It was Mrs. Ed Ten Eyck who saw something in an old magazine to the effect that John was buried in Lamington and the grave has been remembered ever since. . . ." As a matter of fact the whole graveyard has been cared for very well since the days when I first went up and down the road urging people to "climb through the grass" to find Honeyman's grave.

It was really John B. Ehrhardt, editor of the Madison *Eagle*, who showed me the way. "I saw the grave of John Honeyman," he wrote me, "on my way home from the reunion at old St. Thomas's, Alexandria, near Pittstown. I think that before we get together again you ought to see the old cemetery. . .

Actually, there is no reference at all on the marker to Honeyman's having been a colorful spy."

Here, then, is John Honeyman's story as it was given to me long, long ago by the late William E. Blackman, a descendant of Honeyman who had spent much of his lifetime gathering information about the spy, with which, as he once said, he had proved beyond a doubt that Honeyman was not a Tory as some of the experts were wont to hint.

John Honeyman was born about 1729 in Armagh, Ireland. He was conscripted into the British army in 1758 and served under General James Wolfe. He first came to notice aboard the frigate *Boyrie*, when Wolfe was a young colonel in the days that followed Braddock's defeat and when the memory of the massacre at Fort William was very much alive. Honeyman was on the deck one night, somewhere in the St. Lawrence, when his quick action prevented Wolfe's fall down a companionway. The colonel thanked Honeyman, said he had saved his life, made sure of his name, and commended him to General Abercromby.

Subsequently, Honeyman served in the attack on Louisburg, after which Wolfe, commended for bravery, was made a general. He became a member of Wolfe's bodyguard, remaining at the general's side through the defeat before Quebec and, later, the daring climb of the Plains of Abraham. Honeyman was only a few paces away when Wolfe fell, mortally wounded, and he aided those who carried the valiant commander away, as he himself expressed it to Judge Van Dyke.

The judge explained that he had been a boy with sensitive ears when he first listened to John Honeyman tell his story in Griggstown and Lamington. Honeyman, he said, remembered all the wartime scenes with remarkable clarity, even when he was ninety and frequented the old store in Lamington. With the surrender of Quebec, and later Montreal, the war was over and Honeyman was discharged. After several years, and without warning, the young Scotch-Irishman turned up in Philadelphia, carrying his discharge papers and a letter from General Wolfe, the one in which he had been asked to serve as bodyguard.

By this time Honeyman was working as a weaver and had, in

the interval of peace, married Mary Henry, a young and comely girl from Ireland. However, with war clouds gathering again, it was only natural that George Washington should want to meet Honeyman. It is known that there were several interviews, and it may be safe to assume that the removal of Mrs. Honeyman and the children from Griggstown in 1776 was part of a plan.

Washington and John Honeyman talked at Fort Lee, not long before the retreat into Pennsylvania. "The interview was hurried," wrote Judge Van Dyke, "but continued long enough to adopt a plan of operation. John Honeyman was to act the part of a spy for the American cause in that part of New Jersey with which he was most familiar. As he was a Scotch-Irishman, who already had been in the British army, witnessing its triumphs, it would not be considered strange if he still adhered to their cause." He was further to act the part of a Tory, "and quietly talk in favor of the British side of the question. In the capacity of butcher he was to commence some trade with them and furnish them cattle and horses when their armies came into the State, which was certain to speedily take place.

"This course he was to pursue while he resided within the American lines, so long as it should be safe to do so, and if danger at home became too threatening, he was to leave his helpless family amidst its angry foes and go over with the British lines, there to continue his occupation as butcher, and to supply the British with cattle."

Thus Honeyman was to learn the enemy's plans, the strength of his position, and when important things were to happen. As soon as he could "learn anything with reasonable certainty, he was to venture, as if by accident, and while avowedly looking for cattle, so far beyond the enemy lines as to be captured by the Americans. Washington was to offer, if need be, some reward for his arrest, but always with the imperative direction that he should be taken alive and brought before him in person, his object being not only in some way to protect his agent, but to receive his communications in the absence of all listeners, and then to devise some unsuspected means for him to make his escape back to the British lines."

If the fable that John Honeyman was a Tory can be traced to anything it is to the understanding, put abroad in the ranks of both sides, that Honeyman had capitulated to the invading forces. Honeyman, his wife, and General Washington were the only ones who knew the true story. Honeyman saw the Commander in Chief in November, prior to the Battle of Trenton. A month later he was moving along with the British so that, aware of the conditions that existed among the Hessians and knowing that they would celebrate Christmas with even greater relaxation, he saw the need of immediately contacting Washington.

"With a large cart whip in one hand and a rope in the other, a rather greasy-looking coat on his back," wrote Judge Van Dyke, Honeyman started out "in search of cattle" along the banks of the Delaware River. He spotted two American soldiers before they spotted him and, making a show of chasing a farmer's cow, allowed himself to be caught, as the horsemen believed, with great difficulty. There was an exciting chase, a few stumblings on the ice, and then amidst protests that he was but a poor tradesman eking out a living for his family, Honeyman surrendered, with two pistols at his head.

"The butcher was firmly bound with his own rope and mounted behind one of the troopers," says the record, "while the other rode by his side with the other end of the rope fastened to his saddle-bow. He was taken across the river and borne in triumph to the headquarters of Washington, with some demonstrations of satisfaction. The Commander had already admonished his troops to look out for such a person, who was understood to be dangerous, to arrest him if possible, and without fail to bring him to him instantly." The ruse had worked.

Honeyman was, above everything else, a clever actor. He was the center of a convincing scene at Washington's headquarters in the field. "Washington," wrote Judge Van Dyke in the record that Blackman discovered and rearranged, "was unusually grave, but spoke calmly to the spy, telling him that it was painful to see him in such a plight; that he had heard of him before, and that for some time his troops had been trying to arrest him."

Then the general cleared the room. The private interview lasted half an hour, after which the guards were recalled, told to stand outside the door of the log-house prison, and instructed to make ready for a court-martial in the morning.

"Late in the night, when all were quiet and the camp asleep, except here and there a guard whose tramp could be plainly heard, a fire was observed to be breaking out in a dangerous place. It was small and could be extinguished in a few moments if done at once. No one was near to do so. The guards, who were awake, hesitated for a moment, but flames ascended rapidly, and then they instinctively rushed to the fire. In a short time it was subdued. They now returned to and remained at their posts till morning. . . ."

I always have wondered who started the fire to draw the guards away from their post. At the same time, I have wondered why, as a matter of routine, the guards did not look inside the log house on their return to see if their prisoner was still with them. When morning came the prisoner had vanished. "The camp was soon in great commotion. Washington seemed exceedingly angry. But three days afterward the latter was with his army in Trenton, the city with its Hessian occupants being captured. Rahl was slain, and the country was saved." Judge Van Dyke ended with a triumphant note of his own.

Thus it is reasonable to assume that the butcher-weaver of Griggstown and Lamington had supplied the necessary information to achieve the victory at Trenton. This I had said long ago and I repeated it for the benefit of Miss Anna, sitting there on the steaming steps of the porch of her little house, up the road that used to be an Indian trail.

"I'm always glad to know about John Honeyman," she said quietly, pushing back her wispy hair and then folding her hands in her lap. "You see, the Sutphen family sometimes has its reunions at Sullivan's Grove, which even I know is a part of where they fought and planned to fight the Battle of Trenton. Goodness, it's been all of eight years since I went to a Sutphen reunion. We'll have to do something about that."

That was when she told me that the graves of John Honeyman

and other notables of the Revolution were up in the churchyard. That, also, was when she covered up her revelation, startling at the time, with expressions of chagrin over the condition of much of the burial place. Soon after, the grass was carefully mowed and things generally spruced up. "What happened to John Honeyman after that?" Miss Anna asked me suddenly, as if she didn't know.

I told her that much of the story had been written before in little books and publications difficult to find and that I could not understand why Honeyman, as a name, was as unknown as some of the exploits of the spy whose life was quickly adapted to become one of James Fenimore Cooper's best novels. "All I've tried to do is supply some of the family's own details," I said, "as well as something of the countryside through which the man moved. John escaped over the ice and into the British camp, where he told a wild and incoherent story of his amazing escape. Colonel Rahl scolded him for needlessly exposing himself and then asked many questions. When Honeyman said that conditions in the American camp were pitiable, the commander of the Hessians decided that there was nothing to worry about. John once again became the wandering butcher and pushed off toward New Brunswick."

What happened at Griggstown, later to become a port on a canal linking the Delaware with the Raritan River, is anybody's guess—beyond the dramatic climax of John Honeyman's adventures, the truth of which was not believed in spite of the most convincing proof. Why, otherwise, would the Honeymans have hurried off to another home, up Lamington way? For some reason Mary Honeyman and the children had returned to a house which, some say, is still at Griggstown, others that the house's whereabouts always was as uncertain as those of the man who caused all the rumpus. Once John Honeyman's activities had become known, he went down in the books of his home town as a "British spy, traitor, and cutthroat." Suddenly, one midnight, his house was surrounded by a mob.

Many of these men foolishly assumed that with the war drawing to a close he would return there, so they demanded the right to search every nook and corner, threatening Mrs. Honeyman and the children and making wild threats to burn down anything that might serve him as a retreat. Faint rumors of all this came from some of the old canalmen near Griggstown, and the record of one of these excursions goes like this:

"His wife protested that she knew nothing of John's whereabouts, and seemed grieved at his misconduct, but this only increased the demand and tumult. She soon after unlocked the door, and, waving her hand, asked the crowd to listen for a moment. They became quiet, and she inquired who was their leader. The answer, 'John Baird,' came from all directions.

"Now John Baird was one of her well-known neighbors, a young man only eighteen years of age, of stalwart frame, unshrinking courage, and exceptional character, who had from the first espoused the cause of the Colonies with all the energy and enthusiasm of youth. He was afterward in the service and came out of it bearing the title of Major. In his old age he received an honorable pension from the Government.

"When the wife of Honeyman heard the name of Baird her apprehensions subsided, for she knew him well, and knew no harm could come to her or her children so long as he controlled affairs. She handed him a paper and asked him to read it aloud to those outside. He did so after first looking it over himself."
The paper which he read was this:

"To the good people of New Jersey, and all others whom it may concern.

"It is hereby ordered that the wife of John Honeyman, of Griggstown, the notorious spy, now within the British lines, and probably acting the part of a spy, shall be and are hereby protected from all harm and annoyance from every quarter until further orders. But this furnishes no protection to Honeyman himself. George Washington. Commander-in-Chief."

The mob moved off, the story goes, and John Baird gave the important letter back to Mrs. Honeyman.

"So the John Honeyman of Griggstown and Lamington was the Harvey Birch of *The Spy* of James Fenimore Cooper," said a man in the Lamington store of Fred Nelson Anthony, where

I continued to put together the details of the Honeyman story, within sight of the Honeyman tombstones, almost lost in those days under tall and tawny grass and brambles. "I wonder why and how he came to Lamington."

My own feeling about Honeyman is that the gossips at Griggstown continued to growl or, perhaps, made their feelings known even more eloquently by saying nothing at all but achieving their purpose with stares, nods, and shrugs. When John Honeyman's pension came through, as it must have after the long and tedious processes of recognition had been completed, he moved north to Lamington.

"Near the Lamington river," wrote James P. Snell in his *History of Hunterdon and Somerset Counties*, "about two miles south of Pottersville and half a mile from Vliettown, on the farm now owned by Mrs. William H. Vliet, lived during the later years of his life, John Honeyman. . . ." There follows much of the story I have given you, Snell basing his narrative on information credited to A. V. D. Honeyman. "During the war he resided in Griggstown and was a weaver," says this record, published in 1881. "Having a wife and seven children to support, he was necessarily kept in moderate circumstances; but, as a result of his valuable services to Washington, he received, it is believed, compensation sufficient to purchase the two farms he owned in Bedminster township." These farms were paid for, family historians including Judge Van Dyke declared, and Honeyman owed no one. "I remember hearing my father and mother conversing about this property," wrote the judge, "which they valued at $11,000." Judge Van Dyke was John Honeyman's grandson, I was informed in Lamington.

One farm, the homestead, included more than two hundred acres; the other, one hundred sixty-six. The first cost £500, the two more than $4,000. "He never made this money in weaving, his real occupation," Snell pointed out, stressing the fact that John Honeyman's services to his country must have been highly valued, indeed, for in those days this was a lot of money. John resided on the homestead farm from the time he left Griggstown in 1793 until 1822, when he died, a man of ninety-three with many precious memories as well as the gift of keeping much to himself except when the youngsters gathered around him in the store and begged for a story.

Mary, who has gone down in folksay as John's first wife, but in other records as his one and only, went to a grave beside him at Lamington. She died in 1801, age sixty-three.

Fred Nelson Anthony, the Lamington storekeeper who came home from Rutgers University, hung his diploma on the wall, and became proprietor where his father had been, just down the road from where his grandfather George had the corner smithy before and after the Civil War, said there was a lot more to Lamington than met the eye and that the Honeymans knew it all. The last time I saw Miss Anna Sutphen, she sent me on my way to find out more, talking of a lot of things almost at the same time—the need of green vegetables in one's diet, the care of the graveyard, Horace Greeley and his white suit, and the reading of a melancholy poem:

No one hears the door that opens,
As they pass beyond recall;
Soft as loosened leaves of roses,
One by one our loved ones fall.

Fenwick Lyell, a cabinetmaker on the Nut Swamp Road in Middletown, where he had a little shop on the King's Highway, achieved distinction although he never put his own name on his work. In Lyell's second account book, Ledger B, on view at the museum of the Monmouth County Historical Society in Freehold, is the following entry: *May 3, to 2 Sopha frames—thirteen pounds, twelve shillings; May 28, to 1 large pine table—one pound, eighteen shillings; January 25, to 1 pair Knife Cases Veneers found—sixteen pounds.* At the top of the page, dated 1809, is the startling heading: "Duncan Phyfe, debtor to Fenwick Lyell."

II

The Wonderful Auger of
Ananias Lutes

Once on a crisp December morning I went up along the Lamington River in search of the tracks, or at least the trace, of Ananias Lutes.

I thought that perhaps if I looked more carefully in the graveyard at Fairmount, or in the cemetery higher up where tombstones on the horizon prod into the sky, I might find a marker graven with his arresting name. After my first journey, however, I had to report that Ananias seemed to have been buried as obscurely as the tools of his trade were supposed to be. The story had gone around that Ananias had provided that no other man should use his big auger or anything else that was his.

For, you see, Ananias was a pumpmaker, as celebrated in the country along the borders of Somerset and Hunterdon as was Paul Bunyan in lands that are far away.

Inasmuch as the Birds, or Burds, and the Pickles, or Pickels, were prominent among the friends of Ananias Lutes, I began my researches in the then-weedy churchyard of the old Zion Lutheran Church in Oldwick, once New Germantown. As a result I came upon what is one of the most curious epitaphs in New Jersey, as well as a cidermaker by now as remarkable as was Ananias, the pumpmaker, in his day.

The epitaph adorns the grave of one of the many Pickles, in the graveyard that is north of the church which, not long after,

106

celebrated its two hundred fiftieth anniversary. It reads like this:

Me Feebel race
Has run A Pace
My Dwelling Place is here,
This stone is got
To Keep the spot
That men dig not too near.

Above this rhyme is the inscription: "In Memory of Baltes Pickel, son of Frederick Pickel, who Departed this Life March 1766 in the 20th Year of his Age." It is apparent that the stonecutter was not certain, for some reason, of the exact date of the young man's death—I say this because the stone is in the country where sermon texts were graven as sermonizing memorials with great particularity and with no concern for expense. The man who copied the jingle or evolved it for the occasion lost himself so completely in his work that he almost forgot the second "e" in the word here and, what is more, evidently put too many "o's" in spot and then had to use his chisel as a kind of eraser. There are many stones now beyond the ones that Baltes or his family knew but men as yet have not come "too near."

I came away with this sinister consideration translated into rhyme because, almost within a stone's throw of the village of Oldwick I came upon those, as I knew I would, who concluded that I had made up the rhyme myself. One of the younger men at the cider mill said as much but the cidermaker himself, Isaac Hildebrand, was noncommital.

Concerning Ananias Lutes, however, he had much to say and what he said corroborated most of the stories told about the venerable pumpmaker. "I knew him as a boy—when I was a boy, that is," Isaac told me. "His shop wasn't far from the schoolhouse and we used to watch him at work and carry his tools for him whenever we had a chance."

Ananias had been pictured to me as a man of medium build with a face as burnished and hairless as was his head. He was usually good humored, especially when there were children around. The son of Henry Lutes, he was one of the Fairmount pioneers and early in life had learned the wheelwright's trade. "His first shop was across the road from the home of John Pickle, not far from the Fairmount Methodist Church," Isaac Hildebrand said.

"I've often wondered if his shop wasn't a lot like this," he went on, indicating the whole of the apple-fumed cider shed. "This had been a wheelwright's shop here in New Germantown, which before that was Smithfield, when I bought it. The wheelwright's name was Bebeheiser and he turned out wagons, sleighs, coffins, and other things with just about the same skill. You see, he was the village undertaker in addition to everything else. Why, when I bought his shop I fell heir to his hearse as well."

The hearse vanished long ago, for Isaac Hildebrand has been pressing apples for cider at the same Oldwick stand since 1901. "Been at it lots more than fifty years," he said. "Began in the days when my principal piece of equipment was a one-horse treadmill."

Ananias had a partner whose name was Salter Bird. Together they turned out wagons and wheels, but the specialty that Ananias liked best was pumps. "After the time he was up the road near the church," Hildebrand said, "he moved near the schoolhouse and by now that's just a field at the corners of two old roads. Schoolhouse burned down long ago. His shop disappeared, too, after Ananias went away, but somehow his house stood there, boarded up, for a long while after that."

There is every indication that Ananias was the strong man of the area. Freeman Leigh, in his recollections of the neighborhood, privately printed after his death, said that "it was always the delight of the school children to stop and see him work and they were always welcome. Strong and mighty must have been his brawny arms in order to twist by hand his giant auger three or four inches in diameter its entire length through the center of a green oak log eight or ten feet long. But this he did to make the stalk of his pump. He made good sale of these to farmers around about and the remains of a few 'Ananias log pumps' may yet be seen."

I searched for them, as I told Isaac Hildebrand, who, with the help of his family, keeps on making cider until the season's apples are beyond use. Then, just about Christmas, the Hildebrands take off for Florida. "Maybe he used green oak some of the time," Hildebrand told me, "but I remember him best using chestnut. Chestnut trees are gone now, except for the dead stumps up in the hills."

According to one legend, one of Ananias's fingers had been amputated at the second joint and the sight of it always served as an excuse for Ananias to tell the children how he had served as his own surgeon to remove the infection of a felon: "Used my own chisel for the job."

Until I began wandering these hills the big mystery about Ananias, I concluded, was the whereabouts of the giant auger with which he made his celebrated pumps. "He boldly resolved," wrote Freeman Leigh, "that no one in the locality should succeed him in his favorite trade so he made away with his implements. They may be buried in the huge rocks nearby or in the depths of some abandoned well. All this remains a mystery. It would be a good quest for the small boy to seek the mysterious auger so strangely missing."

I had heard rumors that the auger and a bag of other outmoded tools had been found in a shelving of rock along the Lamington River and this, among other things, is what drew me back that brisk December morning. Then came the report that a similar find had been made in the ruins of a house that had come tumbling down on its contents in a dooryard carpeted with moss through which ran a little stream, not far from one of Ananias's old log pumps.

I found the ruins and the moss and even the stream. But there was no sign of a pump. Then came the tale that Ananias Lutes was buried near a place called Owltown, made famous for a time by Joe Lee, the Owltown fiddler. By the time I heard that, Joe was remembered only as a name and Owltown's whereabouts had become a matter for argument. However, there were those who said their parents and grandparents had remembered that Joe and Ananias were good friends.

"Owltown," it seems, was "that portion of Fairmount which lay just north of the farm buildings of Mr. John Pace on the Farmersville Road, midway between that road and the Middle Valley Road farther north." At one time there had been a cluster of houses, and the best story I have heard is that the hamlet gained its name from the owls that haunted the place. It was in Owltown that Joseph H. Lee lived, fiddling for the benefit of the folk who lingered to hear him, from the days that preceded the Civil War until his death in the 1880's.

If this information is accurate, Joe died before Ananias, who passed to his reward between 1885 and 1890, to be followed in a matter of days by his horse Shang, his familiar companion when log pumps had to be delivered.

Freeman Leigh's notes said that the location of Joe's grave was more certain than that of Ananias's and could be found in the "northeast corner of the new Presbyterian cemetery" where, it was hoped when Freeman was writing, a stone would be erected by the government. It was good to discover that Joe's grave had been marked with the simple stone customarily placed on the graves of old soldiers and that the hill served as a vantage point from which a traveler might look down on the hills Joe and Ananias knew so well.

"In the first place we must know that Joe Lee loved to fiddle for the very sake of music," Freeman wrote, and I think I know what he means if the neighbors of my youth can remember the boy who arose at six each morning to annoy them with scales and arpeggios on a violin which was not, I must say, as scratchy as most. Joe reminded Freeman of Zenophilus who, he said, lived to be one hundred five because he was kept active by his own tunes.

C. Watson Apgar, who had known both Joe and Ananias, said that the fiddler played his best when all alone, pretending that he had a vast audience, which he may have had—if you believe in the unseen as much as I do. "Then, too," the record goes on, "Joe was fond of fiddling for others, at the dances which followed the apple cuts, sometimes at the schoolhouse for the children, at other times in private houses. One person tells me of his fiddling at her father's house and then having one of her sisters recite that ditty which was said to be so pleasing to the ageless musician's ears, surely not because of its content:

> "Joe Lee is a fine old man,
> Washes his face in the frying pan,
> Combs his hair with an engine wheel
> An'll die with the toothache in his heel."

This is but a slight variation of the "jumping rhyme" used by many of the rope-skippers in many areas of the country, and I'll wager Joe Lee liked it because it "fit" any number of the dance tunes he played.

Joe, unlike Ananias Lutes, wore a full, sandy beard. There was usually a twinkle in his eye and he never was at a loss for a sharp and witty rejoinder. Watson Apgar has said that Joe had an answer for everything and that when he didn't know the correct reply he made one up.

Move in any direction throughout the middle of New Jersey and you will arrive on Schooley's Mountain, by one road or another. When Schooley's Mountain Springs was drawing people from places that were particular about the kind of neighbors they wanted in summer, Joe Lee and a neighbor, John Convil, would make the trip up there together. Joe would fiddle his way into the hearts of the colony and John, especially skilled in bagging woodcock, would sell them and make his keep at various inns.

When the Civil War was almost over Joe Lee was drafted into Company E of the Eleventh New Jersey Volunteers. "When mustering-out time came in June, 1865," one of the records discloses, "Joe with a number of recruits was transferred over to the Twelfth New Jersey Regiment and thereby his homecoming was delayed a month." Which would not be very important if it were not said that Joe made the most of his time, playing a fiddle and telling stories branded tall by some who heard them. One story concerned a certain Ananias Lutes who made some of the biggest pumps ever seen.

"Ananias had a bone felon once," he may have said, "and there was nobody he'd trust to take it off but himself. So he got out his big chisel and did the job, just like that, clean as a whistle." Whereupon the soldiers, lounging about waiting to go home, must have asked, "What did he hold the chisel with—his teeth?" Joe would have been ready for that. "Couldn't ha' done that," he would have said. "Ananias Lutes hadn't no teeth to speak of!" And there would have been a roar of laughter as the riddle went unsolved.

There I paused after the first few journeys, fragmentarily piecing together all that I could find about Ananias and his friend against the backdrop of the hills they once had wandered, one with fiddle in hand, the other with an auger of startling size that outclassed other implements that clanked in a sack slung across a brawny shoulder. But my inquiries must have left a trail, for soon I knew for certain that the wonderful auger of Ananias Lutes had not been stolen, or lost, or buried.

For a time I had the auger, with some of the other tools, procured at the end of some fevered wandering—from Somerville, to Freehold, to DeBow Church on the Monmouth Road, to Red Bank, and back through the Ocean County pines. Ananias Lutes did not hide his auger and the rest of his kit in a well or at the bottom of a cave or stream after all, as all the legends say.

Let me begin with the letter that came from a man who was obviously more familar with the legends of Ananias than with the typewriter on which he picked out this thoughtful message over the signature "L. Apgar": "I believe a man named Garret Paff, a wheelwright of North Branch, has some of Ananias Lutes's tools. Mr. Paff died some time in the Twenties but I know he gave a large auger and other tools to a man named Roy Decker, who is of Indian descent. I believe Mr. Decker now lives at Reid's sawmill, or somewhere between Reid's and Freehold, for a friend of mine saw him down that way not long ago and he seemed to be well known. I believe the Freehold post-office could help you find him or, if you wish, you might go down to Reid's mill. It is but a short distance from Freehold. . . ."

The writer, whose first name, Roy Decker later suggested, was Lew, gave no address to which a reply might be sent. However, his note was posted in Somerville. Decker, whose Indian ancestry is manifest in a variety of things, said he thought he had gone to school with an Apgar boy. The name Paff, he suggested, should be spelled Pfaff.

I set out for Freehold and the road to Asbury Park beyond. Few persons in the area, I soon discovered, made much of a response to inquiries about a sawmill and, after all, there are many Reids in the neighborhood, descendants of the Scotchmen who settled there hundreds of years ago. Coupled with the name of Reid, the distinction of "a man with a beard and one arm" always brings response, Raymond Reid told me later, but at this point I knew nothing of either.

I found Raymond painstakingly sharpening the angry teeth of a circular saw, holding the file in a way all his own but with not quite so much artistry as was attributed to Ananias Lutes and his method of attacking a bone felon. The loss of his right arm, he told me as merrily as anyone can speak of such things, was caused one summer when a new pair of gauntlets was being used for the first time. "I had worked in the same operation without any trouble for years," he said. "But this time—well, my hand was pretty well mangled. They took me off to a hospital and the doctors thought they were going to let me get away with a longer arm. Then they found they couldn't."

He actually chuckled. "The beard? Oh that's quite another story. But it's the result of an accident, just the same, a different kind of accident. I had no intention of growing a beard. But, after what happened, I was a local man of distinction. They began to know me, up around these places, as the man with a beard and one arm. It became mighty convenient. I didn't dare shave the beard off."

Mrs. Reid filled in most of the tale. Her husband had complained of a stiff neck, and the pain extended down to his shoulder so that by morning he couldn't turn around. He had no recollection of falling, he told the doctors. However, it was later revealed, after a lot of ineffective experiments, that Raymond had virtually broken his neck trying to save himself from a tumble. "He had to wear a harness for a long time. And then, when he had gradually recovered the use of his arm and his shoulders, very nearly all his friends had seen the beard and had liked it. So we trimmed it up and there it is!"

"But I still take a lot of joshing," Raymond Reid told me. "Even when I go into the gas station somebody will want to known if I lost a bet with the razor people or something."

Or, he ventured gingerly, as well his friends might comment on my own lack of stature—a local saying so good that I put it down immediately: "So tall that he needs a stepladder to look over a stake."

Reid laughed when he saw that I was not offended, quickly adding that the Reids had been in the vicinity well over three hundred years, since the earliest Scotch pioneers of that name set out their plantations. "My father," he added with a chuckle, indicating how many years a full beard can add to a man's appearance, "still lives over Red Bank way—that's where I spent much of my life. He's eighty and he raises some of the best apples in Monmouth County on the farm he's looked after more than fifty-four years."

Raymond introduced his helpers, LeRoy Ulrich and Charlie Morrison, at work among the locust and other logs. They all knew Roy Decker, they said. Roy, being mostly Indian, liked to wander, but wherever he happened to be he could fit in as a mechanic. He had hitched up the tractor that provided the power, or some of it, for Reid's Mill.

"But Roy don't live here," Reid said. "He comes along whenever he has a mind or perhaps when he gets lonely." For my part, I doubt if Roy ever gets lonely. As I know him now, it seems to me that he prefers what to some would seem a lonely life, or at least the playing of a lone hand. When he likes to go somewhere, he picks up and gets going. Plans that take a week to work out are rarely part of his procedure—although he was thinking of going to the West Coast because the doctors had said the climate would be good for him.

"Roy lives down by DeBow Church, sure 'nough. Bet you

don't know where that is," said the sawyer, as if he hoped I didn't.

I knew well enough, recalling the Monmouth Road crossing that went back to the years when I was scouring the woods for stories of New Jersey's oil boom days at Jackson's Mills and Prospertown. "Roy has done a lot of well drilling in his time," Reid said, "but not for oil. You go find his machinery and like as not Roy will be somewhere in back of it."

Soon I was traveling along the Monmouth or Court House Road, the old road that was dirt when I first knew it and now, improved from Mount Holly to Freehold, follows the line of the counties just as it always has.

On that first day, however, Roy was not at home. Two dogs inside the shed behind the house, half covered by a littered grove of scrub pine, greeted my approach but they also gave notice that Roy was elsewhere. I hurried up the road to the house of the nearest neighbor, tucked between forks in the road to Lakewood and Toms River and hemmed in by more fragrant pines. As is always the case in such faraway near-at-hand places, the neighbors knew exactly where their friend was. "He's at Ted Parsons' office in Red Bank," they said, explaining that by now he might be serving subpoenas for the State's attorney-general.

And so the merry chase, this search for the wonderful auger of Ananias Lutes, led next to Red Bank and there, sure enough, I found Decker—a big man, definitely dignified, given to a quiet smile now and then but equipped, more obviously than all the rest, with hard-working hands in one of which I feared mine might be crushed. He said he had a little while to talk before more papers had to be served on witnesses in a case involving the DeBow estate itself. He asked what was wanted and I told him about Ananias Lutes and aspects of the story which, at first, I had thought part of a fable.

"Yes, I have the auger," Roy told me, with simple directness. "I have a lot of other tools that belonged to Ananias, too."

"What do *you* know of Ananias Lutes?" I asked him.

It turned out that what he had heard tallied almost exactly with my information. Ananias was a man of medium build, clean shaven, baldheaded, and of a genial nature, especially where children were concerned. He was the son of Henry Lutes—and the rest followed the familiar grooving. I outlined all of it as best I could and Decker listened, sitting across the table from me in a noisy, smoky luncheonette in Red Bank.

"I know about the story," Roy interrupted suddenly. "A Manalapan man read it to me because he knew I had the augers of Ananias Lutes."

"But how did you get them?"

"Lew had a son, a boy who was a friend of mine. I worked for his father now and then and when the boy died Lew gave me the tools. He said they had belonged to Ananias Lutes but he didn't say how he had come by them. . . .

"If the writer of the letter you got is who I think it is, I haven't seen him for many years. . . ." Since then, Decker informed me in a scratchy note, he had gone in search of the correspondent who, if he had done nothing more, had added a chapter as well as a solution to the mystery. "Alpaugh was the name," he said, "and when I asked for him they told me he had died a few weeks before. Guess I won't be seeing him for a while."

Decker had told me of his travels in New Jersey, and for a time the mystery of the pumps and augers left my mind. Irrelevantly, he remembered to tell me that he had been on the West Coast before, trying his hand at salvage diving. "I did all kinds of diving, just as I do all kinds of drilling around here. But then the State got to ordering well diggers to send in samples of soil and I just folded up. So I don't work at it. I'm an Indian. Indians don't like to take orders."

Roy Decker fingered a button on his lapel, indicating that there had been one interval, at least, when orders had come and been taken easily enough. He was a veteran of the Coast Guard Reserve. Something was on his mind and he exploded it so suddenly that I dropped a fork.

"Tell you what!" he exclaimed, with a rush of good feeling. "I'll give you the auger and some of the smaller ones. I'll be going away and I'll have no use for them, anyway. Maybe they belong in a museum like you say."

116

"But how will I prove that they're the right augers and that Ananias didn't bury them the way people say?"

"They'll believe you." And when I saw the largest of the augers I began to understand why the story of the wonderful auger of Ananias Lutes must have a new ending. Old Ananias must have been, truly, a local Paul Bunyan. How he could have twisted even the smaller augers into green wood by hand, let alone the giant of the array, I'll not even venture to guess.

Perhaps you would like to do the guessing. That is possible now, and Roy Decker, wherever he is, will appreciate knowing that the tools Ananias is supposed to have buried are in a museum. Not long after Decker, the son of a Mohawk mother, gave them to me, I heard that some school children at the foot of Hell Mountain, within earshot of where Ananias used to work, were getting up a small collection of artifacts as an index to the folklore of Tewksbury Township. There the augers of Ananias Lutes, who would love to know about it, have come to rest.

> New Jersey's own variant of *Ten Little Indians* lies in a scattering of tombstones behind the faded outline of a small church just off the road that swerves with Great Egg Harbor River toward Ocean City. The death of Thomas Biddle West, 14, occurred May 17, 1826, "after 50 hours illness." James West, 19, died August 24, 1829; George Jr., 23, September 3; George Sr., 53, September 10; and last of all the mother of the brood, Amy, September 15. John F. Hall wrote in 1899 that the sole survivor of the Wests was Joe, that "people had their suspicions as to the causes of" the sudden deaths, and that this "noted character of Atlantic County" was a man of powerful build, a lawyer with little practice, and one who must have been at the West mansion, at a place called Catawba, when the march of death began. Joe later lived in the old house in "princely style," and "made tours of the state in a manner to attract attention"—taking along silk bedclothing for use wherever he spent the night. One day he drove away and never came back.

12 *⌒*

The Frog War

I don't know when it was that I began to hear of something referred to elliptically and mysteriously as "The Frog War."

As I recall it, first mention of the clash came when I was in the neighborhood of Hopewell, long before I had any notion of coming to live in the vicinity. "Surely," someone said, "you have heard of the Frog War?" It was almost as if he asked whether I had heard of the President or the Cardiff Giant or the Smithsonian Institution. No, I frankly confessed, I had not heard of it.

At this point replies became varied, deliberately vague, and, as I have concluded, cunning and confusing. Many who had no notion at all what the Frog War was were more than ready, as is ever the case in folklore, to give explanations. The going was rough and I heard many stories in as many days. All had one facet in common—a background of railroad conflict.

One informant said that one of the early railroads had imported groups of Frenchmen to lay the rails and that these, in some circles, were still called "frogs." Another, in this case a woman, declared that tracks had to be laid across a certain marsh from which, in seemingly bottomless depths, many hundreds of frogs chorused as the work gang, by torchlight, completed the line on schedule. A few of course—like the late Misses Susan and Eleanor Weart of the ghost-ridden Hopewell Museum—had their facts straight, assuring me that the "war" was "fought" over a certain frog, a section of railroad line where tracks were supposed to cross. Details were lacking at first, however, and it was my feeling that a colorful chunk of folksay lay behind all that was said to be both familiar and evasive.

It was not until Spencer Smith had proved to me that Pennington, recurrently my home town, once had a second railroad station, which remains today almost intact as a barn and chicken house, that the saga of the half-forgotten Mercer and Somerset Railroad began to unfold, and with it renewed references to the celebrated Frog War. We talked of a roadbed that few but surveyors discern even though it still throws property lines off at angles.

This was how I came to trace the disappearing evidences of the Mercer and Somerset in another direction, although I am never certain afterwards just how these clue hunts begin. Suddenly, instead of digging among the bones of buried stations, Burroughs and Woolsey, between what was Somerset Junction and Pennington, I was drawn beyond to Marshall and Hopewell and then beyond, to Stoutsburg, Harlingen, and Millstone. This was where a "spite line" costing $760,246.96 to build, as against a profit of $637.16 achieved in only one of its eight years of operation, gave up the ghost in the face of the failure of its mission—to prevent the operation of a competitive road.

At the beginning there were intervals of wandering through meadows dressed in new spring green, lowlands dotted with the yellow of dogtooth violets. The business of exploring took me up the Stony Brook Road where, although it is less than obvious to one who is driving by, there is the stone buttress of a railroad bridge, as startling as a mountain from the branch of the Millstone River.

Golden sunlight interlaced the waters as youngsters from the neighborhood fished for trout. Here, where once the engines and cars of the Mercer and Somerset had rumbled across open country on regular schedules and connecting at Somerset Junction, boys were growing up unaware that there had once been another railroad or that their grandfathers had changed trains there to go to Trenton and Philadelphia before 1876. The way people had talked of the Frog War at first you'd have thought it something left behind at least from Civil War times.

Beyond the piled-up stones of the bridge tether, the route the line had followed became a rise across the meadowland. Walking along it, Spencer explained that when a railroad is abandoned the dividing lines of property owners go back to the center —this was why a fence had been erected along the middle of the rise. The long "grave," a mound flanked by trees that gave a clear indication of the age of the ancient spadework of construction men when there were no giant shovels or other modern machinery, veered off in almost a straight line to the actual scene of the Frog War.

This, Spencer discovered dishearteningly, had been all but obliterated during the recent years by bulldozers changing the grade of the Reading Company's main line to New York. Here, on the four tracks that the road assumes as it approaches Hopewell, commuters' "dinkies" and streamliners like the Baltimore and Ohio's Royal Blue alike ignore the scene of what must have been a mixed melodrama while it lasted.

Now let me cut back into what remains and must ever be Spencer Smith's own story, the result of the kind of research that only a railroad enthusiast could piece together.

The Camden and Amboy Railroad had been successful for many years in stifling all rail competition between New York and Philadelphia, barring all rival railroads from New Jersey. Its success was due in part to the monopolistic charter granted by the State about 1834, and the rest came as the result of scheming by its owners, sharp practices which safeguarded rights that were earning high profits and yielding extremely poor service.

Typical of the Camden and Amboy's methods was the secret purchase of a controlling interest in the bridge across the Delaware River at Trenton over which the rival Philadelphia and Trenton Railroad gained access to the capital. This little trick placed the Philadelphia and Trenton under Camden and Amboy control. In another move the Camden and Amboy later gained control of the trackage from Philadelphia, through Trenton, to New Brunswick, forcing the New Jersey Railroad, operating through Newark to New Brunswick, to sign agreements by which the Camden and Amboy obtained an unfair proportion of the through fare from Jersey City to Philadelphia. Control of the route forced the New Jersey Railroad into a position of secondary importance.

Incidentally, all Camden and Amboy properties had been purchased by the Pennsylvania Railroad, which acquired in rapid succession several other New Jersey branches, including the Belvidere-Delaware, northward from Trenton along the Delaware River, and the New Brunswick-Millstone Branch. However, exclusive privileges granted under the original Camden and Amboy expired in 1869 and thus competition by other companies was suddenly stimulated.

Competitors built the Northern Pennsylvania Railroad from Philadelphia to Yardley, Pennsylvania, five miles above Trenton on the Pennsylvania side, in the hope that it eventually could be connected with the Central Railroad of New Jersey, running southwest from Jersey City to Bound Brook and then veering off toward Phillipsburg. Thus it was natural that a request should be made for a charter for the Delaware and Bound Brook Railroad.

The Pennsylvania, presumably to show that no such railroad as the Delaware and Bound Brook was necessary to the welfare of residents along the proposed route, but more probably to eliminate the threat of a competing through line, quickly built the Mercer and Somerset from Somerset Junction, north of Trenton, to Millstone, across the river from its existing New Brunswick-East Millstone Branch. As far as Spencer has been able to determine, these two were never joined physically and passengers had to cross the Millstone River by whatever means was available.

Just to get back on familiar ground, dotted as it is by abandoned bridge abutments, crumbling trestles, and clearings lined by trees that obviously once were rights of way, let me run down the route of the Mercer and Somerset, as revealed in the book *Pennsylvania Railroad: Historical and Descriptive*, published by the Pennsylvania in 1876:

"West Millstone, o miles; Hillsboro, two miles; Harlingen, five miles; Blawenburg, eight miles; Stoutsburg, ten miles; Hopewell, thirteen miles; Marshall, fifteen miles; Pennington, seventeen miles; Woolsey, nineteen miles; Burroughs, twenty-one miles; Somerset Junction, twenty-two miles." There are several crossroads towns listed which now deny that they ever had railroad service.

Construction of the Mercer and Somerset was feverishly begun in 1870 and cost $760,000 plus. As Spencer Smith figured it out, this was about $34,500 a mile, definitely an expensive investment just to crowd out a competitor. Stories still current list the Mercer and Somerset as using "bicycle"-type engines—one driving wheel on each side—wheels which, according to the legends, were painted red. One Pennington man told Spencer in 1936 that, although there were adequate stations for the twenty-two miles covered, trains definitely came under the title of ultra-accommodation locals—they stopped whenever and wherever a prospective passenger waved to the engineer. As it was the custom in those days to pin derogatory names on railroads, the Mercer and Somerset is said to have acquired the sobriquet of "Corkscrew" despite the relative directness of its line—but subsequent investigations have so far failed to reveal anyone who remembers such a nickname.

In spite of the building of the Mercer and Somerset, a charter was granted to the Bound Brook Railroad and building began. Apparently this line was built in two directions—from Bound Brook west and from the Delaware River east. It was obvious from the first that the new line would have to cross tracks of a rival line.

Such a crossing was proposed west of Hopewell, where new grading and modern culverts have eliminated all but a slight indentation in the land to show where the "fireworks" eventually were set off. To complicate matters for backers of the Bound Brook Railroad, the Pennsylvania's representatives thrust through the Legislature a measure that virtually placed a ban on grade crossings at sharp angles. No one had any doubt which sharp angle was meant. Thus the Bound Brook line's plan for crossing the Mercer and Somerset had to be redesigned at great expense.

As construction approached the Mercer and Somerset, minions of that road stationed one of the largest Pennsylvania locomotives at the crossing, "parking" it there or running it back and forth to prevent Bound Brook construction men from laying the necessary frog. This continued through several months, with the locomotive in almost constant action without really going anywhere—it was backed onto a siding only when one of its companions, a cousin engine from the Mercer and Somerset, had to get through. If ever there was such a thing as a duel of locomotives, this was it.

"The climax came late in the afternoon of January 5, 1876," Spencer Smith told me. "A Mercer and Somerset train was due and the large sentinel locomotive was backed into its siding, a routine to which it had become accustomed. As it stopped, some two hundred employees of the Bound Brook Railroad, who apparently had been hiding in the vicinity, rushed the locomotive, placing crossties and timbers both behind and in front of it and, for good measure, chaining the locomotive to the rails. They proceeded to barricade the Mercer and Somerset line above and below the proposed crossing point. Then, with professional ease, they installed the crossing frog."

Word was flashed, of course, to Pennsylvania officials, who lost no time in ordering Engine No. 336, something of a jumbo, to run from Millstone to Hopewell and ram the barricade. Spencer Smith says that the eleven miles were covered in fifteen minutes flat. The locomotive hit the barricade with a terrific crash, knocked the crossties aside, rolled thirty feet over ties from which, by this time, rails had been removed, and finally sank in some nice, soft mud just short of the frog.

Meanwhile farmers and other natives who had supported the new road pushed Engine No. 37 of the Central Railroad of New Jersey onto the frog and to a place where it could glower at the disabled engine. No sooner was this achieved than Engine No. 550, another Pennsylvania engine ordered out of Lambertville, put in its appearance under orders to ram the frog from the opposite direction. But the engineer, seeing the other locomotive on the crossing, must have lost his nerve, for he pulled up short.

Excitement steamed up and bubbled over. Men and women and children from all over the area gathered at the scene during the night; the crowd was estimated at fifteen hundred, apart from the rival construction parties. Stories have been handed down that men came armed with squirrel guns, muskets, and even heirloom flintlocks of the Revolution—but I found no one who has given full credence to such an arsenal. There is no doubt that public feeling ran high. Both companies augmented their forces of workmen. Some were Italian, others Irish. Local residents, when they were able to discern railroad officials in the gloom, did some fast fist-shaking now and then just to show their feelings and play safe. There were, however, no casualties—and that in itself is surprising.

Next morning a reporter from a Trenton newspaper tried to reach the scene and spent several paragraphs reporting that it took two hours and twenty minutes to make the twelve-mile trip—by train. The local was so overcrowded, he said, that it had to be split into two sections to make the grade near Woolsey. When he finally arrived, a thousand more railroad men had come in from Jersey City. Both railroads had men lying about in empty cars, each side waiting for the other to make the first hostile move. Tension remained high and, according to the old Trenton *State Gazette*, only the complete control of liquor prevented physical battle.

Counsel for the Camden and Amboy arrived the same day with an injunction. It restrained the Bound Brook Railroad from "meddling" with Mercer and Somerset property. Once this announcement had been made, feeling climbed anew. At one o'clock in the afternoon Sheriff Mount, who had his headquarters in a caboose, telegraphed the governor for troops. Bells rang in Trenton and four companies were rallied. Bells were set to ringing in Lambertville for a fifth. The soldiers arrived by special train on the morning of January 17, 1876, forcing workers back from the property, controlling native hecklers, and restoring order.

Then came the decision of the chancellor. He upheld the Bound Brook Railroad and the affair was quickly ended. Troops rode back to Trenton on January 18. The Bound Brook's line was quickly completed and reinforced here and there, frog and all, and the first train, forerunner of the Reading line to New York, ran between Philadelphia and Jersey City a few days later. Thus the Mercer and Somerset, built for no useful purpose, was of no special value to the Pennsylvania once legal umpires gave the decision to its opponent, and was soon abandoned.

Actually, according to the figures Spencer Smith put together for me, the annual operating losses from 1872 to the time of the line's abandonment ranged from $5,000 to $21,000 per year. Only in 1875 was there an operating profit. Default of interest on the bonded debt led to the road's sale at auction in Trenton in November, 1879. Oddly enough, it was sold to a representative of the Pennsylvania who bid $50,000. "Ties and rails were taken up," Spencer said, "and the right-of-way reverted to the rabbits."

This was the story still churning in my head as we ventured forth later to look at some of the remaining landmarks and, in so doing, conjure up a picture of the line in operation before and after the Frog War. The road's cuts and fills actually are everywhere, unnoted by inexpert eyes. The present Jacob's Creek Road is built on the old Mercer and Somerset right-of-way —the heavy stone bridges it uses give the secret away. I have told you of the bridge buttresses and gravelike fill that I found. Even so, all this was but a prelude to the real discovery.

Having noted the ways in which recent grading procedures for various developments have all but eliminated historic battlegrounds themselves, I moved with Spencer and a few friends on Hopewell where the old Mercer and Somerset station was still doing duty as a house. The street itself was the old roadbed of the "spite line," although few in Hopewell, even when pressed, will admit to knowing any such thing. Noting a building which had all the earmarks of railroad construction, Spencer virtually leaped from the car and hurried inside. Seconds later he came out waving his arms, jumping up and down, and calling out something about a gold mine. I would not have been entirely surprised had he led us to a red-wheeled engine or even the jumbo that had been imported to vanquish all rivals.

The discovery, from my point of view, was even more startling. Here in George Wyckoff's blacksmith shop, a leftover from railroad days, were some of Hopewell's citizens of longest standing. At a card table which I feel sure George had fashioned just for them, four fine old men were quietly playing a game that wasn't whist and, as far as I could discern, wasn't poker either. At one end sat Uncle Billy Wyckoff. Opposite was Bill Hoff. The other two players were Homer Kise and John Moore. There might be a world outside but none in the group was particularly concerned with it.

It came out almost immediately that Uncle Billy had been there when the Frog War was fought and that Homer Kise's father was one of those who had informed the Bound Brook Railroad's representatives that "now is the time to chain down that there locomotive." Homer reached for a thirteen-bladed penknife his father had received as a reward. "They wasn't so hot for these here citations in those days," Homer said. "They gived you things you could use."

Uncle Billy remembered the Frog War well. "I rode to the Centennial on the Mercer and Somerset," he said proudly. "Had a pass and that's the way I went so I could use it." He didn't remember any red wheels on the engines and he didn't think anybody carried squirrel guns to the fight, which never got beyond hot words and legalities.

"Was the railroad ever called the Corkscrew Line?" I asked him. Uncle Billy Wyckoff, who was over ninety when I saw him and will not be there any more, said it "could have been, 'cause it sure twisted here and there, even if the tracks *was* straight." Homer Kise, almost as old as Uncle Billy, told me that in spite of a schedule trains were very irregular. "I used to come down with a horse and buggy to meet some folks in the mornin'," he said, "and sometimes the train would show up, at last, in the afternoon. I know, 'cause I was a boy then, and I got pretty hungry."

126

The play at the table there in the half-dark never faltered. Words were woven into a pattern of smoke and the dealing of cards and the leftover smells of a blacksmith shop. I was content to listen and to wish for a Norman Rockwell. Somehow the lore of the Frog War itself was condensed in the minds of men here in the old shop, littered with so many things that had been forgotten that a railroad battle had become only another fragment.

Somebody wanted to know if the line ever had had any accidents, and Uncle Billy replied that the trains never went fast enough for accidents. In spite of that, it is a matter of record that one Joseph Schmitt was run over and killed near the vanished Woolsey Station on December 10, 1873, according to reports by George W. Ellis, engineer, and Charles Thatcher, conductor. And on November 23, 1874, Michael Lucas, a brakeman, "struck by a bridge near Pennington," likewise was killed. Even when the "spite line" might have made money, compensation payments probably eliminated the margin of profit.

The name of George Ellis, the engineer, cropped up in our talk in the village blacksmith shop, but although I was told that he lived in Trenton I never could find him. Homer Kise said that George Ellis was in the cab of the locomotive whose wheels were chained down as the Frog War began. I suppose it was I who remarked that these old gentlemen must have been in the area a truly long time. That was when Uncle Billy Wyckoff and Homer Kise replied, almost as if in chorus, that there were "only thirteen places in the village" when they first knew what the world was all about.

"About those knives, now," said Homer Kise suddenly, his quiet face revealing nothing of the hand just dealt him. "Knives like this here one with the thirteen blades. Wouldn't be surprised if they're all that's left to recall the Frog War. My father, Bloomfield Kise, got one; Ed Van Dyke got another, and Abe Skillman, for whom Skillman station is named, got a third. You see, those three is the ones that gave the signal that brought action from the Bound Brook's men, hidden there in the bushes."

As for souvenirs, relics of a railroad that used to be, there's another one even more tangible. Spencer Smith has it in his backyard in Lawrenceville. Dug up in the woods near Harlingen, it's the Number 17 milestone of the Mercer and Somerset, discovered when he was walking along the fading roadbed more than ten years ago.

They told me in Tuckerton of the laziest man of whom I have heard in all these journeys. He lived aboard what was left of a leaky boat, drawn up on the muddy shore of Tuckerton Creek. Presumably he did some fishing and clamming, for he was able to scrape just enough together for a loaf of bread, a can of beans, and a bottle of beer when he was hungry. What he liked most, though, was sleep—and sleep provided a problem in such a leaky garvey, for bailing was necessary at unusually frequent intervals. Sizing up the situation in his own way, the man removed his shoes before taking to his bunk, always making sure that he fell asleep on his back, with one foot dangling over the edge. This was important. When the rising tide invaded the wreck and eased up to a height at which the water touched his bare foot, the cold shock awoke him. It was time to get up and bail.

13

The Man in the Iron Casket

Nobody is going to dig up Hezekiah B. Smith and take him somewhere he doesn't wish to be. He saw to that as long ago as 1887.

Kinfolk found out about it after they thought it would be nice to take Hezekiah back to Vermont. They soon discovered that Smithville's namesake had provided for burial in an iron casket embedded in cement between iron slabs. This is why Hezekiah Smith will stay in St. Andrew's Cemetery, Mount Holly, until Judgment Day. That's where his bones will be, at any rate.

I have been followed for more years than I can remember by legends of Hezekiah: the man who harnessed a team of moose to his carriage, the man who built the only bicycle railroad in the world to run between Mount Holly and Smithville, and the man whose broad-brimmed Quaker hat, Lincolnesque shawl, and abstemious habits were in contrast to the well-stocked bar, the gay gaming casino, and the opera house that he built in Smithville. But just as I conclude that Hezekiah B. Smith is as certainly dead as he seems to be buried or that his namesake, Smithville, has made its last show of life, I have to take much of it back.

Only recently a group from a historical society that takes its members to the byways and hedges at least once a year were touring Smithville, six miles from Mount Holly in Burlington County, under the leadership of Nathaniel R. Ewan. Now, Ewan calls this tiny village, or what's left of it, the most colorful of all New Jersey's forgotten towns.

Nothing that is Smithville now will supply more than a suggestion of what there was. Desolation is everywhere. This you will discover when you determine to find out about the tower and its observation platform, long a challenge to the curious traveler.

Many of the sixty or seventy houses that remain are empty and nearly all are in disrepair. The stores, restaurant, and butcher shop that once invited trade on "merchants' row" closed their doors long, long ago. A big warehouse beside the rotting freight platforms offered sanctuary, at the last, to birds seeking nests and nooks that were rarely disturbed.

Abandoned and forlorn in its last days before demolishment, the old casino had forgotten its poker chips and cards. The hollow shell of an opera house, surrounded by forbidding stairs and dark passageways, tried vainly to recall, through a process of association with a rusty gallery, sagging curtain, and empty stage, the well-known actors and musicians whose names Smithville knew by heart. Today's visitors move on furtively without knowing that here small fortunes were made and lost to the tune of laughter and the tinkle of champagne glasses. I walked sadly through them before demolishment cheated an end by fire

The skeleton of a conservatory, weed-grown and roofless when last I saw it, once housed rare and exotic plants. Beyond the gate, still crested by eagles of iron, the menagerie of ornamental animals, relics of Victorian days, was less imposing than that which once had adorned the mansion grounds. Here and there the elements took toll of weather-beaten anatomy and now and then a tarnished dog had vanished altogether, ignoring the lone and watchful life-sized Indian, idiotically content with a tipsy pose.

But the most celebrated statue of them all, almost legendary now, was the likeness of Agnes Gilkinson, whom the inhabitants of Smithville knew as Mrs. Hezekiah B. Smith.

There was, of course, something of a town long before the arrival of Hezekiah, the man who knew what he wanted and who, I am convinced, knew some of its history and how its progress was cursed by fire. Or is it more logical to conclude, in the face of his obviously rigid rule for building—brick walls and iron doorways, iron window frames, iron cupboards, iron shelves, and even iron staircases—that there was fear of an enemy, or enemies, from out of the past? Whatever the explanation, it is clear that, although Jacob Parker won his fight for water power and a milldam two miles above Mount Holly in the early 1780's and although a gristmill had been added under a chain of owners, including French & Richards—the latter a member of the distinguished Batsto family—accidental fire was more effective than the Revolution in curtailing operations.

Almost as important as the early mills is the tradition that Revolutionary activities were centered in the vicinity of the village, a legend based on well-defined lines in military formation that indicate remains of entrenchments. History admits that minor clashes marked the movement of small detachments, especially around Mount Holly and New Mills, now Pemberton, and it is more than plausible that these lines were part of the defense plans of 1776. Century-old trees, reaching up through mounds of earth, substantiate the antiquity of these diggings at Smithville.

The first of the disastrous fires came in 1839, according to a discovery made by Nat Ewan exactly a century later, when two of the original buildings of an imposing factory group were still in service. Ewan found the account, touched upon in quaint simplicity, in the *New Jersey Mirror:*

"It is with great regret that we state the Calico Factory, situated about two miles above Mount Holly, belonging to Messrs J. L. and S. Shreve, took fire on Tuesday last and was reduced to ashes. The loss was placed at from 15,000 to 20,000 dollars with no insurance." But if the town was called anything but Shreveville before it became Smithville, no one knows about it.

This earlier designation came when Jonathan L. and Samuel Shreve, young men from Springfield Township, decided to give up keeping store in Black Horse, now Columbus, to become pioneers of the calico trade. The Shreves took title to the French & Richards holdings and whatever they built disappeared with the fire of 1839. A subsequent group of buildings which appears on a map of Smithville drawn in 1856 shows bleach and wash houses, dye and dry houses, printing rooms, and color shops. I mention all this because the site of this establishment is lake bottom now, part of the enlarged millpond that furnished water power for H. B. Smith's machine company operations. The second calico factory burned in 1856 and the Shreves are believed thereafter to have confined their interests to making spool cotton.

But the Shreves had built a fulling mill, entire streets of picturesque brick houses for the workmen, and the present mansion of the Smiths, a house erected in 1842. With the exception of an addition on the west end, the manorial establishment is as it was in the beginning, geographically and socially the center of the village. In 1846, not long after Benjamin Shreve inherited the company interests of his father, Samuel, the firm engaged as its manager one Samuel Semple, a native of Scotland honored by his descendants as the maker of the first spool cotton in America. If the distinction is deserved, Smithville, still wobbling along as Shreveville, is where Semple did his first work.

Raw materials for the factory were brought by boat from Mount Holly, up the Rancocas from the Delaware River. In order that similar transportation might be extended all the way to Shreveville, Semple directed the building of a canal, but this project was abandoned because of financial difficulties common to all cotton manufacturers of the day. Search for the ruined route of the half-finished artificial waterway will find greater reward, even so, than will belated quests for fragments of two earlier factories.

Sam Semple lingered with the Shreves through darkening days and then, when his salary was long overdue, the canny Scot accepted payment in machinery that he himself had bought abroad. Using this in Mount Holly, first on the site of Hack's canoe headquarters and, later, at Washington and King Streets, Semple & Sons began operation of the S.F.T. (soft finished thread) Mills, a close rival of the internationally famous Clark's O.N.T. Meanwhile, matters up the creek were going from bad to worse. Mr. Semple had declined to buy the whole Shreve enterprise for $225,000 and, on December 6, 1856, according to an old map that went with announcement of the auction, "the valuable Spool Cotton Factory, Print Works, Cloth Manufactory, Grist Mill, Store, Dwellings and fifty acres of land" were put up for sale.

This was where, for $23,000, Hezekiah B. Smith, the enterprising Yankee, came in. And this is where the name of Shreve, except for tombstones of the brothers and their sons, loses identity with Shreveville, now a forgotten town except for an ageless fingerboard not far from Burlington.

Hezekiah, who had begun with a small shop in Woodstock, Vermont, soon added the operation of a turning mill. Possessed of an inventive mind that teamed up with that rare companion, business ability, he transferred his interests to Lowell, Massachusetts, in 1847, quickly branching out as a maker of woodworking machinery. This venture provided the surplus capital with which to acquire Shreveville and all that therein remained. However, although something of a Midas touch was evident as Hezekiah set about establishing what was to become one of the largest woodworking machinery plants anywhere in the country, it was said that he had guarded against possible failure by depositing a sizable nest egg in a Lowell bank. So, with the stage set, he let it be known that Shreveville was no more, that Smith of Smithville was to be reckoned with from then on, and that any who needed planers, molders, sanders, band saws, mortisers, sash and blind machines, lathes, vises, and other specialties must come to him.

Predicting new applications of mechanics that were to become, before he died, indispensable operations, some of the departures covered in early Smith patents were as startling as the man himself. More practical than Darius Green, Hezekiah B. persisted in his support of air navigation and, all of seventy years ago, began production of the model of a flying machine, actuated by a propeller similar in principle to an autogyro.

He experimented with a mechanism applied in the center of a long line shafting which would, under sudden stress, allow either section to revolve independently of the other. This departure, in its perfected development, became the differential of every automobile. Legal minds involved in the memorable suit of Henry Ford and General Motors were more than aware of Smithville, gathering there during the litigation to ascertain the extent to which the contested patent had been pioneered by this man Smith. All told, Smith is credited with forty patents, some improving existing machinery, others involving new mechanical equipment.

Immediately upon Smith's arrival in New Jersey, Smithville began to emerge. Extensive additions were made to the old Shreve factory. New houses were begun. A new brick barn, with a brick and iron tower that commanded a view of the countryside and was to become Smithville's best-known monument, was built beside a new gristmill. Then came a boardinghouse of hotel proportions and with hotel appointments, a new school, and a costly warehouse in which every type of machinery could be crated and stored, awaiting orders and shipment. At last came the elaborate opera house and impressive ballroom. To the old Shreve manor, which had become the home of the new lord, Hezekiah added stables and coach houses, a huge glassed-in conservatory, a stone-walled deer preserve, and the miniature casino with its gaming rooms and dazzling bar.

Hezekiah Smith, personally modest and retiring, welcomed the sensational, fantastic, and grotesque, if the departure would in any way advertise his business and his town.

Thus it was that the H. B. Smith Machine Company began manufacture of the new Star bicycle, contracting with the inventor, George W. Pressey, on a royalty basis. In contrast to the conventional bike of the times, Pressey's featured a ratchet-drive mechanism with the small wheel in front, early models fifty-six inches high tempering road shocks with solid rubber tires. Intense rivalry developed between the Star and the older Columbia and so it was that Hezekiah arranged competitions for speed and skill. By now no one remembers that the world's champion speedster on a bike was Charles Frazier of Smithville, who achieved his record on a Star. Not long after that Smith built a bicycle track down the hill from his home and if you care to look for it today, it is still there in a tangle of briers.

Profits that came to the Smith company in the manufacture of bicycles remained intact chiefly because Hezekiah B. decided that the field was limited and that it would be more fun to try a new sideline, the making of Axminster carpet looms. Such company officials as William S. Kelly, vice-president, Charles Chickering, treasurer, and even Bradford Story, superintendent of shops, may have frowned on such plans and policies but, dominated by Hezekiah, the company at one time made some of the first roller skates. When the millpond was considered too small, Smith enlarged it, adding more turbine wheels and a big steam-power plant. When storekeepers failed to stock what Smith thought his people needed, he took over the biggest staples emporium and leased it, on shares, to many operators.

When rumors of financial worries came, the Smithville Beneficial Association was formed. When a captious critic said that Smith kept the best music for himself, old Hezekiah B. organized the Smithville Brass Band which, incorporated in 1876, became one of the best-known organizations in the State, and he registered no complaint when the band, at the zenith of its popularity, was accused of spending more time in horn-blowing than in building Smith machines in the shops. Deciding to run for senator, Smith built a big golden chariot and rolled away with his traveling bandsmen spurred on by his own campaign tunes. Now the band is only a memory but its stand, on the slope below the mansion, is its monument.

Not all Hezekiah's ideas proved practical. However, he enjoyed each brain child as long as it lived, and when one went wrong he willingly paid the price of his pampering. His brick barns allowed so little air that the hay and grain he stored became moldy before they could be used. The schoolhouse, with its narrow barred windows and iron door, allowed so little light that its class had to move to better quarters. The gristmill was too modern for its own good and only the deer and caribou, prizes of Smith's big-game hunting expeditions, remained docile in the private zoo.

Two moose, anxious to go places and see things, were painstakingly broken to harness driving, and for a few months Hezekiah B. delighted in frightening horses and spilling neighbors into roadside ditches. Then, after he had been named defendant in several lawsuits, he sold his moose team and acquired ponies.

Hezekiah Smith's staff was impressive, made up of men of unusual ability. Paradoxically, however, in his leisure he sought out the company of well-known men whose reputations were not above reproach—petty politicians, society outcasts, wanderers with sporting instincts, who were quick to take advantage of his Smithville hospitality. The entertaining of these visitors became a noisome, nightly routine, until Hezekiah B., as temperate as ever, was induced to enter politics. His election to Congress in 1879 was followed by the winning of a seat in the State Legislature in 1883 and 1885. But for the most part he was an easy mark for clever men who knew how to spend his money.

Smith of Smithville had come to New Jersey accompanied by a most attractive young woman whom he introduced as the former Agnes Gilkinson.

Agnes soon made her own reputation as a thoughtful hostess, and Hezekiah B. was ever proud of her social superiority in contrast to his own homespun background.

In 1883, with the death of Agnes, however, there came a marked change in Hezekiah. Inconsolable for a long time, he ordered from a famous sculptor in Italy a marble likeness which was erected on the front lawn, shielded by a little roof of familiar and traditional iron.

"This intimate bit of monumental evidence of the deceased Mrs. Smith," Nat Ewan wrote me not long ago, "was long a center of attraction for the morbidly curious."

Visitors peered through the gate, between the boxwoods, at the counterpart of the hostess who was dead, at Mrs. Hudson, who had become a more mobile housekeeper and could be summoned to play the piano, at Professor Pieterse, who, a pupil of Ole Bull, played the violin, and at old Hezekiah, who came out now and then to look upon the statue.

"I ought to know," Ewan said, "because the professor, who was rescued from obscurity on a Fall River Line boat, gave me my first violin lessons."

136

After Hezekiah's death, Pieterse died in obscurity, still advertising for pupils who never came.

Following the death of Agnes, Hezekiah B. wrote a voluminous will in which he provided that his ample fortune be used for the establishment and maintenance of a boys' mechanical school. This will, contested immediately after his death, gave rise to a lawsuit which set slanderous tongues to wagging all across Burlington County.

Enough of Hezekiah's family affairs. I prefer to remember Smithville as it must have been, or to think of the village in association with the Hotchkiss Bicycle Railroad, perhaps the most remarkable transportation system ever devised to bring workmen to a factory on time, its strange vehicles using the Star ratchet device to skim along atop a fencelike track that crossed the Rancocas at least seven times.

This venture, too, was a failure, although Joe Wolfrum, when he was postmaster in Mount Holly, showed many of his friends some of the fence-top bikes that demanded, for sheer safety's sake, the full courtesy of the road. When the "bicycle railroad" failed, Hezekiah was in his iron casket, hardly remembered as the man who made an early airplane or an early automobile, the New Englander whose strange genius seems to have died with him.

Smithville, still the scene of unsung manufacture but otherwise a mere shell of its former glory, is teetering on the edge of its own iron grave.

14

The Black Doctor

Doctors are always borrowing the book. My yellowing copy of the *Early Recollections and Life of Doctor James Still* is ever in professional demand. They never ask for the volume personally, nor do I understand how some of them discover that I have it, tucked away on my modest shelves of Jerseyana, unless it is through something I have written or by some medical grapevine of which I have no knowledge.

These requests usually come in through the intervention of a friend, or sometimes the friend of a friend. Then, after a reasonable time for reading, my *Doctor Still* comes home, with thanks that are at best secondhand, but with never an added comment. This is perhaps because James Still, like the woman who said she was wife, without benefit of clergy, was physician without benefit of certificates.

So it is time to go along behind the homemade wagon that proclaimed the coming of Jim Still, the Black Doctor. We shall move down the road toward Medford in Burlington County where Dr. Still was best known, first as a woodchopper and then as a man who cured cancer, hip disease, and lesser bodily ills. After that we shall make our calls, along with him, in Eayrestown, Lumberton, and even in Buddtown. That Dr. Still was real is proved not only by his book but by the memory of the late "Doc Ed" Haines, who used to talk of deep-in-the-woods patients as the Black Doctor found them, putting fish into their shoes to make sure the cures would "take."

Between Smithville and Pemberton is old Brumaghim, or even

138

Brummingham, now mere Birmingham, the place where men began digging marl so long ago and where, with holes getting deeper and more numerous every year, New Brandywine has fallen through to China. New Brandywine was the first and best name Birmingham ever had.

Did you see anything of Brandywine Run while you were over there? Or did anyone mention the stream that became the Indian River on later maps? Did anybody tell you about Brummingham Iron Forge, established by Bolton and Jones, perhaps in 1800, or of the time less than ten years later when the proprietors set up at a place still called Retreat? Or did you come upon anyone who spoke familiarly of the Birmingham Inn, built about 1877 on the foundations of an earlier "Birmingham Mansion"?

It is more likely that you met someone who said Birmingham Forge was moved to Retreat to avoid trouble in the Revolution and that without checking on the disillusioning dates you accepted, even as I once did, the convenient and popular tale. Dr. Still or his memory could have helped, perhaps, but without him in the flesh there is little use in seeking traces of the millers and wheelwrights, or even the storekeepers and blacksmiths, who knew Lumberton, Eayrestown, Brummingham, or even Cross-Roads in their earlier days. Last time I went that way a man in Eayrestown told me he was going to tear down the old houses before they fell all in a heap.

Jim Still drove his wagon in Birmingham. He drove to Lumberton, too, sometimes every day when people needed him. Lumberton gained its distinction honestly and has valiantly held on to it, even if its days as a shipping point at the head of navigation of the Rancocas Creek are over—none of the sloops, scows, and other vessels that once sailed away with lumber and charcoal for Philadelphia come there any more. All the good timber is gone from the woods, and charcoal is burned too far away, and anyway you wouldn't get much of a load in a sloop that could get all the way through to the Delaware River now. One of the memorable pioneer landowners here, as far back as 1683, was Robert Dimsdale, another physician. However, although it is true that Robert bequeathed his name to Dimsdale

Run, it does not follow that he had anything to do with the celebrated crossing of the creek called Belly Bridge. Recent signs have made it "Bally Bridge."

Before 1795 Lumberton had no more than a dozen houses, perhaps a meetinghouse, and a blind preacher of renown named Solomon Gaskill. By 1844, however, the village was boasting of a well-stocked store, a glass manufactory, a sawmill, a Methodist church, and forty-five dwellings. With another ten years came the Burlington County Iron Works and a little fleet of at least twenty ships that operated regularly from forgotten Chambers' Landing and Coles' Wharf, loading stations said to have been built in 1790. I recall newer landings and stub-end pilings of early piers up and down the stream from the bridge, but there's no regular commerce now on the creek that used to be a river called the Northhampton.

Lumberton intermittently has been a shoe town with four shoe-making companies doing very well as late as the 1880's, but only one persisted until recently. "I recollect my father bringing me a pair of new shoes from Lumberton," Jim Still wrote, long years after. "In trying them on they did not prove a fit, so he took them back to change them, at which I cried sadly."

Medford's earlier identities were Shinntown and Nebo. The crossing retains little of its eminence, either as the seat of Medford Township's government or as the base of Dr. Still's errands of unparalleled mercy. The Doctor of the Pines was at least forty years too late to prescribe for the famous divine who fell ill while visiting Medford in 1814.

Bishop Asbury, making his second call in two years, was "most dangerously sick and had to be put up at Brother Sale Coate's" to the great distress of such faithful souls as Mercy Huff, Polly Middleton, Hannah Gosling, John and Keturah Moore, the Whites, the Kirkbrides, the Engles, and the Brocks, whose kinfolk are still in the neighborhood where new streets and new houses of brand-new towns are springing up in all directions.

Suddenly, with an unexpected twist in the road, we have come upon James Still, son of the freed Maryland slaves, Levin and Charity Still. Born in Washington Township, later Shamong and now Woodland, Dr. Still was the brother of Peter Still, whose story, *The Kidnapped and Ransomed*, is a book the doctors never ask for, and also a brother of the even more celebrated William, author of *The Underground Railroad*. Jim Still, who first saw the light of this world at Indian Mill, now Indian Mills, in 1812, is perched on the crossboard of a vehicle made by the same hands that fashioned the crude medicine chest, a cigar box, and the restoratives inside it.

"I had no wagon to ride in so I made one," Dr. Still summed it up in his *Recollections*. "The body was of rough pine boards. The cover was of muslin, made by my wife, arranged over old hoops. . . ." This obviously was a Jersey wagon, New Jersey's own variant of the Conestoga, small-scale. "She went to John Edbert's drugstore in Medford, and bought lead-colored paint, and painted the body of the wagon. The top was left white. I was then ready for work."

And what a work it was, a work that never had its equal along the faded roads and among those who had been told that because they were poor they would die. Remembering the house where his brother was born, Jim Still recalled a small structure of logs, "one story high and an attic, with one door and a large fireplace, but no glass windows." "People were poor in those days," he adds, "with no stoves to heat their houses, nor carpets on the floors. Women wore short gowns and petticoats. Six or seven yards would make a gown to be worn on First Day, as it was called."

I am not certain where my abiding interest in folk cures began. Sometimes I have thought that it was when I walked the fields with Uncle Tilden Estlow, at Wells Mills, as he gathered teaberries and then some bearberry leaves with which to make a tea to guard against kidney complaint. At others I know I heard of Dr. Still at an earlier time as I searched for and talked with those I could find who admitted that he had treated or cured them. Dr. Still was fond of telling those who were cured not to talk to others about it, and his patients kept their word. Where and when Jim Still's own persistent concern began is more certain.

"It so happened," he wrote, "that Doctor Fort was called to our house to vaccinate the children, my brother Will being about six months old at the time. The doctor performed the duty, and I have sometimes thought that the virus being inserted in my arm must have taken better than usual, for the sting of the lancet yet remains. From that moment I was inspired with a desire to be a doctor. It took deep root in me, so deep that all the drought of poverty or lack of education could not destroy the desire."

Little Jimmy Still played a game of doctor with his childhood friends. "Among the children I procured a piece of glass," he said, "and made the virus of spittle; I also procured a thin piece of pine bark, which I substituted for a lancet. Thus was the little acorn, which was intended to become an oak, thrown into the thicket, not knowing that it should ever again be seen or heard from but there was one, unseen, who cared for and watered and protected it." Here the Black Doctor revealed a reverence for an aspect of his cures. Dr. Still concluded always that he was guided, that his hands were doing the work of a Force that was near but could not be touched, and that he himself knew nothing of the medicines specifically required for the sicknesses that came to him for relief.

There were years of waiting, years of privation, years in which Jim Still's one delight was "in playing about the yard and looking forward to the time when I should be, like Doctor Fort, riding about healing the sick and doing great miracles. These thoughts would come over me with an enrapturing sense." Dr. Still wrote, musing with something like surprise on the remembrance that he never longed for toys, that he took no interest in "childish sports," and that when he was eight or nine rough work like chopping wood, gathering rails in gloomy cedar swamps, or bending double from one day's end to the other in the gathering of huckleberries and cranberries in season did not deter him. He pressed on beyond circumstances and hard times when there was little clothing and less food. "Often we would not see meat in weeks," he disclosed. And once he was so hungry that he leaped upon Jacko, the family cat, compelling the animal to disgorge the morsel stolen up the road.

Jim Still confounds all adherents of book learning when he says that the most he ever received in any school at all was three weeks of reading, writing, and arithmetic. "We went to school only in bad weather," he explained. "Our school books were the New Testament and Comly's Spelling Book, in which we learned everything that was useful for a man to know. The teacher taught us grammar in those books, and taught us how to pronounce everything improperly, and we knew no better."

Charity, Jim's mother, was a "stanch Methodist," usually tired, and Levin, the boy's father, seemed to conduct his course in family education from a single passage in the Scriptures—the twenty-fourth verse of the thirteenth chapter of Proverbs—in which, wrote Dr. Still, wincing at the thought, his whole soul was wrapped up: "He that spareth the rod hateth his son; but he that loveth him chastiseth him betimes."

There were still a few Indians in New Jersey when Jim Still was growing up, men and women who refused to recognize the abandonment of Brotherton, at Indian Mills, the first and last Indian reservation in the State, or who returned quietly because they didn't like upper New York. "Our nearest neighbors were an Indian family, the name of whose head was Job Moore," wrote the Doctor of the Pines, as more and more of the down-country people seem to have called him. "The eldest son was named Job, and he and I were very social. We played together, and fished and hunted when opportunity would permit." But Indian Job, the father, was often drunk, a terror to the neighborhood until he was run over by a wagon "carrying a cord and a quarter of green oak." After that Job's ghost continued to keep hair-raising appointments.

"I recollect one night that his son Job and myself went to meeting," wrote Dr. Still, "and as we were standing outside of the door we heard a shrill shout, which seemed to come from the graveyard where Job"—six feet three inches of sinister Indian—"was buried. Young Job said to me, 'That's Daddy.' "

The years went by, just as the scrub oak, the laurel, and the stunted pine have gone. "Can it be that I ever will become a doctor?" was the old question that returned, over and over, as rhythmic in its beat, sometimes, as the sound of wheels on a low, brushy road. "If so, how will I obtain information, or to whom shall I go? I know no black doctors and white ones will not instruct me and I have no means to defray my expenses at college. As I chopped wood, thus would I muse, wishing the time to roll around when I should be a man." The musings went on, the questions persisted, and Jim Still became a man, and was bound out for three years on the farm of Amos Wilkins because Charity Still had so many children she didn't know what to do. They persisted among the smells of a glue factory, when the young Negro found work in Philadelphia, and mingled with the chores of more farm work for Josiah Thorn at Fostertown and Ellisburg, and in the face of romance and tragedy.

Jim Still literally sang himself into his first marriage. His wife was Angelina Willow, a young Negress who worked at Thorn's. "I had made up my mind long before this," Dr. Still wrote about years after, "that I never would marry, but the more I talked to her the more strongly I became conscious of the meshes of love environing me. I then learned four love-songs, and sung them every day, first one and then the other, sang them until I got married, and have not sung them since. The names of two I still remember, the others are long forgotten. 'Barbara Allen' and 'James Bird' are the two which have not escaped me." I think I know one of his songs but this is only surmise. Beyond that, the memory is gone with the wind that soon carried Angelina away and, not long after that, their little daughter, Beulah. Meanwhile, Jim Still had bought a patch of brushland, not far from the Cross-Roads that would someday be his, almost stick for stick.

There is something of the picture of St. Paul on the road to Damascus in Dr. Still's account of the sudden lifting of his burden, in the midst of the natural dejection that followed his wife's death. "What to do in this forlorn condition I did not know," he wrote. "I secluded myself from all company, I walked the woods and road alone, ate but little, and grieved bitterly. . . . I sold most of my goods, reserving a bed, a few chairs, a table, and some other articles, which I left in my house. I then walked about, mourning for one who could not come to me, but to whom I could go. So I determined to go to her. I prayed much. . . . One day I was meditating and praying fervently when all at once the light of life shone over me and the Spirit of God filled my soul. I was transported with joy and peace unspeakable. I looked around and it really seemed to be as if the trees, the sky, and the atmosphere, were all singing praises."

Since reading these words for the first time I have examined with the greatest care the lake and bathing area between the place that was Cross-Roads and the Quakertown that was Vincentown: Ballinger's Mills, later Cotoxen, was Jim Still's Damascus Road in August, 1838. "I have passed the spot many times," wrote the Black Doctor, "and I never have neglected to offer up my supplication to God for his bounteous goodness."

In the time of mingled poverty and ecstasy that followed, James Still moved swiftly. He looked after two aged Negroes, Delilah Johnson and Charles Lopeman, in his home; he worked for Nathan Wilkins and Moses Livesey; and he began looking for a second wife. "There were many difficulties attending single life," he admitted in his book. "I considered that it would be better for me to have someone to tell my troubles to." Chosen as a good listener was Henrietta Thomas, who lived in the home of Robert Woolston, at "Vincenttown and she, being like myself, with no home, none but the kitchen of someone else, was not long in making up her mind." Not long after that Jim Still bought equipment "from William Jones, near Mount Holly" and began the preparation of distilled sassafras roots and essence of peppermint. The sale of these to Charles and William Ellis, Philadelphia druggists, provided the means of arrival in a bookstore at the right moment for the launching of a never-forgotten but repeatedly delayed career.

Jim Still shuffled uncertainly into the shop that was somewhere on a corner of Chestnut Street, in Philadelphia, as he remembered it. He asked the man behind the counter if a medical botany was for sale. The reply was in the negative. Then appeared "an old gentleman dressed in Quaker garb." "Has thee a notion of studying medical botany?" the stranger asked the shy Negro. "Yes," Jim told him. "Then," he answered, "thee must never give it up." Turning to the storekeeper, the old Quaker asked if he knew where such a book as was wanted could be purchased and, if my deductions are sound, the rival shop to which Jim Still was directed was Leary's. There the young unorthodox physician-to-be was able to purchase his medical botany and later, at a herb store, a book of formulas recommended by the proprietor, Dr. Thomas Cook.

"I did not know," wrote Dr. Still of this interval, "that the time had come for me to practice. I made up some tinctures for my own family and one of my neighbors was known to it. One of the daughters of this neighbor developed scrofula and he had me visit her. I gave her medicine which soon cured her. I thought it no great thing, for it always seemed to me that all diseases were curable, and I wondered why doctors did not cure them. This case was Mary Anna Carson, daughter of Abraham Carson. The neighbors began to call on me, and I administered to them with great satisfaction.

"As I was engaged with my distilling I did not find time to attend to medicine. One day, as I was coming along the road, I saw a hedge of sassafras growing by a fence. I went up and asked the lady if Mr. Glover was at home. She replied that he was but not feeling well, was lying down. I told her I should like to see him. She went in and presently he came out. 'Good morning, Mr. Glover,' I said. He returned the compliment, and then lay down on the ground. I was in a hurry, and not wishing to annoy him I said, quickly, 'Mr. Glover, I called to see if you would let me dig the sassafras roots along your fence.' 'If you cure me of the piles,' he answered, 'I will dig them up and give them to you.' 'I do not want you to dig them,' I said, 'but I will cure you if you will let me have the roots.'" Jim Still got his sassafras roots and the patient was cured.

Dr. Still borrowed a little wooden mortar and an Indian pestle with which to pound herbs. "It did not occur to me at this time," he explained, "that I was practising medicine. I thought that I was but doing a friendly service to a fellow-being" even though "people were beginning to call upon me so

146

much that it interfered with my business of distilling." It is clear that up to this point, at least, the services of the Doctor of the Pines came free.

In 1844 old Charity Still came down to Cross-Roads, searched out her son in his brush-patch house, and told him about John Naylor's daughter, who had been seriously afflicted with scrofula from her first birthday. John Naylor brought his daughter and boarded her at Abe Carson's while the treatment was in progress.

"He told me," said Dr. Still, "that the doctors said she could not be cured, and that they refused to do anything for her. She was, in reality, the most distressing case I had ever seen. Her neck and breast were ulcerated, and so swollen and sore that she could not raise her hands to her head. . . . In two weeks from the time I began treatment of her case, the child could comb her hair."

Jim Still was warned, thereafter, that he would be fined for practicing medicine without a certificate if he persisted in continuing such ministrations. "Thinking over the matter, I concluded to go to a lawyer and get his counsel," he wrote in his *Recollections*. "Accordingly, I went to John C. Ten Eyck, of Mount Holly, and stated my case. He took but little notice of me, as though he did not want to bother with me. I told him I would pay him. I asked him if I was finable for practising without a license. He told me no, but that I could not collect for medical services without a license. 'You can sell medicine,' he said, 'and charge for delivering, and then you can collect it just the same as for anything else. There is a fine for giving prescriptions, but you don't give them; you sell medicine and there is nothing to stop you." Mr. Ten Eyck probably knew all about the Black Doctor before he arrived in the office.

On that basis the Doctor of the Pines began his work in earnest. There was William Springer's daughter, victim of "hip-disease" for seven years. "I attended her with good success, and he paid me, manfully. This was a great help to me, and he and his family were well pleased to find the daughter cured."

The little gray wagon now gives way to a more impressive vehicle, "a new rockaway wagon bought of Thomas Lee on time." The circuit was eddying out, calls were becoming more numerous, and the success of the Black Doctor became known along the byways and hedges. "I was paying off my debts and my practice was increasing. Every two weeks I went to Jackson Glassworks, to Waterford, to Pump-branch, to Tansborough." Then there were journeys to Brummingham, to Eayrestown, and to Buddtown. Weary from travel, worn from the brainwork that went with every diagnosis, Dr. Still came home, night after night, to find his house filled and surrounded by more patients.

Among them were men and women who had been ineffectually treated by well-schooled medical men who had warned their patients never to visit "that nigger." In one of the many instances Dr. Still told the story in detail: "I was sitting in my office one evening when a man came in, introduced himself, and asked if I was the doctor. I replied that I was, upon which he said that he had a very sick daughter, and wanted me to go see her. I asked him how long she had been sick, and he answered, 'Eight weeks.' 'Who is attending her?' I asked. 'Dr. B. of Medford and also Dr. T. of Moorestown.' 'What is the matter with her?' 'Typhus fever,' said the distraught father, quoting one of the doctors. 'Well,' said I, 'I shan't go.' 'Why?' 'Because you have two doctors and I don't intend to interfere.' 'I will go and see Dr. B. tonight and discharge him; then will you go?' I said, 'Perhaps I will.' 'Well,' said he, 'I will come and see you tonight, or in the morning, and let you know. She is not at home, nor can we get her there. She is at Cross-Keys and the doctors have blistered her all the time on the legs and she must die without some change.'" Cross-Keys is now Fairview, not far from Taunton.

The girl's father returned next morning with the report that he had discharged the Medford doctor, who, Dr. Still remarked later, "would rather hear of her death under my care than otherwise." In spite of little cooperation from the young woman and less from her mother, the Black Doctor made an examination, provided some of his homemade medicine, and effected a cure in less than a month. "In two weeks," he reported, "they could move her home, where she soon got well, to the delight of all her friends."

So it was with Mary Sooy of Eayrestown, whose house, when Dr. Still arrived, was encircled by wagons and carriages of weeping friends and relatives who had decided that after a seven-year illness poor Mary must die. So it was with Margaret (revealed merely as the wife of Mr. T, presumably of Medford), whose case had been variously pronounced dyspepsia, liver complaint, consumption, and stomach disorder, and then, given up by all but Jim Still, was privileged after his treatment to live more than sixty years. So it was, incredible as it may seem, in cases of cancer, dismissed as incurable by physicians who in derision said, "Go see Black Jim—*he* will make you well!" Which is exactly what Dr. Still did, in numerous instances, always, as he said, with the Guidance of God.

"I have treated cancers in every stage of their growth," he wrote, "and though some were obstinate and incurable, I have had many good results." I have talked with several men and women who have said that they or members of their families had been cured of cancer and lived much longer than the Black Doctor himself. Dr. Still said: "I think many more would have been cured, but it seems persons afflicted with cancer become very irritable, and in a great measure lose that proper control of themselves that is necessary in all bad cases."

This, I presume, is where my doctor borrowers end their reading. If that is so, then they have come far enough to take note of the Black Doctor's "recipes" for sudorific drops, emetic powder, cough balsam, and other remedies using such old-fashioned ingredients as saffron, Virginia snakeroot, pleurisy root, and even the lowly skunk cabbage. They have become aware of at least the manner in which the doctor concluded his examination, perhaps a hundred times a day, in that little office last used as a dwelling near the Cross-Roads.

"I think I can do it," he would say. Quiet caution, a reverence for the Unseen, and courage were all rolled into one in his tone. Patients replied, like the young woman who had come all the way from Philadelphia for a cancer cure:

"We like Doctor Still all the better for answering in that way. It shows he makes no pretensions. I think he had better be allowed to try."

All that was the Black Doctor, even the boxlike office that adjoined his home not far out of Medford, is for the most part forgotten. A new developer of overnight towns, unaware that Burlington County already has a Georgetown within a few moments' ride, has given sprawling acres of streets and split-levels the questionable distinction of Georgetowne. Unremembered by the crowd or not, the spirit of the Doctor of the Pines remains benevolent among the ghosts of those to whom he gave a longer life.

In the beginning One Mile Run, Three Mile Run, Six Mile Run, Nine Mile Run, and Ten Mile Run were all coach stops on the road from Princeton to New Brunswick in country settled by the Low Dutch in the 1600's. Clifford Nevius, of Franklin Park, told me about the cockerel that once adorned the steeple of the pre-Revolutionary Dutch church at Six Mile Run. He said it was in Bound Brook, in the possession of the Voorhees family. He had tried unsuccessfully to get it back. Failing that, he had obtained permission to make a duplicate, even to the gunshot marks made by the British soldiers who had used it as a target. It has been said that some of the marks were made by Indian arrows, long before the British started shooting. What, I wanted to know, did a rooster on the roof signify? "Truth," replied Clifford Nevius. "It goes back to the cock that crowed when Peter denied his Lord."

15 ᴄᴄᴄ

Nobility in the Pines

W hen I went first to Chatsworth, the road through to New
Gretna was hard-surfaced only as far as the cemetery. The way
over from Tabernacle was equally bad, a twisting Burlington
County trail of drifting white sand that sooner or later compelled
adventures with ax and shovel. When I went Down Jersey in
those days with Doc Crate and Jack Sperry and Howard
Shivers, ropes and jacks and chains were standard equipment.

Those were occasions when Willis Buzby himself presided
at the Chatsworth store and when Squire Warner Hargrove
emerged from among the snake-skins that festooned his Pemberton and Browns Mills offices to guide me along to a land where
all the stories sound tall.

The squire began appropriately by introducing me to Willis
who, he said, was "King of the Pineys." Willis would laugh and
wipe the stain of tobacco juice from the corner of his mouth,
but he never denied the distinction. Almost at once he would
call in someone to take his place behind the counter and take
me up the road to where Levi Parsons Morton, vice-president
of the United States from 1889 to 1893, played host to royalty,
nobility, society, and international bankers at Union Forge; to
the "Princess House," with walls still covered with scarlet cloth,
an ornate hideaway in which an Italian prince was born; and
to Speedwell Furnace, where Benjamin Randolph, cabinetmaker
of Revolutionary days, fashioned a chair which eventually sold
for $33,000.

In more recent times, with Willis Buzby in his grave up the

road we had traveled and with his son Jack presiding in a far more orderly emporium, a hub of unequaled friendliness and the best stories of the vicinity, I have had the opportunity to tell busloads of invaders from the cities that none of the old stories was tall and that the newer varieties are just as credible. Willis was the kind of friend who would shut up shop and bring help for a car bogged down on a cranberry causeway, as he once did for mine, no matter what the hour.

Although his Woodland Country Club is far less now than the hole in the ground it remained for almost twenty years, when the bricks of broken steps leading down to an empty lake were its last solid testament, Levi Morton had been there, sure enough; and Mrs. Buzby, Jack's mother, told me of fondling the baby prince, son of Prince Mario Ruspoli, in her arms. As for the Randolph chair, made by the man who fashioned the small desk on which Thomas Jefferson scratched out the Declaration of Independence, I have the confirmation of Nat Ewan, who knows an authentically old house when he sees one, even in the clearing that remains since the untenanted ruin has crumbled away.

Experience has taught me that the tallest tales are told not by people who live in Chatsworth or Jones' Mill or Tabernacle, but by those who live in other parts of New Jersey or, for that matter, in other states. These seldom bother to find out the truth firsthand, or as close to firsthand as they can get by now, for their curiosity about names on roadsigns is stunted by distance and inertia. It is far easier to enlarge on gossip, to conclude that all backroads people are dull, shiftless, and not too particular about baths. It is much simpler to decide that forgotten towns are as dead as the men and women who first knew them or that a few of us who go beyond cellar holes and broken dams deliberately piece together fragments of stories that no longer can be confirmed or denied.

Once in a while I meet a man who knows Chatsworth and Shamong Township only in deer season, who will laugh at the thought that Chatsworth people are industrious with a versatility that exceeds anything in his office experience. Occasionally

152

a writer will confide that he is waiting for the day when I portray my Piney friends "as crusty as they really are." Then I see red and discover all over again that the knowledge of the wilderness claimed by many who say they are hunters is actually superficial and the man who so often confuses realism with dirt never has been south of Trenton or Asbury Park or off the new roads that have changed so much.

Linger in Chatsworth for a day and you will get a bagful of contradictions—at least, that is the way it used to be: Everett Applegate, and his outdoor sawmill; Francis Estlow, who has been buying and storing sphagnum moss, raked and baled by hard-working "mossies" year after year; and men in their seventies like Jesse Estlow and Jack Ritzendollar, who picked an average of one hundred pints of blueberries every day.

In the Pines there's a job for every season and in every season men and women adept in several routines, their skills bred of experience, take their choice. No one is ever baffled by the lack of equipment. Whatever is needed can be made from something that is available, from a sphagnum moss baler to John Bowker's huckleberry sorter, using a long piece of window screening that separates poor berries, bits of leaves, and twigs from the best grade that roll quickly into the box. This is the land of family industry, and I always go back to the Bowkers of one generation or another as something of an index. I have seen Ruth Bowker, nine, Shirley, seven, and Nancy, five, expertly helping John with the picking in the woodland thickets and then taking time out to watch John's wonderful machine sort a daily stint of six crates, twenty-four quarts to the crate.

Money is rarely a primary consideration. An honest dollar is made whenever and wherever the opportunity comes. Even so, Jesse Estlow and Jack Ritzendollar, father of Mrs. Jack Buzby, weren't faring too badly one day when I saw them, the oldest residents in Chatsworth, picking cultivated blueberries at ten cents the pint. They had gathered one hundred pints apiece. "That," said Jack proudly, "is about an average on good days." And when Jesse and Jack "just didn't feel up to it" they turned to other things. "That's the best thing about living down here,"

Jesse said. "Nobody's really lazy. It's just when he gets tired of one thing he goes to something else."

With the "mossies" the going hasn't always been as even as that but then, as Sammy Ford once told me in Green Bank, "when you don't feel like gathering pine cones that the florists use in lots of ways we don't even know about, two dollars for every thousand well-shaped cones at a time, you put on your boots and with a wooden rake you've made all by yourself you go tramping down to the cedar swamps." Throughout the hot summer the people of the little towns and at the edge of the Pines, sometimes whole families bent on making a living and having as good a time as they can doing it, go "swampin' " with "tater" rakes, home-fashioned grapnels, or even wooden "drags," for the moss that is then dried and baled and shipped to floriculturists all over the country. Only the new generation would use a word like "floriculturists" instead of flower growers.

Once I went "mossin' " with the Bowkers of another generation just to see the whole operation. I'm glad I did. I haven't seen a "mossin' crew" at work in the swamps for a long time— although now and then I see crudely lettered signs advertising moss for sale and indicating that the same routines still persist where, in spite of incursions of one sort and another, the moss always seems to be ready if the gatherers want it.

And so, against this rich backdrop of moss and berrypicking and rustic ingenuity, I shall tell you of the days when the Chatsworth Country Club had its day, not only in actuality but in *Town and Country* magazine, when the elite of New York and Philadelphia knew Chatsworth on the Jersey Central in ways that I never can, when an enterprising doctor bottled "health water" to be used at the projected and "documented" Pine Crest Sanitarium on the rise of Apple Pie Hill, and when an Italian prince was born at Shamong in the gentle air scented by cedars and pines and cedar water. I shall tell you, too, of a newspaper called the Paisley *Gazette*, published up the road toward Tabernacle to promote a village called, not only in that boastful publication but also in lavish advertisements far away, "The Magic City." The name was far more appropriate than any of us thought when we heard it first—"The Magic City" was so truly magical that it vanished almost as soon as it "appeared."

There is the counterplot as well. I wonder if the author of the resplendent article so well illustrated in *Town and Country* came home with tongue permanently affixed inside his cheek. I wonder what the "chief of staff" of the projected sanitarium would have said if he had lived to see some of my friends of the area make good use of the "health water" in batteries of their cars. And I wonder what became of all the people who purchased lots and even considerable acreage in Paisley and whether title to the land, probably questionable then, was not sold several times over in that transaction, if not frequently since. The land of Paisley indeed had its own varieties of legerdemain.

The late Albert LeDuc, who had not yet retired as the fire warden of countless acres of that wilderness, found a copy of the Paisley *Gazette* as well as a copy of *Town and Country* for July, 1901, at the home of his aunt, a house which itself was a survivor of the village that died aborning. It was long before Willis Buzby played one of his trump cards, an old photograph of the Woodland Country Club, formerly the Chatsworth Club, as well as a soft-hued prospectus of the "sanitarium" which, when I saw it, was only a ramshackle house with countless bottles of "health water" stacked up in the cellar.

When Willis Buzby was "King of the Pineys" at the crossroads store, laughing his way through life as far as I could tell and forgetting the bills of those who owed him the most, he made it his business to relieve my incredulity about many things. When repeated journeys to the former vice-president's woodsy retreat, already a hole and a clutter of bricks, or visits to the "Princess House," distinguished most of all by a lovely staircase smashed by vandals and desecrated by those who were storing sphagnum there, failed to infect me obviously enough, birdlike Mrs. Buzby would interrupt her attentions to customers to mix great names and impressive titles in her recollections.

"Certainly the prince was here," she told me time and time again, as if she were a mother hen clucking over an unusual baby chick. Then, in the midst of other voluntaries, she would

155

suddenly notice the uneasiness of a patron who had heard all this before or wasn't interested anyway. Then she would go back to filling an order of ordinary things like bread and milk and canned goods.

I remember Mrs. Willis Buzby with something like reverence whenever I look from the windows of the store on a crossroads which always seems the same. There have been changes, of course, but they have come with such subtlety that they have seemed neither obvious nor important. In the story, as it was told and retold, the prince was only a count sometimes, but the details rarely varied. The prince's mother? Her name had been de Talleyrand. His father? He had been an attaché at the Italian embassy in Washington. It was all very honorable and the best I ever heard in the way of explanation for the birth of a young prince in Chatsworth is that his mother expressed a sudden abhorrence for the boat trip home.

"I held the prince in these arms of mine," Mrs. Buzby assured me, "these very arms."

The magazine article authenticates the whole interlude of faded elegance and now, when doubters appear, I dig among my scattered treasures for the precious proof.

"The estate of Chatsworth was owned," according to one of the more important paragraphs of the old *Town and Country*, "by an ancestor of the Marquise de Talleyrand-Périgord and the Princess de Poggio-Suasa, two charming American women who were the daughters of Joseph David Beers Curtis." The Woodland Country Club brochure, replete with persuasive photographs, contents itself by saying that the prince had "married an American lady who, among other possessions, owned seven thousand acres of land in the then little known pine forests of Southern New Jersey."

"Being but slightly informed regarding this property, the Prince and Princess went on a tour of inspection to satisfy their curiosity as to its probable use and value. Arriving at the little village of Shamong"—now Chatsworth—"they immediately noted a soft, dry, balmy atmosphere, different from anything they had hitherto experienced in this latitude. . . ."

156

To make a long story far shorter than that of the word artist who wrote the prospectus, the prince and princess decided to build a "villa" where, in due time, they "gave frequent house parties to their titled friends and others well known in society both here and abroad.

"The conditions were so ideal," wrote the brochure specialist, in pages of text and reproductions attesting the lost beauties of the landscaping of Shamong and its lake, the elegant appointments of the dining room and its manor house, and the roomy atmosphere of the villa's restful lounge, that it was suggested among friends of the Ruspolis "that a country club be organized and proper accommodations provided, which suggestion was immediately carried out."

A site was quickly chosen on the lake shore and a building was erected which was, from all accounts, a faithful reproduction of the country seat of the Duke of Devonshire in England, an estate called Chatsworth. So, even though the country club has become a bulldozed clearing, the successor of a hole in the ground, and even though the "villa" was burned out not long after one of my visits, you know now why the old Indian name, Shamong, bowed out quickly to the fleeting though impressive elegance of Chatsworth, except for the name of the township itself. To the Indians, I understand, Shamong meant "place of the horn" and reference was probably to deer antlers.

The renaming of the town came as recently as 1901, when the Chatsworth Club was formally organized "for the mental and physical cultivation of its members, and the protection, increase, and capture of all kinds of game and fish." The new establishment became, the historian assures us, "popular among its 'Set' and shortly boasted seven hundred members, through the able efforts of Albert Morris Bagby, who headed the organization committee."

Bagby must have been a persuasive sort, for soon Levi Parsons Morton was president, with John E. Parsons as vice-president, and the roll sparkled with such names as Astor, Collier, Depew, Drexel, Archbold, Morgan, Armour, Gould, Stokes, and Vanderbilt. Wall Street titles soon began to run their proprieties against the brocades of nobility in such personalities as Prince Brancaccio, the Marquise de Talleyrand-Périgord, Baron Raymond de Sellier, Don Giovanni del Drago, and the Countess de Laugier-Villars. All this, from what records there are, went on for six or seven years, a period in which most of those concerned may have concluded that Chatsworth could have been a much safer place in which to preserve the best names of crown circles than in Europe.

Finally Prince Mario, with others of his titled friends, was transferred to another embassy and "the Club was less frequented by those whom only an atmosphere of royalty could satisfy." This was where, it is now evident, the backers of the Woodland Country Club, successor to the Chatsworth, came in.

I have tried to explain all this to some who have wandered the wilderness with me, standing on what used to be the remnants of steps that led down to the lake, where once there were island pergolas, or climbing to an even more impressive perch beside the drive, where carriages brought passengers from Chatsworth Station, a depot that has become drab, lonely, and even boarded up, although it maintains some of the architectural extravagances of its period. Here is at least one visible reminder of days when money and fashion descended to the platform "two hours from New York, one hour from Philadelphia, eighteen miles due west of Barnegat."

The feeling haunts me, however, that few believed that ivy ostentatiously imported from Kenilworth Castle once clung to the walls of the Chatsworth Club, that fried chicken in abundance was a standard item on the menu of the manor house, and that here, where only the sighing of the pines and the flash of passing deer join occasional picnickers in interrupting the heavy quiet, there were billiards, golf, trapshooting, and other sports, including those with gay attire who came by Pullman to bask in the scented sunlight.

Mrs. George L. Kirkland, Mrs. George Vanderbilt, Mrs. William C. Schermerhorn, and Mrs. Edward S. Willing, of Philadelphia; Mrs. John L. Gardner, of Boston, and the Morses, Townsends, Drexels, Dyers, Palmers, and Whitneys, of New

158

York, were by no means the kind whose names could have been ill-used in a magazine of reputation. They and many others were, assuredly, a part of Chatsworth's yesterday, even as Willis Buzby maintained from the beginning.

The paths the buses never take up Apple Pie Hill were lovers' lanes "formed from an old cranberry canal." More than hope lies buried in the pine needles and evidence of recurrent forest fires around the site of the Pine Crest Sanitarium. This establishment, beautiful on paper, was to have been operated at Harris, once the loading station of Harrisville's paper and now less than the crossing of a wagon trail across the Jersey Central's tracks. I gaze again at the portrait of Levi Parsons Morton, head of the celebrated L. P. Morton & Company, and remember that this was the Levi who was born in Shoreham, Vermont, in 1824, the man who figured prominently in the Alabama Claims case against Great Britain, and the vice-president who later was elected governor of New York.

I sought out the facts of Union Forge, across the road from the bulldozed clearing that is truly a hole filled with all that was left of the burned-out clubhouse, and I found that William Cook, of Chesterfield Township, was there in 1800, making bars from pig iron hauled from Speedwell Furnace. Charles S. Boyer, in his *New Jersey Forges and Furnaces*, said that William Cook, Sr., was assessed for fifteen hundred acres of unimproved land in 1806, land valued at $200 per hundred acres, "and for two forge fires." Three years later, with the property listed in the names of Cook and his son, there was "a forge and a slitting mill." On Horner's *Map of New Jersey*, issued in 1855, the Union Works is shown as a furnace although tradition indicates that it always was a forge.

"The site of the forge," wrote Boyer, "is on the road from Chatsworth to Vincentown opposite the ruins of the Chatsworth Club House and is well marked by a dam and 'sheeting,' still in a good state of repair.

"This forge, which was a small one, made bar iron, using pig iron from Speedwell Furnace, and was operated for many years. No authentic details as to its subsequent owners or date of abandonment are available. The water power was in 1843 used to operate a sawmill."

By the time I first went to the site of the forge in the mid-1930's there was but the slightest reminder of an old dam and some slag and ironstone farther on.

The Paisley *Gazette* presents convincing sketches of the Paisley Inn, the villa of Miss Marie Hager, and the main building and engine house of the American Mattress and Cushion Company. Then, suddenly, I remember finding burned tufts of mattress filling and the charred stakes of building lots where the Magic City is reported to have begun its rise, built on hope and credulity and a monthly newspaper published "on the corner of Fifth and Main Streets, Paisley, Burlington County, New Jersey." And I remember that if it had not been for Willis Buzby and Squire Hargrove I would have missed the stakes and burned filling altogether. However, the "villa" of Miss Hager bears a striking resemblance to the house of Albert LeDuc's aunt, which is even less than the blackened ruin it used to be.

Realizing by now that the truth along the low roads of New Jersey is stranger than the strangest of fiction, I hurry on to Speedwell, a slag pile over the New Gretna road from what used to be a beaver dam, but a setting, nevertheless, for the incredible history of Benjamin Randolph's $33,000 chair. I used to pause by the roadside and point to the house the beavers built; I used to gesture up the hill to where the shell of the Randolph house stood so long, in defiance of the fires that swept through the woods or could have been started by vagrants; then I would pick up a handful of slag for the collections of my companions. By now only the multicolored slag is left and one has to dig for that.

Speedwell Furnace was located three miles south of Chatsworth and on the east branch of the Wading River. A title survey made in 1865 shows that the original survey was dated 1760 in the names of Thomas Lawrie, Daniel Randolph, and William Hendrickson. "Just before the Revolution," wrote Boyer, "it passed to Daniel Randolph, who soon built a sawmill thereon, long known as 'Randle's Mill' or 'Randolph's Mill' or 'Speedwell Mill.'" In 1778, Daniel sold the mill and tract to his brother Benjamin, who was living then in Philadelphia and who set out stone markers at the corners of his land. I have seen one of these, carefully lettered "B.R. 1785," although I doubt if I could go back through the thickets and find it again, any more than I could show you the surprisingly large Randolph house of which Nat Ewan took one of the last photographs. By 1779, Daniel Randolph had opened an inn, first in New Jersey's Allentown, then in Freehold. Benjamin, stating that he could not supervise the mill business properly, advertised it for rent.

"Tenants came and departed," Nat Ewan told me once, "but in 1783 Benjamin Randolph decided on an active interest, going down to Speedwell, building a furnace, and erecting the large and impressive dwelling beside it." No one wants to admit that he rebuilt a furnace which was there already.

Although the operation of Speedwell as a furnace seems to have been colorful enough, with such names as Joseph Walker, John Youle, Mark Richards, and Sam Richards contributing something to its history until the arrival of James McCambridge and the Whartons, the story of the chair is the most incredible. In the book *Philadelphia Furniture: 1662 to 1807* there is a paragraph which touches lightly on the subject, referring to a group which "includes a set of chairs originally made for John Dickinson, and a wing chair, the latter an heirloom of the descendants of Benjamin Randolph and reasonably attributed to that craftsman." If the wing chair can be accepted as Randolph's work, the reference concludes, "then this highboy and lowboy are from his workshop. Unfortunately there is no analogy whatever in the carving."

This word of caution doesn't bother me particularly inasmuch as in New Jersey there were several craftsmen, perhaps as good as their masters, who served as jobbers for experts like Duncan Phyfe, who received all the credit. What is more, Nat Ewan has assured me, after considerable research on the problem, that the chairs did not "descend" through the family of Randolph but through the descendants of his second wife, Mary Wilkinson Fenimore, daughter of Nathaniel Wilkinson of Springfield Township, also Burlington County.

"Randolph," Nat has said, "died at Speedwell Furnace, of which he was the owner, in 1790. By the will of his widow, dated 1816, the six sample chairs in question are thought to have been included in "the remainder of my household goods which I bequeath to my son, Nathaniel Fenimore." This disposition of the chairs is indicated further by the fact that all six were located in succeeding generations of Nathaniel Fenimore's family. The last private owner of the wing chair was S. Stockton Zelley, of Philadelphia, whose mother was a descendant of the Fenimore line. From this point on the tale should be Nat Ewan's own:

"Mr. Zelley, while of course aware of the family connection with the chair for some generations, had no conception of its value or historical background. Its identity was disclosed only by the accidental discovery of this long-missing relic by an expert in antiques. Immediate efforts to buy the chair were unsuccessful and advancing prices were offered over a period of several months.

"Finally, the owner was more than satisfied with what he thought was a fantastic price, one thousand dollars, and his comments on what he referred to as his fancied ability to exact from a dealer a preposterous figure were to have an amazing reaction. The chair passed through various collectors and, upon the death of its famous last owner, Riefsnyder, was offered for sale in New York. Together with other pieces of Randolph's work, the furniture was sold at auction, and a record price of $33,000 was actually paid for this one lone wing chair."

The chair is in Philadelphia's Art Museum. There it attests to Benjamin Randolph's skilled craftsmanship and recalls that he was a member of the elite First City Troop and that he saw service at Princeton. More famous as the man who made Thomas Jefferson's desk, Ben Randolph is the man I hope you will think about as you look across a lonely clearing where once the Randolph house stood. In its last days the house had been rudely altered by those who had lived there, never aware of its history, and not long before the fire that destroyed it was inhabited during the deer season by hunters.

Think of the chair, Vice-President Morton, the old Chatsworth

Club, royalty in the Pines, a baby prince—think also of the backroads sawyers, the "mossies," and the berrypickers who, with their homemade gadgets and homespun ways, continue to keep life as uncomplicated as you and I would like it to be.

Samuel Morse has gone down in history as the magician of the telegraph. However, the family of Alfred Vail, living in Morristown, argued that Alfred had done much of the work and had been given no credit. After Vail had died in January, 1859, and was buried in the cemetery adjoining St. Peter's Church, Morristown, a stone was erected with the name and dates and the line *Asleep in Jesus*. One morning the rector of the church discovered that a stonecutter, presumably working carefully at night, had added something more. The additional lines read: *Inventor of the Telegraphic Dot and Dash Alphabet*.

16

The Hidden Land

We have come to a country where clam and corn fritters are often *flitters*, where wasps are *waspers*, and where the industrious ant, depending upon its size, is either an *antymire* or a *pismire*. This is the land where old men and old women pronounce names like Nescochague as if the "g" were the "ch" in chocolate, a hand-me-down, some say, from the Lenni-Lenape. This is where you say, after a while, Fork-*ed* and not Forked River or strip-*ed* and not striped bass.

Friends of mine along the shore say that this business of making two syllables out of one goes all the way back to Elizabethan speech. I have asked many woodjins, charcoal burners, and baymen why it is Fork-*ed* River and not Forked and their replies are either jocular or evasive. The superintendent of the State Game Farm at Forked River told me that he had once cornered a gnarled old native with the same inquiry, only to have another question tossed back at him: "Why do you say nak-*ed* baby?"

This, too, is the country in and around the vast Wharton Estate, estimated to be about one hundred thousand acres of pines and scrub oak and swamps and little rivers, called the largest privately owned tract of land east of the Mississippi until New Jersey purchased it for three million dollars in 1955. The trouble with many stories of "the Pines," and particularly the Wharton tract, has been that some people are prone to inject so much that isn't there and take away so much that is. In this fabled and foiling wilderness, mostly in Burlington but partly in

Camden and Atlantic Counties, truth needs no artificial coloring.

Not long ago, at least by implication, such places as Mount Misery, Worthless City, Double Trouble, Fooltown, Ong's Hat, Bedbug Hill, Caviar, and Hog Wallow were grouped as belonging if not to the Wharton Estate, then at least to "the Pines." Much was made of the Richards family and its management of the forges that now are ghost towns; and Charles Read, the genius with the Creole wife, was forgotten altogether. To make matters worse, the people who live in or around "the Pines," known through the years as "Pineys," were "analyzed" by a social scientist who made a survey in 1913.

Mount Misery, once called *Miséricorde* by Frenchmen imported to grow grapes, is far away on the other side of the Lebanon State Forest, where an old outpost of the forgotten Civilian Conservation Corps has been turned into a Methodist youth camp. Double Trouble is an extensive and successful cranberry plantation across the Forked River Mountains in Ocean County, now readily accessible with the completion of the Garden State Parkway. Fooltown was the sobriquet of Georgetown, with mail delivered from Columbus, once Black Horse, and not far out of Burlington City. Ong's Hat, with a dying but still lofty oak in a clearing where all these wanderings began, is just inside the Lebanon Forest or as close to "the Pines" as the world outside can get without taking over. Bedbug Hill, and with it Alligator Ridge, is far up what is sometimes called "the Court House Road," quietly connecting Mount Holly and Freehold. Caviar by now is crab-catching Bayside, down in Cumberland on Delaware Bay. Not all crossroads or clearings with lingering peculiar names are either in "the Pines" or the Wharton tract any more than all New Jersey's ghost towns are in the south.

New Jersey purchased the Wharton lands in a desperate search for water—and water was what Joseph Wharton had had in mind when he bought the first part of his holdings in 1876, for $14,000. Before that an industrial empire of iron, glass, paper, charcoal, lumber, and some small shipbuilding had come and gone, but the story reaches back long before the Richards family.

Much earlier there had been Charles Read, the sailor turned statesman, a many-sided genius who established ironworks using Jersey bog ore at Taunton, Etna, Atsion, and Batsto. Taunton, sometimes spelled Tanton by its first proprietor, is with Etna now Medford Lakes, a well-developed community begun as a summer retreat by city folk but now home to an ever-increasing population. Neither Taunton nor Etna is inside the lines of survey for a watershed. Batsto and Atsion are well inside, however, and while Batsto remains the best possibility for the restoration of a complete colonial forge village, Atsion also has retained its ironmaster's mansion.

Inside the irregular Wharton lines, extricated from a tangle of property involvements over the years, are other towns or at least clearings pockmarked with cellar holes that used to be towns. Among these are Quaker Bridge, Bulltown, Washington or Washington Field, Hampton Furnace and Forge, and Martha Furnace. Just outside, by accident or design, are Speedwell Furnace, Green Bank, Hermann City, Waterford, Chesilhurst, Jackson, Indian Mills, Tabernacle, and South Park. No doubt Chesilhurst and Waterford were as startled to find that parched New Jersey had bought land virtually in their backyards as New Jersey was to learn that its purchase included a healthy stretch of the old Tuckerton Road, a trail over which Charles Read rode from Batsto to Atsion on the earliest stagecoach route from Philadelphia to the seashore.

By now Quaker Bridge has lost every vestige of its houses, its tavern, and the bridge that was built without a nail. The houses and the tavern were gone when I first went that way but the bridge was intact, a narrow crossing demanding courtesy at either end and with railings that spread apart like the sides of a wagon. Even so, Quaker Bridge remains a botanical shrine simply because it was here, in 1805, that the *Schizaea pusilla* (curly grass) was found. "Over the name hangs an aura of interest in lands you may never see," Hollis Koster, Green Bank naturalist, told me not long ago. It also was at Quaker Bridge that John Torrey, of New York, "remained two days at Thompson's Tavern" and was, as he reported in a letter to Zacheus Collins,

166

of Philadelphia, under date of July, 1818, "very well entertained." Cedar water, white sand, and endless groves of pitch pines would be Torrey's lonely entertainment now.

As for the wilderness beyond, land watered by the sometimes curiously spelled "Poppose," Tub Mill, and other branches of the Wading River, even Mr. Torrey admitted that there were moments of anxiety, just as there were every time I traveled through from Atsion, Atsayunk of the Atsayonk Indians. "After we had left Quaker Bridge," he wrote, "we fared pretty hard. Some places called taverns that we put up with were not fit for an Arab. At a place called Ten Mile Hollow, or Hell Hollow, we expected to sleep in the woods, for it was with difficulty that we persuaded them to take us in. This was the most miserable place we ever saw; they were too poor to use candles" and had "no butter, sugar, etc. A little sour stuff, which I believe they called rye bread but which was half sawdust and a little warm water and molasses, were all we had for breakfast. For supper I could not see what we had, for we ate in the dark."

I have had companions on my wanderings down the Tuckerton Road as it pushes on through Atsion to Batsto, and many of them have disagreed as to where Ten Mile Hollow was. There were days, in the beginning, when with the land all around drained and dry, one of us had to walk ahead of the car, making sure of the depth of the blackish water with a stick. In recent years I have made no attempt to go that way—on foot it might have been a long journey and comparatively safe, but no automobile could have come through unscathed. But there always has lingered with me the challenge and the thrill of traveling east of the flowering wastelands through which Audubon rode in a produce wagon on his way farther south, a journey described in "Great Egg Harbour," an episode of the third volume of his ornithological biography.

Although it would be less than whimsy to advocate preservation of a Tuckerton Road that is barely visible, a trail with turnouts like those used by the rolling and rumbling coaches, crowded with valiant travelers on their way to Tuckerton when it was Middle-of-the-Shore or Little Egg Harbour, is part of a more cautious dream. Quakers, who needed it to make their way to Quarterly Meeting in the old Tuckerton Meeting House that still stands, at last after years of casualties in crossing the Batsto River there built the bridge with pegs and fitted timbers. Along the Tuckerton Road, leaving Evesham or Marlton and striking out through the woods to Taunton and Dellett's, there was something of an added challenge in the stretch beyond Quaker Bridge, and it may be so once again. For here is the lonely land north of where necessity developed one of the earliest toothless cranberry scoops, used in gathering *true*, or upland, berries, divided by the natives into classifications like *boggies* and *staggers*. Like so many tools of the neighborhood, the scoop was born of isolation and evolution from the first picking by hand to Rob Ford's use of a basket and cloth-covered paddle—and then, almost overnight, this device of a Green Bank genius whose name is unknown.

The discovery in Burlington County of Charles Read's farm record book helps gauge the full stature of the man who had his fingers in every social, economic, and political pie during the three decades prior to the Revolution. A friend of Benjamin Franklin, collector of the port of Burlington, secretary of the province, speaker of the Assembly, member of the Council, justice and for a time chief justice of the Supreme Court, colonel of the Militia, a commissioner appointed to treat with the Indians, a farmer and owner of one of the first fisheries on the New Jersey coast—this is the man who pioneered in iron and walked the trail that was to be the Tuckerton Road.

Charles Boyer in his *New Jersey Forges and Furnaces* devotes almost forty pages to what he calls "The Charles Read Enterprises" and stays on the subject of iron from the moment that Charles Read began acquiring land in this area of Burlington County, about 1751. Taunton Furnace and Forge, or Tanton or even Tintern Furnace, "was started by Charles Read in 1766-67," says Boyer. "On Faden's *Map of the Jerseys*, published in 1777, it is shown as 'Read's Mill.' It was in active operation in 1768, when Charles Read advertised for three indentured servants who had 'run away from Tanton Forge.' In the following

168

year 'Colliers and Forge men' were wanted, the former to begin work by March 10th."

Etna, or Aetna Furnace, now Medford Lakes and the second on the string of Charles Read's ventures in iron, also was built in 1766-1767, and was active during the following year as shown by various advertisements in the newspapers, seeking master colliers, molders, and stocktakers, as well as "a middle-aged woman not subject to Liquors." In 1765, John Estelle obtained permission to build a dam across the Atsion River in order to float logs from his sawmill, and almost immediately Charles Read acquired the Estelle tract, building a forge there in 1767-68. But by the fall of 1770 Read was advising the public that he was "very infirm and not able to stir much" and therefore desired to sell his one-half interest "in these works, called Atsion Forge or Bloomary." Subsequent sales or withdrawal by Read should not imply the failure of the works—as a matter of fact, there are stoves and other products that came from a later period. One of these stoves was in the Crosswicks Meeting House last time I wandered that way. Another is in the Broad Street Church far away in Bridgeton.

There are many persons who live in Medford Lakes and as many who live in and around Taunton who would do no more than stare in perplexity if asked about the sites and operations of the forges or furnaces there. The story is far different at Batsto, still being referred to in 1768 as "the new furnace at Badston, near Little Egg Harbour."

There was, as I have told you, something of a settlement called "The Forks" about a mile below the place that Charles Read singled out for still another furnace, perhaps with the thought that he could persuade the fishermen and lumberjacks of the village to work there. At any rate, he went to his uncle by marriage, Israel Pemberton, at the place he then called Whitcomb Manor and persuaded him to sell. Read obtained permission from the Legislature to build a dam across the Batsto Creek or River—once, I am told, it was called Batstoo, for that, or a word that sounded like that, meant "bathing place" to the Indians. Then came Colonel John Cox and Thomas Maybury;

but Joseph Ball, a wealthy Philadelphia Quaker, was there when peacetime operations gave way to wartime munitions and sent William Richards, his uncle, down as manager in 1784.

John Cox was a Philadelphia merchant who took an active part in all the proceedings that preceded the Declaration of Independence and all the repercussions that required the courage of a stanch patriot. He became a member of the first General Committee of Correspondence and of the Council of Safety. In June, 1777, he was at Batsto, reporting obvious preparations of the enemy, off Chestnut Neck, to sail up the Mullica River and put out Batsto's fires. The colonel announced that he was throwing up some hasty fortifications in this unprotected area, but these were far less than adequate. "Had adequate protection been provided for this famous harbor, which was used by the American privateers against British commerce," wrote Boyer, "the massacre at Chestnut Neck . . . would undoubtedly have been averted and many of the Tory raids on the inhabitants along the shore would have been prevented." Chestnut Neck and its prize ships were burned, but Batsto held to its work.

That work in 1775 included "a great variety of iron pots, kettles, Dutch ovens, and oval fish kettles, either with or without covers, skillets of different sizes, being much lighter, neater and superior in quality to any imported from Great Britain—Potash, and other kettles, from 30 to 125 gallons, sugar mill-gudgeons, neatly rounded, and polished at the ends; grating-bars of different lengths, grist-mill rounds; weights of all sizes, from 7 to 56; Fullers plates, open and close stoves, of different sizes, rag-wheel irons for saw-mills; pestles or mortars; sash weights and forge hammers of the best quality; Also Batsto Pig-Iron as usual, the quality of which is too well known to need any recommendation."

Early in 1776, John Cox agreed to make at Batsto a large number of cannon balls for the Council of Safety of Pennsylvania, contracting to deliver them by water at Philadelphia. With British ships all along the New Jersey coast it became impossible to keep this part of the agreement. "On May 16," the record reads, "the Council of Safety directed that a letter be sent to John Cox, Esqr., requesting him to send to the city, by wagon, all cannon balls he had made for the Council and informing him that he would be allowed the difference between land and water carriage." The correspondence that passed between officials and John Cox or his agent, Joseph Ball, should be plucked from the *Pennsylvania Archives* someday and made a part of one continuing Batsto story. Ball, who became sole owner of the works in about 1781, sold again to William Richards.

New Jersey has never fully appreciated the importance of Batsto, every detail of which can be thoroughly documented. Said Charles Boyer:

"So important were the Batsto Works thought to be that, when Colonel Cox, who also at the time owned the Mount Holly Iron Works, petitioned the Assembly for the exemption of his ironworkers, that body, sitting at Haddonfield, on June 5, 1777, appointed Cox, who is styled 'Proprietor and Conductor of said Works,' to enroll a company of fifty men and two lieutenants, with himself as captain, and exempted this company from military duty except in case of invasion by the enemy.

"After the destruction of the property of the inhabitants in the vicinity of Egg Harbor Meeting House (Tuckerton) by the British expedition under Captain Ferguson in October, 1778, it was planned to proceed up the river and destroy the ironworks at Batsto. The objective was abandoned when it was learned that Pulaski's Foreign Legion was encamped in the neighborhood. The British did, however, surprise a picket post and massacre about forty men before Pulaski, who was half a mile away, could marshal his forces for a determined attack."

The remarkable thing is that much that was Batsto, also spelled Batstow in the past, is as it always has been, except for the unnatural quiet. No one goes to the old store except by express permission of New Jersey, and then he may see among other things the darksome figurehead of an old ship, one of hundreds that could reach the busy twin villages of Pleasant Mills and Batsto in the last great days. The old Richards manor house, with its thirty-six rooms and a stairway that winds straight up into the tower, remains high on a shaded knoll, restored and maintained by Joseph Wharton and kept intact for so long by his heirs, the Lippincotts of Philadelphia, the city of which Joseph became mayor and in which he helped establish the Wharton School of Finance and Commerce at the University of Pennsylvania. The store, the "big house" that had been Whitcomb Manor, the old barns, and the mills beyond them went unscathed January 23, 1874, when a spark, presumed to have come from Robert Stewart's chimney, set fire first to his house and then, before the flames could be checked, to most of the village.

There are few in Pleasant Mills, with its paper mill converted into an artistic summer theater, or in Batsto, the almost intact forge village of patriot days, who will tell you much about the Reads, or Colonel Cox, or even Colonel William Richards. The reticence of the very few who may know something bespeaks a frame of mind I have learned to share. Now I hide my customary enthusiasm, and merely say that Colonel Richards, the man who seems to have been caught while wandering out of bounds and so was suspected too quickly of Tory sympathies, was truly a naïve and good-humored gentleman who, judging from his portraits, was usually in need of a haircut.

He was a fellow of "wonderful energy and enterprise," according to the records, and beyond that was the sole owner who "lived like a prince" when, as one of six uncles and aunts, he inherited Joseph Ball's estate. But I prefer to concern myself, usually, with the grave of Jesse Richards, his son, in the shadow of a white and spotless Methodist church dedicated by Bishop Francis Asbury in 1808. The huge, pyramidal stone, the largest in the Pleasant Mills graveyard, is barely adequate because Jesse, it seems, was "very large and powerful, weighing close to three hundred pounds." Even before the death of the colonel in 1823, Jesse had succeeded his father as master of the manor and from the impressive house on the hill "ruled Batsto as his father had done with great energy and success for thirty years." This was the period when the estate was enlarged and given many more facets of industrial advance in the making of glass, some pottery, and little forges seemingly everywhere, adding companion ventures in lumber, farming, and the building of ships. All was well in Batsto until the coming of the railroads, looked upon by even some of the Richardses as a solution of many problems but actually a fatal counterattraction.

The fires at Batsto went out in 1848 and the heart of Jesse Richards in some measure died with them, even though new operations had sprung up at such other Richards centers of activity as Weymouth, Martha, Hampton, and beyond. There Jesse's sons—Thomas, Samuel, and the second Jesse—met the new competition as best they could but, beyond that, fell prey to their own diversity. I recall such stories as the one about the Quaker captain David Mapps, who sailed away with an empty boat rather than carry a cargo of Colonel Richards's best munitions, which, he bellowed, were "the devil's own pills."

I first went to Atsion with the late Jim Armstrong, who proudly pointed out that the old house of the iron superintendents had pillars on the portico that appeared to be wood but were not wood at all. They were Jersey iron and stamped at the bottom with the "P" of Phoenix Furnace. I first went to Martha Furnace with Warner Hargrove when there were mountains of slag that had not yet been carted off for fill on the roads, when there still was evidence of the houses in the clearing, and when the great dam was visible not far under the water above the pool where the big pike awaited a tempting lure to their liking.

Martha Furnace, according to the account book of Isaac Potts, "went in Blast" and made its first casting in September, 1793. Then followed different blasts until 1797. "Thus," wrote Charles Boyer, "we can definitely fix the date of the establishment of this furnace. In the tax duplicate for Little Egg Harbour Township for 1797, Isaac Potts is assessed for 2000 acres of unimproved land and a furnace. The furnace was named, as was common custom, after his wife, Martha. On some old maps, the location is marked Martha-Calico, a combination of the name of the furnace and the village near by where the workmen lived."

There is no certainty that Isaac Potts lived at Martha. In 1797 when his tax bill came in he was living on Arch Street, between

Sixth and Seventh, in Philadelphia. "Isaac Potts & Co.," declares Boyer in a footnote, "were important iron factors in Philadelphia, and are mentioned in the *Durham Furnace Papers* as of Green Lane Furnace (Forge) in 1783 and as large buyers of pig iron from the same furnace during 1785-1786. Isaac Potts (b. 1750, d. 1803) operated a sawmill at Valley Forge from 1768 until near the close of the century, and, at one time, lived in the old house which Washington used as a headquarters during the memorable encampment at that place." Martha Furnace, whose products included pig iron and castings, hollow ware, cannon wheels, shot, sash weights, "spiders," sugar kettles, nine-plate stoves, fire-plates and fireplace jambs, is a story by itself.

If the road between Atsion and Batsto, part of the old Tuckerton Road, has been grown over with the years and made almost impassable in extended areas by floods and other friends of heavy weather, then the road that once led into Martha Furnace from the Chatsworth-New Gretna Road is hardly discernible to any but those determined to reach one of the most important furnaces of New Jersey. Martha was inured to setback and difficult to defeat. In June, 1813, the furnace and its warehouse were destroyed by fire but within two months it was "back in blast" with bricks for the stack hauled from Speedwell and with bellows parts from Hampton and Atsion in action on a new site. Here, where the paths may turn back even a jeep, it is hard to imagine that sixty hands were employed for long hours every day, that family-wise there was a population of at least four hundred in from forty to fifty houses, and that seven hundred fifty tons of iron castings were turned out every year.

In 1822 the heirs of Joseph Ball conveyed the furnace to Samuel Richards, who in 1841 conveyed the Martha tract to Jesse Evans, and he in turn sold it seven years later to William Allen and Francis French. After the abandonment of Martha Furnace as an iron-producing center, the charcoal phase of the operations persisted until 1848. Perhaps this is why, when the soil is "kicked up" almost anywhere in the vicinity, the sand is found to be unnaturally black, although I have heard of invaders with surplus mine detectors discovering much more than charcoal close by the dam and in what, it must be concluded, was the actual location of Martha's chimney.

The first mention of Hampton Furnace was in May, 1795, when Clayton Earl conveyed to William Lane and John W. Godfrey, both of Philadelphia, "for a consideration of four thousand pounds, one half part of and in all that Certain Furnace called Hampton Furnace and also of and in all that Certain Sawmill" *known* by the name of Unknown Mill. The other half was owned by Richard Stockton of Philadelphia, but was sold by his heirs to Garret and William Ashbridge by 1797. Tom Gordon wrote that "the Hampton Furnace and Forge at the head of Batsto River is now in ruins" and later he said that at least the real estate involved was part of the extensive holdings of Jesse Richards, whose son-in-law, William W. Fleming, had inherited in 1860. By that time "every vestige of the forge had disappeared."

Although many people forget that here in the boglands Joseph Wharton is remembered for his odoriferous "fish factories," making fertilizer offshore, this is not where his story really begins. After his purchase of all the land that by 1876 had become known as the Richards Estate, Wharton assigned Brigadier General Elias Wright, a veteran of the Civil War, to buy up whatever he could in and around the tract whenever it became available. The general went ploddingly at his pleasant task, which, I understand, continued through more than thirty years. One of Wharton's plans was to pipe water to Philadelphia, but Philadelphia wanted the property as well as the water. And New Jersey, realizing that vast quantities of water were within its reach, began negotiations which culminated in the purchase. Ever since then survey crews, with headquarters in the Green Bank State Forest, have been continually at work trying to untangle property titles involved in formal and informal transfers.

To its redounding credit, the state of New Jersey has at last made up its official mind about what to do with Batsto. The whole task of transforming it from a pitifully neglected stepchild of the state's past to a New Jersey Williamsburg, so to speak, will take a long time and a lot of money. But the first step has been taken. The Assembly has voted an initial appropriation of $75,000 (handsomely increased to that from an original pittance by some far-sighted assemblymen). This is good news indeed, and those who have long believed in the preservation and restoration of a wonderful chapter in New Jersey's past are happy people. All who had a part in this constructive outcome are not only delighted, but proud.

What there will be, I cannot tell. Will someone remember that Charles M. Peterson lived in the never-never land at "The Forks" and there wrote the earliest American novel of New Jersey, *Kate Aylesford?* Will someone remember that Francis Asbury, first Methodist bishop in America, gathered herbs and preached and dedicated the church at Pleasant Mills while a guest of Jesse Richards? Will someone think of Jesse as the stanch Church of England man who was also the ironmaster who operated forges and furnaces, who liked to argue with Scotch Presbyterians and Swedish Lutherans, who employed Quakers and Methodists as "a pleasant mixture," and who built St. Mary's Church down the road for his Roman Catholic associates? Will someone remember the delicate pink of the Indian moccasin, the gay yellow of the prickly pear, or the sticky deceptions of the sundew, safe until now in their own secret hideaways of Wharton land? I hope so.

17 ✑

Glass Past

In the rolling country of Salem County, where patches of white partly conceal ridges of brown and yellow beneath the feeble warmth of a winter sun, I paused beside a small, insignificant crossroads. Far in the distance was the hazy blue of woodlands on the horizon, with snake-fences and lines of frozen brambles wandering downhill toward Cool Run and the headwaters of the Alloways Creek.

A country wagon trail climbed down at the other side of the surfaced roadway. Across from the rough and crusted fields that seemed to be hollowed with unexpected dips and cavities, there was a farmhouse. Before it, on an angle, was a mailbox bearing a name that sounded Polish. A woman appeared, a woman in mannish dress among a lowing herd, cows that were restless because it was past milking time and the warm barns had not yet been reached.

I often have wished that a photograph had been taken then because I could even now persuade you that the picture was taken overseas. But no cameraman made progress beyond the first reaches of the dooryard. The reason was simple enough. The woman had deserted her chores long enough to get a shotgun to lend emphasis to the gibberish with which she shooed us away.

I protested vainly that I was looking for Wistarburgh, and have wondered time and time again what she thought I was saying. It was clear that she didn't know that here, more than two hundred years ago, by the side of the Alloway-Daretown Road, had once been a thriving village, founded by other and more amenable foreigners intent on an industry that gave it distinction in the New World. This was the site of the earliest of the successful glassmaking villages of the colonies, political football in days when pioneers were building toward a nation's independence. Here where I saw cows crowding together was the "glass house" itself. In the stone and brick used in building the farmhouse there is evidence that they were collected from some earlier structure, surely the foundations of the Wistar manor house which once commanded an impressive view from the promontory, rare on the plains that slope gently toward the Delaware River.

Wistarburgh was founded by Caspar Wistar, whose glassware in authentic preservation is to be found but rarely nowadays. There is but one piece of true Wistar-ware, I always have been told, in the Metropolitan Museum of New York. Wistar purchased the land for his famous establishment from one Clement Hall; it was a tract of about one hundred acres two miles from Alloway and six from Salem itself.

Caspar Wistar came to America in 1717, a native of Heidelberg and son of Johannes Caspar Wistar, electoral huntsman of the forgotten Duchy of Baden. Following his arrival in Philadelphia, Wistar worked at various jobs for a few years and in 1725 became a member of the Society of Friends. Shortly after, he married a young Quakeress in Germantown, Catherine Janson, and two years later a son, Richard, was born. This was the Richard who was to have a part in his father's glassmaking dream, realized and made to flourish through forty-one years. It was not until 1780 that conditions compelled this same Richard to close his father's celebrated enterprise.

With the rise of the colonies there came a natural demand for table- and glassware. In 1738 quantities of sandy soil favorable to the manufacture of glass were discovered in a country described as lining the highway and connecting Salem and Pilesgrove. It also had been noted, at about the same time, that the Alloways Creek—then curiously spelled as "Aloes"—was navigable as far as Thompson's Bridge, a crossroads village near Salem in Salem County.

Caspar Wistar made an agreement with James Marshall, a sea captain, to transport to Philadelphia, for the sum of fifty-eight pounds, eight shillings, four experienced glassmakers. These men took ship at Rotterdam and through the years a controversy has waxed and waned as to whether the newcomers were Belgians, Germans, or Dutchmen.

Wistar, having worked hard to finance his undertaking, engaged most efficiently in carrying out his preparations, contrary to so many of the little glass manufactories that sprang up in later years. This is what makes the transition to a cow pasture so unusual—in many instances there is more to show for the smaller Jersey glass towns that existed only a few years before their workers went off in search of better working conditions and better sand than there is to show for Wistarburgh. Caspar signed four experts—Caspar Galter, John Halter, John Wentzell, and Simon Greismeyer—to show and use their glassmaking formulas, with all expenses for living, for the employ of servants, and for all sorts of conveniences cheerfully paid.

Whatever nationality the original four were, they arrived safely and began work for Caspar Wistar, who, with the actual beginning of his operations, became known far and wide as Caspar the Palatine. Just as I have wondered how much the sea captain Marshall knew about the Marshalls of Marshallville, another forgotten glass town on the way to Cape May, so I have reflected on the village of Palatine, not far off, asking if there may not be some connection with Wistarburgh. In fact, such a reference to the celebrated glassmaking pioneer appears in the records, bearing the date 1740, and it is supposed that by this time the business was highly profitable.

Its success, however, was chiefly indicated in papers and incidents of the day, as well as in the political machinations that preceded the complacent years of colonization under England's rule. Much attention seems to have been focused on Wistarburgh by the collectors of His Majesty's customs, and even Benjamin Franklin was a party to a subtle system of misinformation and concealment which gave far from a true picture to the mother country.

Franklin, in writing to his son, William, then a governor of New Jersey and not yet the declared Tory that he was to be revealed, advised that the king should be told nothing of the glass operations. Specifically, he advised that reports to the crown should state but briefly that a "glass house" was progressing, experimenting in the making of "coarse window glass" and bottles, but adding that "duty fine glass" could still be imported profitably from home. In 1768 this propaganda belied the real situation, and it is permissible to conclude that Wistarburgh's success was kept secret from the overseas agents who should have been more suspicious concerning the curtailment of imported glass in the face of such contradictory reports. It is possible, of course, and quite probable that these agents were wined and dined and "bought off."

The bustle and activity of the glass house had built up a goodly community that must have been evident enough, with a large plant in operation every day and with shallops carrying its products down the creek from Thompson's Bridge and beyond. A shallop is a small open boat with oars or sails or both. Workmen's houses stretched along the road as far as the eye could see, I was told, although the last time I was in the neighborhood there was but one lone house that had the appearance of reaching back to those days of lost glory.

Advertisements in contemporary newspapers were filled with news of runaways, bound-out boys and men who had fled from "Mr. Wistar's Glass House," indicating one of two things: either conditions of labor could have been better or many of the workers used Wistarburgh as a mere way station into a new country. At the same time, young women of Philadelphia and vicinity who disappeared, apparently in the company of young Germans in bright blue coats with shiny metal buttons, were frequently reported to have eloped with employees of the Wistar establishment. Many of these runaways changed their names, I am convinced, to set up many of the smaller glass towns that sprang up over a wide area of Down Jersey with varying success. In many instances I have learned all I thought could be found out about this forgotten town or that, only to have clues come tumbling out at the end indicating that here, too, was a venture in glass with all the rest.

These advertisements ran like this:

"TEN DOLLARS REWARD. Philadelphia, April 18, 1770. Run away from the Subscriber's Glass-house, in Salem County, West Jersey, a Dutch Servant Man, named Adrian Brust, about 27 Years of Age, 5 feet 7 or 8 inches high, of a pale Complexion, has short light Hair, two Moles on his left Cheek, and on his right Temple a Scar, also on one of his Feet, near his Ancle, which is but lately healed, and the Shoe mended where the Cut was. Had on when he went away, an old Felt Hat, a lightish coloured Upper Jacket, with Brass Buttons, this Country make, about half worn, with a Patch on one of the hind Flaps, where there was a Hole burnt, and under one with flat Metal Buttons, both of frilled Linsey, Leather Breeches, grey Yarn Stockings, good Shoes with Brass Buckles, a good Shirt, and generally wears the Bosom Part behind. He has been a Soldier in Portugal, and came last Fall from Lisbon. Whoever takes up said Servant, and brings him to his Master, or secures him in any of His Majesty's Gaols, so that his Master may have him again, shall have Ten Dollars; if taken in this Province, or Jersey, and Sixteen if in any other Province. It is supposed, he is lurking about this City, as he crossed the River at Gloucester Ferry early this Morning. If he be enlisted for a Soldier, and any Person will make Proof thereof, he shall receive Six Dollars Reward. He can speak but little English."

This notice, signed by Richard Wistar, indicates several things that were common in those days. Perhaps they were forerunners of gossip columns in that they involved indentured servants who had records, slaves believed to be with child, serving maids who were admitted frankly to have run off with needed farmhands posted as too good for them, and so on. Clearly Adrian Brust's master took extraordinary note of his physical appearance. He made it equally obvious that knowledge of the young man's whereabouts was important, even though his return to service could not be obtained. However, while many such fugitives were apprehended and returned, there seems to have been a more or less general conspiracy to cooperate with the underdog, especially if names had been changed, legally or otherwise.

It must have been about 1760 that Wistarburgh attained its zenith. In the early 1760's there poured from Salem County a constant stream of flasks, demijohns, sweetmeat and preserve jars, spice jars, mustard pots, snuff canisters, medicine "phials," tubes, and globes, all in such colors as light green, golden amber, opaque white, and smoky brown.

My guide to the site of Wistarburgh in days before the reign of the lady with the shotgun was Joe Sickler, historian, teacher, author, and for some little time postmaster at Salem. I know very well that without Joe's help I could not have found the place, or, having found it, would have believed all the stories of its vanished wonders. Surely there was nothing then to indicate that any town, let alone an important one, had ever been at what by now is an even more obscure turn in the road. But Joe, armed with such a miscellany of facts as he had picked up in his own researches, as well as through family connections with the Wistar place, moved about, pointing to such evidence as could be found with unquestioned authority.

Joe's great-grandfather, Theodewald Ziegler, soon became Caspar Wistar's trusted friend and coworker. The name was Ziegler then, not Sickler. Later on, for reasons that must have been practical enough, Theodewald became David and Ziegler became Sickler. And Sickler it has remained to this day.

Another family identified with the rise of Wistarburgh was named Laurentz. It was in the Laurentz house that the first Roman Catholic Mass was said in all Salem County, some Jesuits coming there under the George II interdiction.

Thompson's Bridge has become the town of Alloway, sometimes spoken of as Alloways or even Allowaystown by some of the older people. I have been told that Thompson, one of the Wistar managers, moved to the east and took over the inn at the Alloway corner and was followed by those who had no intention of lingering among the clattering shutters of a ghost town.

Cornelius Weygandt used to say that the art of Wistarburgh was virtually extinct and that the craftsmanship began to lose individuality when families like the Stangers, or Stangeers, moved away from the Alloway neighborhood, to Glassboro, Clayton, and beyond. It was almost in the "beyond" that I came upon Miss Isabella Stanger, namesake of the Isabella Glass Works, operated by her father, but that was at New Brooklyn. There only the weather-black but nonetheless picturesque workmen's houses recall a little "glass house" truly born of Wistar's ways.

Tom Gordon makes no reference to Wistarburgh as a town or to Wistar's Glass House as the center of activity in either Upper Alloways Creek Township, Lower Alloways Creek Township, or Alloways town which, in 1830, when he was putting his *Gazetteer* together, owned up to "from 70 to 80 dwellings, 2 taverns, 4 or 5 stores, 1 Methodist and 1 Baptist church. The Messrs. Reeves have here 2 very powerful saw mills, engaged principally in cutting ship timber and a valuable grist mill on the Alloways creek," the paragraph goes on. "They employ from 75 to 100 horses in drawing timber, etc., to their works." There is no slightest bow to Wistarburgh here, or in the description of the townships where the villages listed are Allowaystown, Quinton's Bridge, and Guineatown.

However, the *Historical Collections* of more than a century later makes up for the omission with its own description of the township called Upper Alloways Creek. "Alloways creek, which runs through the township," reads the description, "derives its appellation from an Indian chief, named Alloways, who lived in this country at the period of Fenwick's arrival, in 1675. The township was early settled. About the year 1748, a German Lutheran church, called Emanuel's, was established at Freasburg [now Friesburg], the constituents of which are believed to have been all Germans. Their names were Freas, Trollenger, Meyer, Hahn, Born, Wentzell, Mackassen, Heppel, Ridman, Dillshoever, Sowder, Kniest, Tobal, and others, with their families. These people worked at Wistar's glass-works, 2 ½ miles

183

above Allowaystown, which are said to have been the first glass-works established in the Union."

Fragmentary as Wistarburgh's story remains, and elusive as its precise location seems to be, it must lead all others when the great story of New Jersey glass is written. Through the years from that first visit to a town which more than a decade ago had vanished utterly except for glints and flashes on the ground that were clues to bits of bottles, chapters of a present-day industry that overlooks its romantic past have thrown long shadows across my path. At Bulltown, now another uncertain clearing back from Crowleytown on the Mullica River; at Green Bank, keeping alive the memory of Herman City with a cluster of houses and a country store; at Jackson, or Jackson Glass Works, visited regularly by the kindly Black Doctor on the road from Berlin, once Long-a-Coming, into the Pines; at Tansboro, Williamstown, Hammonton, Eayrestown, and Lebanon, now a state forest but once another name, Lebanon Glass Works, that I can well remember on rickety signs—I have pieced together more than a notion of what a wonderful saga there could be.

"Why don't you do it?" some of my friends have asked me, whenever I have tried to enlist a more expert hand for the special task.

"For more reasons than I can tell in just a minute," I usually reply. "First of all, the one who does it would have to have spent much of his lifetime eating and sleeping and breathing glass. I'm not the one. I'd always be afraid that I had left somebody or something important out of the reckoning altogether. There was a glassworks at Marshallville and another at Estelville, and the one that was called Isabella was, I think, very important. And I'd want to bring the Clevengers at Clayton into it, for they're the only ones I've seen operating with the old Jenny Lind and Log Cabin and other molds they inherited."

At Green Bank, where bits of old Jersey glass can be found any day in the fill around the small but picturesque Methodist church beyond one of the loveliest houses on the Mullica, the Forman place, some of the first clues came in corrections of my spelling of Kate's Pewter, or Katesputah, as the name of a

184

nearby run or stream. Long ago Rod Koster wrote that on re-opening Aunt Hattie Ford's store on his return from war service in England, he had found but little time to investigate the early years of William Sooy. "But I found out that Billy was co-owner of the Green Bank glassworks and was buying as well as selling the glass of Samuel Crowley at Bulltown between the years 1852 and 1857," he told me.

"Do you recall the name, Kate's Pewter, that bothered us so?" he asked. "Well, among the papers I have gone over so far is what they call a true copy, dated 1842, of a warrant of a survey granted one Daniel Smith, of Burlington, by 'Societies of 100,000 acres in the Western Division of the Province of New Jersey' in the year 1762. The name here is spelled 'Cakes pruto' and some of us have it figured out that this is the English approximation of a lost Indian name. I can smile now at the folksay that developed through the years around that name, Kate's Pewter. For a long while they had me convinced that Kate, whoever she may have been, had buried some precious pewter beside the stream that took her name, still lettered out as Katesputah on regional maps and surveys. Katesputah Run is mentioned in more than one description of the little glass plants that grew up and grew down in a widespread area."

Then another patient searcher for neighborhood information, caught as I have been by this land of scrub oak and laurel and stunted pine, came upon listings which described very quickly the kinds of bottles that were made in Green Bank where today the glass factory is as gone as Joe Mulliner, hanged on Gallows Hill, Burlington, and buried on his widow's land by the river up the road. Vials were "common," "wide-mouthed," and "Prescription." Others were fashioned for Harlem Oil, Stoughton's, Turlington's, Godfrey's, Lemon Acid, and inks. Price lists of various types prove to be an index to a short history of patent medicines—Ess. Peppermint, Bateman's British Oil, Opendeldoc, Cephalic Snuff, Calcined Magnesia, Balsam Honey, Long Cologne, Macassar Oil, and Bear's Oil. Long Cologne described the size of the bottle, I'm sure, rather than the quantity to be used.

All kinds of bottles were made at Green Bank and other little glass towns to which the workers, like gypsies, moved almost overnight according to demands for the products and the sources of sand and other ingredients. There were bottles for "Caster" Oil, for Mineral Water, for Blacking or Varnish, for Scotch and Moc'ba Snuff, and Druggist's Packing—all names that are exciting far beyond the age that produced them. Hollis Koster, Rod's brother, who has emerged now and then from an avalanche of papers left in a forgotten garret at Green Bank by William Sooy, has concluded that the Green Bank glassworks rose, prospered, and fell between 1850 and 1855. That was usually the way of "the little glass houses" that followed the days of fame of Wistarburgh—they rose, used all the glass sand available, and then moved to a new location, lock, stock, and barrel, almost with the precision of a circus.

I often wonder how antique specialists spot glass as Bulltown or Williamstown or Winslow glass and I suspect that much of their information is a matter of testimony which often is none too dependable. Not until I came upon an early advertisement of the Winslow Glass Works of Hay and Company was I sure that the same plant that made window, sheet, and coach glass also made bottles for wines, porter, and, as the "per fifty feet" price list revealed, "all kinds of holloware." Not until that list turned up had I seen any accurate picture of New Jersey's own covered wagon, the "sheet-topped wagon" that has been sung about in the old cranberry-picking song. Linked with glass is almost every facet of life in a lost land.

Stories of the glass house at Herman, or Hermann, City are unusual, but like all other tales of glass they begin with people. Talk to old men at Charcoal Point on the Mullica and they will tell you that this isn't Charcoal Point at all but Crowley's Point and, further, that if you wait until the wind is right after a northeast storm you will see the skeleton of an old ship, the *Argo*, emerge from the river mud. When Herman failed, because of a depression in the glass market rather than any failure of the glass house itself, the skipper of the *Argo* saw no sense in sailing a cargo of glass out of Great Bay and on to New York. He had no expectation of being paid, so he scuttled the schooner. Not until recently did the *Argo* "turn up," shipping Martha iron.

And there is always one more story as good as or better than the last. Not so long ago someone downcountry told me that Andrew Etheridge, long ago the caretaker of the vast Wharton Estate, wanted the stone and brick of the stack of the glass plant that pointed skyward at Herman. I know it was there, for Aunt Hattie Ford used to show me pictures of it. Etheridge offered a spotted cow as the purchase price and got the chimney.

Long ago I met Constant Ford at a corner in Williamstown and took him along to see some of the smaller glass houses he had known, or at least the clearings in which they had once operated. And it was Granny Sutts who brought new color to the fading picture of Winslow and the Winslow jar, once as famous as Tansboro's Mason jar, as she talked in her little house wearing her hat because, she explained, the wood-burning stove wasn't everything it ought to be. Constant died not long ago in his nineties and Granny has been in her grave these many years—but to them, as well as to so many others, I owe the memories of Jersey glass that I have done my best to piece together, to bring alive once again the Wistarburgh that used to be. For, after all, Wistarburgh was, on a larger plan and in more of a pioneering sense, the mother of all the little glass mills, even if there is now less than a cow pasture to prove it.

Clyde Cheesman came around one night with an old book inscribed with the name Stanger. Clyde's father had been a glass blower and one of his eyes had been bad since the time there had been a spurt of molten glass. "All we knew was glass, as we grew up," Clyde said, "and I wondered if the name Stanger meant anything to you."

It meant more than something, I told him. It was an instant reminder of Wistarburgh, of the young men who had worked there and dressed in blue coats with brass buttons, of the flaxen-haired girls in Philadelphia who had run away with them, of bottles, flasks, and "phials" that had been taken for granted for so long and now were treasures almost without price, and of the little clearings and rain-black and sometimes empty houses

187

in the woods in villages that shared the glass sand they couldn't spare for Sandwich ware to become seemingly more famous.

I was once again in a farmhouse kitchen, with begonias filling the windows, sweet potatoes in a large bin beside an old-fashioned stove, a workbasket and some sewing on the pine table. As if it had been but yesterday, or even that morning, the one who asked me in was not Miss Stanger. "*This* is Miss Stanger," she had said quickly. "Aunt Isabella's ninety-four. I'm her niece, Mary Newkirk. You won't have to talk loud—she isn't deaf."

Miss Isabella told me that she was the Isabella of the Isabella Glass Works, that she was the daughter of Thomas W. Stanger, who died in 1894. "Where you lost your way," she explained, "was Broad Lane. The glass house ran in two places, you might say—the main one was over there in the field where they've been doing all the plowing again, although it's too early for it. The other was across the old cranberry bog around the bend of the road. Just over the road from the bog there used to be the big manor house. That is where I was born. One night it burned down. Somehow the sawmill up the road went the same way.

"There's a bottle from the old factory up there in the cupboard. Lift it down and show the young man, Mary. See, my name is on it! Burned into the glass. Isabella Glass Works, it says. That's *my* name. Father called the plant after me when I was a girl. There were three girls, though. There was Frances, Mary's mother—Mary looks after me here. Elizabeth died as a child. And there's me." Miss Isabella laughed to herself. "Father was one of seven brothers. They all came from Germany to work for Richard Wistar, Caspar's son. Wistarburgh, they said the place was. . . ."

Isabella Stanger fondled the markings in the glass bottle with bent and bony fingers. She pushed back old-fashioned spectacles into hair that was singularly black and drawn straight back. Suddenly I knew that beyond any shortcomings of the clearing near Salem or the protective interruptions of an angry woman with a gun, or even the hurried reference of the *Historical Collections* to founders of Glassboro who were no less than "Stangeer & Company, seven brothers," I was reaching across the years to

188

America's earliest glass. I was saying, as if I had memorized it from the *Pennsylvania Journal* of October 11, 1780:

"The GLASS MANUFACTORY in Salem county, West Jersey, is for sale, with 1500 acres of land adjoining. It contains two furnaces, with all the necessary Ovens for cooling the Glass, drying wood, etc. Contiguous to the Manufactory are two flatting Ovens in separate Houses, a Store-House, Pot-House, a House fitted with tables for the cutting of Glass, a stamping Mill, a rolling Mill for the preparing of Clay for making of Pots; and at a suitable distance are ten Dwelling houses for the workmen; as likewise a large Mansion house, containing six rooms on a floor, with Bake-house and Washhouse: also a convenient Store-house, where a well assorted retail Shop has been kept above 30 years, is as good a stand for the sale of goods as any in the county, being situated one mile and a half from a navigable creek where shallops load for Philadelphia, eight miles from the county town of Salem, and half a mile from a good mill. There are about 250 acres of cleared Land within fence, 100 whereof is mowable meadow, which produces hay and pasturage sufficient for the large stock of cattle and horses employed by the Manufactory. There is Stabling sufficient for 60 head of cattle, with a large barn, Granery, and Waggon-house. The unimproved land is well wooded, and 200 acres more of meadow may be made. The situation and conveniency for procuring materials is equal if not superior to any place in Jersey. For terms of Sale apply to the subscriber in Philadelphia. RICHARD WISTAR."

All that, every vestige of it, is gone. So, by now, is Miss Isabella. I'm glad to remember that for some reason I tiptoed away.

Glass Present

The latest general guidebook committed to the function of leading the way to places along the main and secondary roadways of New Jersey, past and present, dismissed Clayton, Gloucester County, with a scant three lines. Clayton became "a bustling little community of fresh painted houses and well kept lawns dependent on its several small industries. The town," it was added, "was settled before the Revolution."

All the while there was, and remains, a little industry on which Clayton doesn't depend in that sense at all but which reaches back to the Jersey glass of long ago. I don't call it an industry. To me it is an art or one of the crafts kept valiantly alive by one of the surviving Clevengers, who nowadays calls his friends together each winter, makes enough bottles and other items to fill a lingering demand, and then closes down.

Tom Gordon, in his reliable *Gazetteer*, makes no reference to Clayton at all, unless it was disguised in his day behind an alias among the post towns listed for the county in a time when the county of Camden as yet had not emerged—"Absecum, Bargaintown, Camden, Carpenter's Landing, Chew's Landing, Clarkesboro, Glassboro, Gloucester Furnace, Gravelly Landing, Haddonfield, Hammonton, Jackson Glassworks, Leeds' Point, Longacoming, Malaga, May's Landing, Mullica Hill, Pleasant Mills, Smith's Landing, Somers' Point, Stephens' Creek, Sweedsboro, Tuckahoe, and Woodbury." I have listed these places in their original spelling because of the changes that have come in three counties that were made of one.

Absecum has lost its Indian accent and now is Absecon, a far cry from the very first Absegami. Carpenter's Landing is Mantua, which in the early days of railroads was a junction on the Pennsylvania side of the river. Clarkesboro now is Clarksboro and Long-a-Coming has become Berlin. As for Jackson Glassworks, there is no stick of evidence, not even a glitter in the sunlit sand—only the name of the Jackson Road recalls that glass was blown there in quantity in earlier days. In Tom Gordon's day there was at least enough of which to write: "Jackson Glass Works, post office, Gloucester County, by post route 156 miles from Washington Capital, and 48 from Trenton."

The writers of that guidebook made little apparent effort to disclose that Clayton, within the memory of the living, was Fislerville, even as they concealed the fact that Franklinville was, in the beginning, Little Ease.

In the pages of the *Historical Collections* there are two Franklinvilles, at least. The first, up in Essex, had even in the days of John Barber and Henry Howe succumbed to a newer name, Spring Garden. The other is the right one. Franklinville, once Little Ease, is identified as the possessor of a fine hotel, a sawmill, a few mechanics, and about a dozen dwellings. Glassboro, up the road, gained a full paragraph in 1844. From Chew's Landing, now Chews, quantities of cordwood were shipped in days when Hammonton was Hammondtown and when Kresson was Pendleton—both were blowing glass.

John Carey, father of a son celebrated in American labor activities, brought me something of the Clevengers of Clayton story many years ago and I have gone back whenever I could for what usually turned out to be a new chapter. Nine years before I first went there, I was told, the glass trade had been at a standstill. That was when three brothers—William Albert, called Allie, Tom, and Lorenzo, called Reno—began fixing up a shed back of the old Clevenger homestead in Clayton. John, who lived in Glassboro, suddenly came upon details of the saga—how three men, born and reared in the Jersey glass business, had put together bricks and mortar and some sheet iron, making the best they could find serve as a rough kiln. Soon they had two serviceable furnaces and had developed a glassmaking routine startling in its revival of one that had been all but forgotten in its backyard simplicities.

When I was down last time, Allie, the only active survivor of the three Clevengers, was still directing as many native Jersey glassmakers as he could find. "But as many as I get," he told me, "there will be only six weeks of work." When I went back to renew an old friendship with something of the warmth with which he and his brothers had renewed the trade of their ancestors in the making of line-for-line and curve-for-curve reproductions—if, indeed, reproductions can be made from inherited and original molds—Allie's voice was a little sad: "During the war was something like. Now the importers prefer what they can get from Europe. We can make what's wanted in only a little while, no matter how original the work is. It's too bad. These old glassmen should be kept working until they want to stop."

Reno, who had been at work when I first went to see the Clevengers, was sick and I went into the house to see him. He hadn't blown a bottle in four years and he was more than upset about it. To stop work, for him, was to break a link in the chain. He was on a couch from where, he told me, he could see "all the company that comes." Many visitors wander in. Allie and the men who worked with him never let intrusions disturb them. They quietly keep to their routines, never wasting a motion, and calmly asking a stranger to move a little to the right or left if he or she gets too close for comfort. I well remember Reno as he used to be—a rosy, white-haired, robust village blacksmith of a man.

Tom Clevenger had died before I met Allie and Reno, at John Carey's suggestion, but he had been a part of the trio which with infinite patience had assembled the old molds of the family and its partners to fashion pieces of glass which at once recalled Wistarburgh, Marshallville, Lebanon Glass House, and all the little glass towns that used to be. For all the fame that Clayton had in Fislerville glass, inheriting a glass trade that readily moved from place to place, the Clevenger boys grew up in the business elsewhere. Reno was born at Winslow when there was more glass and less railroad junction there. Allie had worked with Reno in many of the glass towns that started up "wherever the glass sand was good." When I first saw Allie at work he said that he was almost fifty, the youngster of the family, and that he had lived in the old house there all but a half year of his life.

People say that the days of truly ancient Jersey glass are over, that the dozens of little glass towns that flourished a century or more ago were doomed by machine methods and inferior sand, that authentic pieces repose either in the top museums or in collections worth thousands of dollars.

Clevenger pitchers, bottles, and jugs would fool all but the experts, but that isn't why they're made that way. They are made as they are because this is the only way the clever Clevengers know—and that goes back a long, long time, perhaps "three, four, five generations if you take time to figure it all out." Although the Clevengers get but a small fraction of what the retailers in the cities charge, they figure that what happens after a sale is made is none of their business. "We work for ourselves," Allie told me, "and that's what we like. And perhaps at the same time we prove that beautiful glass can be made the way it was in the beginning and that reproductions made by the old molds are just as good now as ever they were."

I remember seeing glossy automobiles bearing New York license plates drawn up at the curb outside the plant, which would not readily arrest more attention than a chicken coop from any but those who knew what they wanted. I remember stories, too, of the Clevengers selling dozens of Jenny Lind and Log Cabin bottles for what they said they were worth, knowing full well that invaders from across the Hudson River would recoup the price per dozen in the retail sale of a single item. "We never fooled anybody," Allie always said. "If they were fooled by other people, we couldn't help it. We couldn't run after every bottle we sold here and tell its story. But now, when prices are lower, so many have forgotten just where Clayton was and still is."

From one way of looking at it you might say that Allie Clevenger drops a little carefully selected sand into his crucible, waves a wand over it, and draws forth a variety of objects which, for both use and beauty, put to blush fabled achievements of the most modern Merlins. From a practical side, you list the tools, the very same as were used in New Jersey's first glass houses, even in days when Jersey sand was shipped to Cape Cod for the making of Sandwich glass. These, principally, were the furnace, the pontee, and the blowpipe. Subjected to intense heat, so that when you look through the furnace door all you see is a molten mass, the medium becomes ductile and is drawn out in tenuous threads, then rolled, skillfully twisted, molded, and cut at will. It yields even to the slightest breath of the blower who, like Allie Clevenger, puffs down on the pinkish bubble inserted into a mold at the end of the blowpipe.

I watched Allie and his friends in motion one day, each a mobile piece in a machine almost as old as anything known in the Jerseys. The man at the furnace, an old hand in the trade with a story all his own, selected a pipe from those racked against the wall of the kiln. He passed it to Allie after cooling it with water. Allie rolled the molten bubble on a long brown stone. As his good companion held the mold open, Allie blew down and the mold closed. Then the last of the Clevengers moved to the bench and became part of the picture I had remembered from visits in other years.

Arts have had their deaths and they also have their resurrection. Things have been said about bog ore, cedar mining, Jersey clay. Now, quietly and off by itself, hand-blown glass still lives on its second wind, hoping that the day will come when a land will again appreciate its own. With the return of the only art or craft the Clevengers have known, the old half-forgotten vocabulary of the Jersey glass house has come back, at least in Clayton: all aboard, the order to begin or quit work; batch, the mixture of soda and sand of which the glass is made; bench stones, resting places for pots inside the furnace; blast, the ten months, now reduced to six weeks at Clevenger's, when fire is in the furnaces.

"You'd know what a blower is," Allie said, taking a few minutes off, "but would you know a blowover? This is a bottle finished by grinding its mouth on a stone. A bounty jumper is a cylindrical mold such as we have a lot of here. A bull is glass unfitted for use after the melt. . . ." I have wondered if Bulltown, the glass town just off the Mullica River, might not have been given its name that way. "The carrier-in? He's the man who takes glassware to the annealing oven. Cullet? That's just waste glass. Flip-flop? That's just a bladder of thin glass used as a toy."

When I first met the Clevengers, I heard someone talk of the gaffer. Sensing some new departure in folklore, I learned that the gaffer is the man who finishes a bottle by putting a mouth on it. A gatherer is a man who takes the glass from the pots. A lazybones isn't what you'd suspect—it's an iron machine used for resting iron bars when the furnace is being cleaned or repaired. Cleaning is frequent in even the smallest of orderly glass houses. One day, just after I left, all hands were going to turn in for the cleaning of the main kiln.

The presser is the man who presses glass in the mold. Allie called it a pontee and I spelled it that way. Later, digging into the notes of Francis Baisley Lee, I found that he spelled it puntey.

"A snapper-up is the boy usually employed in the plant," Allie explained patiently, "and there are no boys learning the trade the way we learned it. Perhaps the stories of the glass men have chased them away. I was a snapper-up when I was eight. Worked for forty-five cents a day and a day was ten hours. Then, when I'd get home, like as not I'd get sent over to New Brooklyn or Franklinville for coal oil if the family was fresh out."

In Allie's hands shears are manipulated with the skill of a dressmaker, clipping glass at just the right place and time. Naturally, the men working with Allie Clevenger are deft in every phase of the business. One minute they're shearers, then master shearers, then mill hands, then hands at the glory hole— that's the small furnace in which ware is finished. A necktie in a Jersey glass house is an imperfect bottle, wrinkled at the neck. And a Henry is a lie, and the legend is that the term came up from Millville way and was originally associated with a notorious liar there.

The first time I saw the Clevengers at work they were making pitchers simply because they needed some. A shed and the cellar of the Clevenger home, both fitted with ample shelves, have been stacked almost constantly with what the Clevengers have on hand after the furnace blast is over. Last time I was down Allie and his remaining associates were making all kinds of things—ash trays shaped like giant petunias, tall pitchers with ornate handles, and many other items. "I keep going and I keep the men I know going, loading up the shed and the cellar and the yard because I want these old fellows of the trade to have as much as I can get them," Allie said. "I wish it could be six months or longer. They're real men, they are." As a matter of record, you will go a long way to witness such a show of warm friendship, perfect synchronization, and unusual harmony in men who fit each motion to another's, each operation to that of the man beside him.

Unique among the array of Clevenger products are the celebrated "Log Cabin" whisky bottles, first made in 1840 for the E. C. Booz Distilling Company. Until I went to Clayton I had thought that a booz bottle gained its name from the contents, not from the container or the distiller. These bottles, however, shaped like an old-fashioned log cabin with a neck like a miniature chimney, were products of southern New Jersey, and from there went all over the country.

Originals are scarce and in demand by collectors, I am told. Clevenger reproductions are deceptive to all but the connoisseurs because the Clevengers acquired or inherited the very molds that had been used for the originals in Clayton when it was Fislerville. Add the same time-honored methods and routines and you have a "Jenny Lind" that appears as old as any Jersey bottle to be found or an "Eagle" small-size quart, with a spread monarch of the sky on one side, thirteen stars above it, and a large bunch of grapes on the reverse. And there are small-size pints, also reclaimed from oblivion by the Clevenger clan; they are called "Benjamin Franklins" and have a portrait of Franklin himself on one side and a full-rigged ship on the other. Camphor jugs and old Jersey pitchers, on every hand the first time I went to Clayton, were only part of the variety in the days when I went back, a part with its own background of charcoal from Chatsworth, cabins lit by rags dipped in saucers of grease, and shoes put on only after a boy's feet had been well greased with hog fat.

"Whose feet?" I asked Allie. "And what was the point?"

"They were my feet. They had grown too fast for the last shoes they got for me. The only way I could get 'em on was by using hog fat. And another thing from the old days, we used our own money, just the way they used shinplasters in the bog ore towns. Take a look at this."

Allie Clevenger's "funny money," as the workers since have called it, bore the name Fislerville in one corner, and the date, January 15, 1863, in another. Each piece was good for five cents, although in size it resembled a dwarfed five-dollar bill. "Fislerville Glass Works" was inscribed across the middle under a trademark upholding the name "Moore Brothers & Co.," operators who, according to Allie, made Clayton most famous. Then he produced from another pocket a coin, good only in the store of the Whitney Glass Works in Glassboro. "Some of these men worked for the Moores," Allie told me. "Don't look surprised—they're older than you think, some of them. Albert Schneeman over there—he's been at it wherever glass was cooking in the old ways: Medford, over in Pennsylvania, down in Virginia, it's been all the same to him. Otis Coleman, now," he said, pointing, "he's almost seventy-two but he's been working in glass since he was a boy."

Albert told me he was sixty-nine, but he appeared much younger. Agile, nimble-fingered, he worked expertly, with concentration and yet with time for a laugh. "Started in glass when I was nine," he said, "just as most boys I knew did. That was the big business of the neighborhood then, and it was expected that you'd go into it just as soon as you could. When I was a boy, this here was Fislerville, not Clayton."

Frank Schlagle, called "Groundhog" by companions who seem to have had a pet name for every fellow worker, told me he had been "in the glass mills since I was eight." Albert broke in to add that when he was a "snapper-upper" he walked three miles to the glass house and three miles home at the end of a ten-hour day. "Then, like Allie's ma, mine would like as not send me down to Franklinville because we were out of kerosene."

"My father burned charcoal for Manus Dellett," Allie said suddenly, and then, there in Clayton, after so many years of patient and often impatient inquiry, I knew where the name Dellett had come from. Dellett used to be on the old and faded-out Tuckerton Road used by the first stagecoaches that lurched their way to and from the shore. No one living in the neighborhood ever had explained it beyond saying that the house on the corner once had been an inn, a place where the horses were changed.

"That, you see, puts the family down Chatsworth way," said Allie. "Called it Shamong then, they did. But in 1869 my father was down to Winslow, the town that was known everywhere for glass long before the railroads made it a junction. They built it up only to let it fall apart. The railroads did that with a lot of places. Guess they couldn't help it—cars and trucks came along before they knew what was going on."

Somebody pulled out an old picture, a fading photograph of the men and boys who worked in Fislerville's heyday of glass. As the men in the Clevenger circle began picking out those they remembered—and there were few they missed—I was amazed once again at the good feeling that must have prevailed in the little industries and the towns they built, with money good nowhere else and with stores permitted to sell only to employees. My friends in Clayton knew the ones who had died and, for the most part, what had become of those still alive. "There's Old John Mick," someone said. "And there's Johnnie Bull," called out another. And so it was, as the names were repeated, there in the half-dark of the glass house, out of action for the moment because memories were more important: Ratdog Snyder, Tater Bug Schmidt, and Mary Lib. "Ratdog?" I asked. Then Allie remembered that there had been a Big Ratdog and a Little

Ratdog as well as a Little Rabbit. No one volunteered as to where Mary Lib got his name.

All I had to do when the small talk lagged was to pull out of my pocket another old advertisement, from my collection or lent me by Nat Ewan. One, that of the Whitney Glass Works, established in 1776, proclaimed glass from Philadelphia more than a century later. Another similar display from the seldom remembered *Business Register* gave a full page to Potter & Bodine, specializing in Down Jersey glass and listing for sale such items as private mold bottles, "phials," wine and bitters bottles, handle flasks, mineral water bottles, porter bottles, species jars, and something which from the beginning was really a rarity, "patent hermetically sealing fruit jars." Nat Ewan also has an advertisement of the "Atlantic and Millford Glass Works" of Crowleytown and Millford, Burlington County. I know of no other "find" that has linked together Crowleytown, now a scattering of houses and a point on the Mullica River, and the place that became Pendleton and, today, Kresson.

Nat told me about the Jenny Lind bottles which, when they were in production at Clevengers' in Clayton, stood like soldiers in a row almost everywhere. "Beyond the rather uncommon Jenny Lind calabash bottle," he said, "only a few types of druggists' bottles have been identified as being made at the Pendleton factory. The factory, Charlie Boyer always said, was never very successful, and was sold at sheriff's sale in 1856. Joseph Iszard purchased it for $4,900. Samuel Iszard & Company operated the plant for several years but the works was closed up in 1860." As far as I can determine, the Jenny Lind calabash was "jobbed out" with molds lent to the smaller plants in a typical friendly spirit, but there is no more evidence of a glass house in the Kresson of today, given new distinction by a state highway, than there is of the first Camp Ockanickon that I saw there or of the pool for baptisms that I have been told about.

The dark was descending on the warm and heart-warming circle in the homey and homemade house of Clevenger glass in Clayton. Faces were all around me, or at least in a half circle as in a minstrel show. The dark was descending, I thought as I looked into Allie Clevenger's grim though smiling eyes, in more ways than one. Reno was no longer sick; he had left the circle. Only Allie was there—the "youngster" of the family, as he had said—to carry on.

"I could tell you the names of dozens of little plants," he said suddenly, "that have given up. They had to. They're no match for the market in the land of the Czechs and neither am I. Hoffbauer's down in Vineland is still going, I think, but he may have to close out now, before we do. Glass men have been on half time everywhere, the real old-timer glass men, that is. Of course, there will always be a place for the big plants, and I guess some of us could work in them if we wanted to—but it wouldn't be the same. My father, born down there at Johnson Place near Chatsworth, wouldn't have liked that, no more than I. Neither would the Colemans on my mother's side—they came from Mount Tavern, now only a clearing and a few cellar holes that are filling in."

It was almost dark now but I pretended I could see the photograph they had shown me, the one with all the workers at the plant who had turned with ease from "large Tobias" to "small Tobias" and from "castor oils" to "inks." "Look at all the *boys*," I said, perhaps for the second time. "Some were men before they grew up."

"Don't you believe it," Allie objected. "Lots of 'em never growed up and I don't mean they died. Families were big and boys were expected to work as soon as they could and felt able. That's why a boy dying young was a real hardship in a family."

I suggested that you could tell the boys from the men by the mustaches; those ample lip coverings of the pioneer days were well represented in Allie's prized picture. "That would be a good title for a book on Jersey glass if one is ever put together," I said. And then: "*All the Men Wore Mustaches!*"

"And all the boys wore long pants," Allie Clevenger, lean and wrinkled, came right back. I left it at that.

19

Of Rascals and Trials

The first clue came from forgotten records of the court in John Fenwick's Salem. Afterward came a tale of paralleling sorcery at the end of an unremembered Gallows Road that by now is a principal street in Newton. At some point between, as the hangmen strutted in Burlington and Belvidere, I knew that the *Law of the Bier* was legal witchcraft and that it supplied a link connecting New Jersey with the Saxon kings and the first superstitions of the colonies.

The train of evidence actually started when a friend called me, urging me to tune in quickly on a radio program already on the air. I heard an excellent dramatization of the story of a Salem notable who ate a tomato in public to prove, once and for all, that love apples were not poison.

At the conclusion, when credit lines were read, the directors revealed that they had received considerable assistance from my friend Joe Sickler, the former Salem postmaster who had led me to the site of Wistarburgh. Then I took time out to write a note, expressing my appreciation to Joe for what he had done for at least one little phase of Jerseyana, and that was how I heard about a stack of pamphlets, reprints of something that had appeared originally under the elusive title *Rex et Regina vs Lutherland*.

Joe had entrusted publication and distribution to a small house which had suddenly withdrawn from the publishing field. "People don't like pamphlets," Joe complained, "even if the original was issued in 1692 by William Bradford in Philadelphia. People in New Jersey don't believe there was any slavery here—

that's one chapter that serves as an introduction, maybe, to their disbelief that there was sorcery and witchcraft, too. That's what this was all about. This *Law of the Bier*, or *Bier Right*, was something under which a man could be sentenced to hang depending on what happened, or what most of his fellows wanted to have happen, when he was required to touch the body of a murder victim in public. As far as I have been able to find out, it didn't make much difference what happened. If they wanted to hang a man, they up and hanged him, anyway. . . .

"You shall see for yourself what it is. There is only one copy of the original pamphlet in the world that we know of and that is in the New York Public Library. There is enough superstition, folklore, law, history, and all the rest in those few pages to commend them to those interested in Jerseyana and Americana—but, as you say, people have to know about it and I'm afraid we haven't been equipped to do much about that."

Later I received another letter, in direct reply to one in which I asked Joe for particulars. I knew Salem fairly well from a variety of sources, among them the journals of the first missionaries who called the place Swamp Town and petitioned their superiors, almost from the moment of their arrival, to send them to Burlington or fetch them back home. Now I wanted scenes connected with *The Tryal, Condemnation, Confession, and Execution of Thomas Lutherland* and *The Ancient Law of the Bier*, both of which appear as subtitles on Joe Sickler's rescued book.

"You might look over the Salem Court House again," Joe suggested. "It goes back to 1735 but, for all that, it is not the same." I had not expected that it would be. There are changes obvious even by comparison with the engraving that appears in the *Historical Collections* of 1844, although it is still possible to trace a few lines here and there. "The place where the celebrated murder with which the pamphlet concerned itself," Joe said, "is near the Salem Country Club and above Sinnickson's Landing or, in other words, just where Salem Creek flows into the Delaware in a wide cove. Here the shore line is blown in, filled, garbage dumped, and with a canal that was dug some years ago the contour is completely changed.

202

"You've got to remember, if you really mean to go into this old case, that West New Jersey was quite disorganized politically in 1691-1692. Then, maybe you remember, the year changed on March 25, as far as the legal calendar went—and I should think every lawyer would be interested in that, even if the profession wants to go on saying that the law never mixed with sorcery. Incidentally, that's why farmers still consider March 25 to be moving day."

Old leases ran until New Year's Day. There were no Superior Court judges and the only magistrates were minor, or justices of the peace. Three of these tried Thomas Lutherland: John Worlidge, a scrivener and celebrated cartographer whose house in Salem is still standing; George Deacon, ancestor of all the many Deacons in Burlington County; and Roger Carrary, antecedent of George Connarroe, or Cannarroe, famous Philadelphia artist for whom a street in Manayunk is named.

"Lutherland being convicted," Joe Sickler went on, "the three justices of the peace were afraid 'to wear the black cap' and pass the death sentence. You see, this was the period of James II, who lost his throne to William and Mary. The justices of the peace probably thought that with so much political upheaval they had better 'get organized' in case a new judge came out from England to West Jersey. So they resorted to the expedient of having the assembled yeomen of the courtroom at large vote on whether they, the justices, should pass the death sentence. Then, if a new judge came over, they could say they had supported the petit jury's verdict by the best means they had—public sentiment. The vote of those in court was one hundred to one to hang the man."

I was interested in the folklore of Gallows Hills in New Jersey, not because of any macabre aspects but because great effort has been made to lose them. "For your information," Joe said, "the 'Gallows Hill' on which Lutherland was hanged is well known. It is on Yorke Street, in Salem, at the corner of Kent and next to the Baptist cemetery. This section of Salem, in 1692, was called Angelo's Landing and Gallows Hill was close by."

Another thing vital to remember, he told me, was that at this particular trial the accused had no lawyer and that the sheriff of Burlington County acted as king's counsel. "I do not believe that a similar case exists anywhere in American legal history," Joe insisted over and over. "That is why I have been anxious to bring out all the details and why a reprint of the original pamphlet, it seemed to us, was the best way."

In publishing the pamphlet from notes roughly taken at the trial, the justices of the peace, still playing it safe for posterity and for their own protection, gathered up the proceedings and took them to William Bradford, the celebrated Philadelphia printer, presumably paying him under sanction of Samuel Hedge, son-in-law of John Fenwick, Salem's founder and principal proprietor.

Joe was joined in his search for the pamphlet by the late Frank H. Stewart, historian of Gloucester County. "We spent sixteen years in the hunt," Joe told me. "We found that John Watson mentions the case in his *Annals of Philadelphia*." Watson referred to the Bradford pamphlet, giving the name of the celebrated printer, but added that "the whole points of the trial are too long to be given in this piece; but the facts and proceedings, of an unusual character, are preserved in my MS Annals in the Historical Society."

Joe was disappointed in the manuscripts. Watson had strung together only an outline of the story from the Bradford original, which was evidently still in his hands. "Obviously," Joe Sickler wrote in his preface, "my next step was to try to locate a copy of the pamphlet with the graphic and dramatic title, 'Blood Will Out, or An Example of Justice in the Tryal, Condemnation, Confession and Execution of Thomas Lutherland, Who Barbarously Murdered the Body of John Clark, of Philadelphia, and Was Executed at Salem, West Jersey, the 23rd of February, 1691-92.' "

For a long while the search was fruitless. Then Frank Stewart suggested the Lenox Collection of the New York Public Library. This was more than a good guess, although it was revealed that the item was a rarity even in 1885. Hildebrun, in his *Rare Books and Issues of the Press in Pennsylvania*, published that year, said that "John F. Watson had met with a copy and J. R. Smith of London in his catalogue offers a copy for 7s6d." In his search among stories and legends about traditions Joe discovered that there were discrepancies even in the name of the defendant— Lutherland sometimes appeared as Southerland. But this variation in no way detracts from the tale.

The "law of the bier," or "bier right," classed as superstition as it may be, was so well regarded in old English law that it acquired the titles "law" and "right."

"There is no allusion to it in any of the primitive *Leges Barnarorum*," Joe said, "nor is it referred to in the German municipal codes of the thirteenth century. Yet it was judicially employed in Germany until the sixteenth century under the name of *Bahrrecht*. Thus, in 1324, Reinward, a coroner in Minden, was murdered by a drunken soldier and the crime was brought home to the perpetrator by a trial in which *Bahrrecht* was used. In the year 1601, Bishop Binself spoke of the occurrence as an indisputable fact." A variation of the "bier right," known as the Schein Gehn, was practiced in the Netherlands and in Germany: the hand of the corpse was cut off and then touched by all suspects. When the guilty person touched it, it was expected to bleed. A description of the "Law of the Bier" was included, Joe discovered, in Henry C. Lea's *Superstition and Force: Essays on the Wager of Law, the Wager of Battle, the Ordeal and Torture:*

"The superstition that, at the approach of a murderer, the body of his victim would bleed or give some manifestation of recognition is one of ancient origin and under the name, bier right, it has been a means of investigation and detection. Shakespeare introduces it in King Richard III, where Gloster interrupts the funeral of Henry VI and Lady Anne exclaims, 'Oh, gentleman, see! see! Dead Henry's wounds open their congealed mouths and bleed afresh!'

"The story is well known which relates that, when Richard Coeur de Lion hastened to the funeral of his father at Fontevraud, the blood poured from the nostrils of the dead king whose end he has hastened by his disobedience and rebellion." To which are added other instances, in the poetry of Sir Walter

Scott and in various trials in England and elsewhere abroad. To all of which Henry Lea adds a case in Accomac County, Virginia, *circa* 1680, in which the paternity and sudden death involved in a complex mystery were settled when the suspected man touched the body of an exhumed baby "so that the blud was ready to come thru ye skin of yew childe."

Down in Salem Thomas Lutherland was indicted thus:

"Thou standest here indicted by the name of Thomas Lutherland, late of Pennsylvania and now of the Town and County of Salem, in the Province of West Jersey, carpenter, for that thou didst on or about the twelfth day of November, last past, in the night time, contrary to the peace, Crown and Dignity of our Sovereign Lord and Lady, William and Mary, King and Queen of England, not having the fear of God before thine eyes, wickedly, maliciously, and feloniously enter the boat of John Clark, late of Philadelphia, in the province of Pennsylvania, merchant, then riding near Salem Landing, and didth then and there break open, and feloniously take and carry away the goods of the said John Clark, to the full value of fifteen pounds, eight shillings and eleven pence: and further, thou didth then and there, with force and arms, willfully, maliciously and barbarously, for lucre of the said goods, inhumanely murder and destroy the said John Clark, for both which said facts thou art required to plead, Guilty or Not Guilty."

I am not going to give the full text which is reproduced in Joe Sickler's little reprint with all the oddities and twists of handmade and hand-set type of the period. Lutherland pleaded not guilty to the felony. The accused agreed to be tried by God and country, made objection to four proposed jurors, and then listened to what the clerk had in the way of evidence. Lutherland maintained that he had bought what he was accused of stealing, but there was no record of a sale on Clark's ledger. Asked what he used for money, Lutherland replied, "Thirty-six shillings in Wampum, one piece of eight and two half pieces, nine single and two double bits, and two or three old casks."

One of the justices of the peace pointed out that Lutherland was a little out on his arithmetic, but the accused replied, "I am sure it is as I say, that I bought the goods of John Clark, or I wish the earth may open and swallow me alive." On the second examination, that night, Lutherland added some details which had to do with a canoe, spelled "canow," and an attempted alibi in which he was given dubious support by his wife. Then he was committed and, when he attempted an escape, was caught quickly by the sheriff.

At a subsequent hearing the discovery of John Clark's body was described with considerable gruesome detail. "They sent for the prisoner," says the narrative, and "when he was brought, he was bid to touch the corpse, the which he did do, and wished most execrable wishes, that God would send some sudden judgment upon him if he murdered Clark." Lutherland, who must have known something of the "bier right," was quick enough to point out that nothing happened when he touched the body. "If I had murdered him, he would bleed afresh," he said, or at least these were the words put in his mouth by the justices. "Poor innocent man! Why should I destroy him?"

The tribunal was not satisfied and another inquisition began. Lutherland added more details with the remembrance of the purchase of "some thread buttons," some "mettle buttons for the children," "a knotty canow," and "a parcel of cheese," which had been duly carried home. Witnesses argued that they had seen no such canoe as the prisoner described, that there were numerous lapses and contradictions in his statements, and finally it was the verdict that John Clark came to his death by violence and that Thomas Lutherland was guilty of murder, no matter how the *corpus* reacted or failed to react to the touch of the accused. The coffin was all but fashioned and it remained only for king's counsel to nail down the lid.

Lutherland was sentenced, of course, to be "hanged by the neck till thy body be dead, dead, dead; and God have mercy upon thy soul." He was given five days, according to the detailed statements of the ancient brochure, to prepare for the gallows. On the very first of these days Lutherland sent for the sheriff and made a confession that takes something of a prize for completeness and originality—it would seem that at least one of the justices had a flair for writing, although no one admits to anything of the sort. Lutherland admitted himself to be a rascal of the first degree, that he had a record in England, that he had wronged as many young women as came his way, and of course that he had murdered John Clark. "I confess my great sin of marrying a wife in this country," he went on, "having a wife and child in Claycotton in Northhamptonshire. I have been very disobedient to my parents, a great breaker of Sabbaths, which was the cause of my habit of sin. I had rather go to an alehouse than any church. Pray, young people, take warning of my shameful end; keep the Sabbath truly; go to any religious meetings . . . the devil is always at hand to tempt sinners." It was almost as if the prison chaplain had rewritten Thomas Lutherland's confession.

The point Joe Sickler's pamphlet reprint makes, as he stressed it to me, is that the Law of the Bier was used in Salem in the days of the Proprietors of East and West Jersey. "Don't you see," Joe asked in his continuing enthusiasm, "this was just as much of a psychological test as anything we use today? The reactions of the culprit always have been just as important as anything the corpse could give away—if corpses ever give away anything!"

And there the matter ended—until I went back to tracking down some persistent ghosts: Joe Mulliner, Jacob Harden, Bonnel Moody, Peter Brakeman, and old Uncle Philip, the Sussex sorcerer.

The Mulliner ghost story comes back with almost every spring. Mulliner was the Refugee bandit of the Tuckerton Road. More rascal and thief than anything else, he was one of those roving robbers of the Revolution who stayed clear of the armies of either side, and, as has been said, "had their own fun in between." He was different in that he liked to show off as the reported head of a band of forty ruffians. That was how he was caught at a tavern, now less than a crumble of stones among some cellar holes in a clearing not far out of Batsto—he had a habit of dancing with the prettiest girls he could find and then, with his men who had been on guard outside, vanishing in the dark.

208

The Mulliner story belongs to the Tuckerton Road but there always was a detail that provoked continued investigation. Captured one night when he had stretched his daring just one swoop too many, Mulliner was carried away, tried, and sentenced to be hanged. There is no record of his having killed anybody, but some of his men had and Mulliner, the leader, would be executed as an example to all the rest. Some have said that he was hanged in Burlington, others that he paid with his life, after one of those concocted confessions, in Woodbury. I now have no doubt that he was hanged on Gallows Hill in Burlington, the provincial capital, which Dr. Henry H. Bisbee only recently located under the variant Laurel Hill. This, he says, is "a slight elevation on the west side of Jacksonville Road within Burlington City limits." Then: "In 1781 Joseph Mulliner, an infamous renegade of the 'Pines,' was tried and convicted in the Burlington Court. He was hanged on this hill."

This is important to the record in that the ghost of Joe Mulliner is always "pictured" as wandering along the Mullica, not far from where he was buried on land owned by his wife. This is supposed to give credence to the tale that the rascal was strung up on a convenient limb of one of the buttonwoods that used to stand not far from Bulltown.

The annual "return" of Joe Mulliner to his old haunts at Pleasant Mills and Washington Field usually coincides with that of Jacob S. Harden, the murdering parson of Pleasant Grove, whose grave in a rocky clearing is indicated only by the most general of gestures by the best of guides. Mulliner is supposed to come back looking for money he or his friends are reported to have buried—and I have known men credulous enough to dig great holes along the road that follows the Mullica River, looking for it. What Harden wants is not, as some say, to linger on Gallows Hill in Belvidere.

Jacob Harden was hanged July 6, 1860—for the poisoning of his wife, Louisa—on a scaffold erected in the shaded square of the Warren County seat, after making a confession which was printed in time for distribution to the crowd on hand. Belvidere actually had no Gallows Hill, but one aspect of the hanging is worthy of consideration. *Rex et Regina vs Lutherland* was printed for the justification of the death penalty in the eyes of expected judges from England. I wish I knew how many copies William Bradford printed and whether they were made ready for the morbid who assembled to see Tom Lutherland breathe his last as seems to have been the practice in later years. Every effort was made to obtain, and sometimes "help out with," a confession sufficiently ahead of the date of an execution so that copies of such brochures could be sold by the hundreds in the shadow of the gallows.

One of these bears the likeness of Parson Harden, who seems to have been a handsome devil, and is titled *Life, Confession and Letters of Courtship of Jacob S. Harden*. I have examined its pages carefully in an effort to discover some slightest clue as to why Harden's ghost should come back at all, especially in Belvidere. He had taught school in Stillwater Township and later had been licensed to exhort by the Swartswood Society, a Methodist group. At other times he wandered the Warren and Hunterdon hills selling Bibles and tracts. Louisa Dorland Harden, who had lived with her parents in Blairstown, died in Andersontown, where her husband made his home while preaching at the little churches of the Clinton Circuit, her death resulting from systematic doses of arsenic administered on apples. Since Harden had lived and worked in so many other places, why should his ghost haunt Belvidere? I can only conclude that the visitation may be in protest against the tickets of admission, special trains on "the Bel-Del," and the general carnival spirit that surrounded his execution.

I had been wandering along the Big and Little Muckshaws, streams still crowded by woodlands and rocky glens that were favorite hideouts for Bonnel Moody, another Refugee who was from all accounts a more violent man than Joe Mulliner. One day I stopped at the Cochran House in Newton for some luncheon. Not by way of invitation for comment but because I always like to keep it in sight, I placed my copy of the *Historical Collections* on the checked tablecloth in front of me. The proprietor, always as genial as he is observant, came over and at once spied the book.

"That book," he said, "is older than you are."

I assured him that it was and suggested that he read at least some of the two and a half pages of small type in which the rascality of Bonnel Moody is described. "Following the directions given there," I told him, "I've been looking at Moody's Cave and Moody's Rock. At least I think I have. It's hard to be sure."

"There's an engraving of the hideaway on the wall in the lobby," the proprietor said. "I think it's more likely that he hid out everywhere and he had to—he was the complete villain, you know. Coming up from Kingwood Township, down your way, the British lined him up to recruit for them and do a little spying on the side. He's best known in Newton for the time he walked in on the old jailer in the middle of the night and, taking his key, let out all the prisoners—yes, all that is here." He looked up and said that the Barber and Howe was not among the volumes in his modest collection. "Why the interest in Bonnel Moody today?" he asked suddenly.

"Somebody's got the story going that his ghost is around," I answered, "and I thought a good place to start looking and listening, all over again, would be the Gallows Road."

"Bonnel Moody wasn't hanged—at least he wasn't hanged in Newton," he assured me, then hurried away to show some newcomers to a table. I retrieved the battered book and was about to squint my way through the text when a white-haired man reached out his hand. "May I see it?" he asked, all smiles. "He's right about Moody, you know. This is Spring Street now and it used to be Gallows Road but Moody, I'm pretty sure, got away for all that. Yes, of course he did. Here it is—and don't be embarrassed. You wouldn't find it in a month of Sundays." Then he read from the Barber and Howe: " 'It is said that he and a companion, in attempting to cross over the river to New York, to the English, was arrested at length, conveyed to Morristown, and there hung, as traitors and spies. *This last is somewhat doubtful but still it may be true.*' I don't think it *is* true," the man concluded and added, as he rose, "It's not the ghost of

Bonnel Moody they talk about. It's the ghost of Peter Brakeman. You'll find it all here," he said, handing me the *Collections* and smiling like a conspirator before he walked out with all the authority of Messrs. Barber and Howe. Then he turned, and half whispering from the door behind his hand, he told me clearly enough: "*Peter's the one they hanged, even after he had touched the corpse!*"

I don't know if I had much in the way of lunch that day. I do know that I ignored everything else, even the manager, who continued to hover nearby as if to witness my discovery of something I should have noted, or even remembered, in the light of all that Joe Sickler had learned about Salem. My only solace is that without this peculiarly meandering train of thought with the wandering it entailed from one Gallows Hill and one ghost to another I would not know the denouement even now:

"What is now called Spring-st., because it leads out from the village in the direction of the Big Spring, was formerly called the Gallows Road, on account of a number having been hung along that road. The two most frequently spoken of, on account of the aggravated nature of their crimes, and the peculiarly hard circumstances attending them, are Mary Cole and Peter Brakeman—the former hung on the right hand side of the road, just below Dr. Stuart's residence, by Sheriff Green, in 1811, in what still is called Mary Cole field. . . . Peter Brakeman was hung further down, in a hollow near Moore's Pond, by Sheriff Darrah, in June, 1820, for murdering a pedler by the name of Nichols. . . . It made great excitement at the time of his apprehension and trial. The body of the pedler was disinterred, and taken into the courthouse, to see if he would put his hand on it,—many thinking that if he did, and was guilty, blood would gush forth at his touch. No blood started therefrom, and this was considered, by not a few, full evidence of his innocence. . . . Circumstances were strong against him,—so strong as to require the forfeit of his life."

The story of Uncle Philip, who, quite frankly, should confine himself to familiar ground in Frankford Township, goes frequently beyond the borders. Some time ago a phantom that was at least his double was reported to have a seeming fondness for Sunrise Mountain. Only recently a feeble wraith, bent almost double, was said to be cavorting skittishly around the rocks that border Sunfish Pond, truly a long way from home. All I can do is give you some lines from an account of more than a century ago and bid you to go on, however carefully, from there:

"Some years ago there resided in the northern part of this township [Frankford] a certain Mr. C., more familiarly known among his acquaintances as 'Uncle Philip.' He was of German descent, and his father was among the earliest settlers of the township. Uncle Philip, take him all in all, was no doubt the most singular specimen of human nature the township ever produced. He was an implicit believer in witchcraft, ghosts, hobgoblins, or any other creature of superstition of which he ever heard. . . . He believed that there were 'more things in heaven and earth' than . . . philosophers ever dreamed of, and that the art of magic was indispensable to the development of truths pertaining to the material or immaterial world. . . .

"His perpetual brooding over dark mysterious objects aided in giving a countenance, naturally far from prepossessing, a still more wild and unnatural expression. An artist, desiring to personify superstition, could not have chosen a better model. His long, lank form, bent and misshapen, his swarthy, lantern-jawed, unshaven visage, dark shaggy brows, a deep-set, wild and wandering eye, which seemed ever and anon looking out for spectres—and then his costume, constructed with utter disregard for fashion from the skin of some hairy, uncouth animal, ornamented with its long bushy tail dangling over his shoulders—the whole forming as grotesque and singular an outline as the wildest imagination could conceive. And his manners were quite as eccentric as his external appearance."

There is much more, but from this you will recognize Uncle Philip if and when you see him. There are no reports that he has been seen on any of the Gallows Hills or in the territory staked out by either Joe Mulliner or Bonnel Moody. There is merely the persistent rumor from up on the shore of the Lake of the Mountain, Hidden Lake.

20 ∾

Woman's Town: Port Elizabeth

Now I must take you farther afield, where the folklore of a town belies the tales that historians have been telling for so long—that Haddonfield was the only community in New Jersey founded by a woman. It will be a journey through Camden County's Haddonfield, where I grew up as much as I ever will, to Cumberland's Port Elizabeth.

I hardly know Haddonfield any more. It becomes increasingly difficult to see in wide highways and branches of elegant city department stores and traffic problems the muddy and tree-shaded streets and little shops and people who knew everybody else around, the transition of only a lifetime. Yet in the very midst there remains, attached to an ancient buttonwood in the Friends' Cemetery, a bronze tablet inscribed as a memorial to Elizabeth Haddon, planner and namesake of what to me, in spite of changes, will always be a town.

Elizabeth's character has been celebrated not only by historians but also by Henry Wadsworth Longfellow in his *Tales of a Wayside Inn*. Elizabeth had a husband, John Estaugh, but the girl sent out from England to manage her father's property in the new land was the dominant and more celebrated character.

Beneath a stone too often forgotten in another Friends' burying ground at Port Elizabeth, not so far away today, are the mortal remains of another woman who built a town, a woman who for many a passer-by hides her identity behind the inscribed initials E.B. The legend is that these two Elizabeths were great friends, and that they journeyed to each other's towns in alter-

214

nate years for Quarterly Meeting. Elizabeth Haddon, later Estaugh, was more than likely the inspiration of Elizabeth Bodly, the founder of Port Elizabeth. For when Mrs. Bodly was first married in 1757, at the age of twenty, Elizabeth Estaugh was sixty-four.

Port Elizabeth long ago became, for those who have hustled past the village on their way to resorts far down the coast, just another of the tiny towns that string along a Jersey road. And yet, though its dreams of lasting fame in the ordinary sense were broken long ago, its memories are vividly alive, especially among those who will point out the first lonely trail to "the Cape."

You would not think that in the days of long ago Port Elizabeth was the most important center in its area or that it claimed a distinction in industry, in world commerce, and in social activity beyond the notions of glassmaking Millville, its present neighbor. You would not think that this tiny landing on the Maurice River was a port of delivery, that vessels plied directly from here to the West Indies, or that here were manufacturing enterprises of which there is now little trace or recollection. Such are the facts, however.

When I first went through the town and the farmlands surrounding it, I came upon a blue-eyed, brown-skinned tiller of the soil who told me, among other things, that he and his friends were going to try and put a "more suitable" monument on Elizabeth Bodly's grave someday. My first reaction was one of delight. By now I have different feelings in the matter. Both Elizabeths were quiet, unassuming, and to a large extent self-effacing. To celebrate them in terms of today would be displeasing to them both. I'm sure it must have been Elizabeth Bodly's own wish that her gravestone bear only the initials of her name.

That farmer, whoever he was, told me, too, that Elizabeth Bodly was almost certainly Swedish royalty and that she must have sought to lose herself in a faraway land, taking a deceptive name and hiding in a corner of what was to become Cumberland County. I wrote that down many years ago and so far no historian or folklorist has affirmed or denied the notion. I think my informant was wrong, for the family tree indicates that Elizabeth

215

was the daughter of one John Ray and was born in Pilesgrove Township, Salem County, in 1737, just twenty-five years after Elizabeth Haddon had built her first Haddonfield manor house.

Elizabeth Ray was married to Cornelius Clark, a native of old Burlington, and soon after the solemn ceremony the Clarks went to live on a large tract of land they had purchased on Manumuskin Creek. Calling a little log house their home, four little Clarks were born—Joel, John, Susan, and Elizabeth. Their father died young and their mother, left to fend for herself, her farm, and her children, proved equal to the task, harvesting from the best meadowland in the vicinity.

John Bodly, admiring the assurance and resolute personality that must have mingled with the charm of such a pioneer, became Elizabeth's second husband. There were two more children, Sarah and Mary, and then, almost overnight, Mrs. Bodly found herself a widow once again. For Elizabeth, life was no bed of roses and death a too-frequent visitor. Two husbands had died. Joel, eldest son of Cornelius Clark, married Ann Dallas and died soon after. John, the second son, succumbed to camp fever while in his country's service during the Whisky Rebellion. Susan the elder daughter, married Jonathan Dallas and died a few months after. Mary was married to Theophilus Beesley, who died before his son, Theophilus, later a Salem doctor, reached his mid-teens. But in the face of everything Elizabeth struggled on.

Mrs. Bodly seems to have been a large woman, with coal-black eyes and a smooth complexion, called handsome even in her last years on earth. She was known far and wide as the friend of all and it is probable that in her day there were few who did not know her definition of warm friendship and gracious hospitality. When winter came, the intense cold found many unprepared. Elizabeth cared for as many as she could and the portico of her home was continually crowded by those who were in need.

Picture her, in passing, in her Quaker bonnet and shawl, her grandchildren at her feet, listening as some wayfarer told a tinseled tale of goblins and witches. When such transients departed she would tell her progeny that there was nothing to such stories and that she had listened, apparently spellbound,

216

out of politeness. Her life, eventful, useful, and a triumph over adversity and sorrow, came to an end November 25, 1815, when she was seventy-eight. And so it is natural that her name clings to a Jersey village which in every way was her own.

From the cluster of log houses Elizabeth Bodly founded upon the Manumuskin, Port Elizabeth grew to be a thriving community. She had employed some of the first and best surveyors to plot the town, it was said, and she saw to it that it was bounded by Broadway on the north, Second Street on the east, on the south by Lombard, or Quaker, Street, and on the west by Front Street. In 1789 an act of Congress established a district for the collection of duties on imports to Bridgeton, for a long time called "The Bridge," making Port Elizabeth and Salem, not very different in size, the ports of delivery.

James and Thomas Lee, Joshua Brick, Isaac Townsend, and Stephen Willets were among the first young businessmen to see Port Elizabeth's advantages. They purchased lots, set up houses, and built storehouses for the shipping of lumber and other products of the land. The development was steady and promising. Ships arrived from and sailed to the Indies until the greater facilities of New York and Philadelphia eliminated smaller trading centers. Port Elizabeth in the early 1800's was one of the two leading villages of the county, Bridgeton claiming an equal prominence. Sailormen from far away mingled in the streets with new arrivals, bound out perhaps to the barrel-makers, cobblers, or husbandmen who sought ways of life that were new. Women dressed in costly materials purchased on arrival from the earliest hubs of fashion abroad.

However, even when I first visited Port Elizabeth, it was necessary to make a slow, dusty detour through an iron bridge beside a high mound of earth upon which the new one came to rest as the state highway system was extended—so, I must admit in looking back, it was easier to remember the port that used to be. Port Elizabeth disliked this new evidence of progress, and no wonder. Although the new bridge and roads unquestionably sped traffic on its incessant rush to anywhere beyond, it destroyed forever the venerable aspect of the village.

In 1802, Port Elizabeth set up its own post office in a nest of sprawling dwellings and hotels for the entertainment of armies of pioneering commercial travelers.

No sooner do you start digging for what used to be in Port Elizabeth than you come upon the names of two glassmaking establishments. Christian Stanger opened a hotel at the Eagle Glassworks in 1807. The ground for this plant, traceable by deeds from Abram Jones in 1782, was sold in 1805 to James Lee—177 acres for $2,000. But the factories had been built by Lee earlier than 1799, so a rental basis must have been involved; Lee continued the business, in person and with successors, until 1884— one of the longest records in the industry. Of the glass pits, the kilns, and remnants of the products that were made, there is no sign on the site. Of like sadness, too, is the wanderer's reflection on the Union Glass Works, once on the north bank of the Manumuskin. After a court wrangle and the appointment of Joshua Brick, Isaac Townsend, and Stephen Willets for the fair distribution of the property, there was a fire, and several years after "on a clear still day," as the records say, the ruins tumbled in a heap.

In addition to its commerce, Port Elizabeth was celebrated almost from the beginning as one of the most important educational centers in the country. As early as June 30, 1798, Elizabeth Bodly had deeded to the trustees of the Federal School a portion of "the school lot" on which a substantial building was constructed in 1854. Students came from afar and only the best teachers were employed on the Academy's staff. The sciences, the fine arts, and languages were taught, but as other institutions of learning were created elsewhere and began to gain reputation, the long-celebrated Port Elizabeth Academy for which a Federal School tract had been set aside so long before went into a decline.

When William Donnelly, a Methodist circuit rider who had lived in Port Elizabeth, died, it was Elizabeth Bodly who provided the burial plot without charge. She always had said that "a man of God was a man of God," and that was that. A church had been proposed but had not been built in those early days.

Nevertheless, as you will find in many of these country places, there was a kind of unity, though by no means uniformity, that held all kinds of people together. Mr. Donnelly's work bore fruit, however, and the Methodist meetinghouse, said to have been an imposing building, was completed in 1786. A brick church replaced it in 1827 and this building, surrounded by the burial places of Port Elizabeth's pioneers, was intact when I was there.

This particular graveyard always reminded me, for some reason that I cannot explain, of the quiet apartness from the world that I sensed when I was a boy at Old St. Peter's in Philadelphia, in the cemetery shaded by the giant and historic oak at Basking Ridge, or by the glebe at Old St. Mary's, in Burlington. Here are memorials of men who worked in glass long before the Civil War, of men who died in conflict with the South, and of men who died of yellow fever at New Orleans in 1878. Here lies Joshua Brick himself, with his son Joshua, who died in 1860, and Reuben Willets who, at fifty-seven, was able to claim in the fullness of early American distinction a summing up in the epitaph "He was a good man."

Among early enterprises of its own, Port Elizabeth made the most of two tanneries, one begun in 1799 by John Coombs and Randall Marshall, and another, called the Old Silvers Tannery, in business as early as 1818. Isaac Townsend kept a store. David Lore was proprietor of another and Francis Lee operated a third on Second Street at Broadway. The traveler realizes with difficulty that business of the area revolved around Port Elizabeth in its truly adventuresome days.

I always have heard two explanations for the passing of Port Elizabeth, and for the strange relegation of its business and little industries to the scrap heap so soon after this teeming activity, this preening in prosperity. One puts the blame on the doorstep of pioneer railroad men. The Pennsylvania, lining out its tracks, cut over through Millville and avoided Port Elizabeth, whereupon Millville became the continuing center that Port Elizabeth had expected to be. The other story is that the glass pioneers, seeking tracts of land on which to build larger and more modern plants, were refused property at reasonable prices at the Port and so went farther up the road to Millville. The truth is made up of both stories, I think. On the other hand, I have wondered whether Port Elizabeth, even in growing down, has not retained something that Haddonfield has lost, in growing up.

Before going further into that, let me include a few of the old legends which, in every village, must be chosen at random from the fading miscellany that remains. One concerns the "Negro Exodus" of 1824 when Captain Samuel Craig, who ran a packet between Port Elizabeth and Philadelphia, gathered up two shiploads of Negroes and, bringing them to the Port, hastily transferred them to the schooner *Olive Branch*, on which they were shipped to Haiti. Finding out that the stories that fruits and vegetables grew there without cultivation were false and, what was more, that promises of a new black man's kingdom were sheer imagination, many died in disappointment, grieving for kin who would not join them as they had planned and to whom they could not return. Ned Wright and John Cornish, two of the adventurers, somehow returned as far as Port Elizabeth and rarely missed an opportunity to tell colorful stories of their "escape."

There is one story connected with the "Exodus," the name by which the tragic incident seems to have been known from the beginning, which clings even now to what used to be commonly called the haunted hotel, the hostelry that once stood across the street from the impressive old residence of Colonel Willets. There used to be a filling station here which all but hid the springhouse that belonged to the hotel. It seems that in 1817-1818 the hotel was the center of considerable concern. Every night at dusk there was a terrifying commotion—windows began to rattle and, finally, the whole neighborhood turned out to witness the odd manifestations and obtain, if possible, some explanation.

At last a girl, a servant in the place, was caught as she ran almost soundlessly from room to room, making queer noises, shaking windows, and then appearing before the company with an expression of guileless alarm on her face.

At the time of the Exodus there was a Negro girl working for John Ogden at the hotel. It is known that she sought to sail with the others to Haiti. On being refused permission, she put on men's clothes and hid aboard one of the schooners. I have wondered, through the years, if this was not the same girl who had "haunted" the hotel four years earlier and who, on detection, declared that she had been bribed by an old witch. Legends do more than hint that she became something of a voodoo queen.

When first I went to Port Elizabeth, Mrs. John Willets, the colonel's widow, lived in the old house that was next to the doctor's office on the corner. I found her there, glumly considering the new bridge "wall" but smiling and gracious among the memories of a very old town. With her was her daughter, Mrs. Thomas B. Lee, wife of the physician and one of the Port's celebrated Lees. It was there that I first heard of these forgotten days of a woman's town and of the first families of the Port— the Lees, the Bricks, the Willetses, the Olivers, the Vanamans, and the Strattans. These names will go on in the neighborhood long after Port Elizabeth becomes an old story and the wharf at Bricksburg goes the way of the hotels and the ferryhouses.

I remember going down among the villages that were Elizabeth Bodly's town neighbors ever so long ago, among what I called the marshes and mosquito choirs beyond the Panther and Berryman Branches of the Maurice River. There I found a place called Buckshutem with a story that matches the spelling of the name. When I climbed the old wharf behind the Joshua Brick mansion in Bricksboro, I looked across the river and the flats beside it to where a little white school and a smaller white church flashed in the sun in those days. These, I was told quickly, were in Buckshutem. The name was a challenge.

But Buckshutem had nothing of the distinction that identified Port Elizabeth, nor of Bricksboro which, as Bricksborough, once laid claim to from twelve to fifteen houses at the confluence of Muskee Run and the Maurice more than a century ago. Buckshutem was described in 1832 as "a hamlet, near the meeting of the Buckshutem creek with Maurice river, Milleville t-ship,

Cumberland county, containing eight or ten dwellings, a grist and saw mill, and store."

In writings of that day Buckshutem Creek is pictured as "a fine mill stream." But the millers of old have gone, the mills themselves have crumbled into forsaken or dried-up mill streams, and even in a place such as old Eayrestown the houses and store long empty on Main Street have been followed by the celebrated mill in complete dissolution. Neither the church nor the school in Buckshutem is as old as the town. My first questions about them were at a farmhouse where a phonograph of surprisingly ancient vintage was wobbling a popular song out of tune. A woman who told a child to end the music until she found out what I wanted informed me that there had been a Buckshutem ferry. But she pronounced it "fairy" even as a man farther down the road had talked of soot as "sut."

I was directed to what then was known by everybody as the old Mayhew house. Patty Mayhew, last of the Mayhews to own a wide domain along the river, died in 1932. Patty was born and died there, and when I went down the owners were Leslie Woodruff and his wife—Mrs. Woodruff said she was a cousin of Martin Mayhew and that they were keeping the house in the family. They said the house went back to Revolutionary times but there was little enough to prove anything like that twenty years ago. The Woodruffs, who said that their "house was a hundred and fifty years old, at least," were the only ones there who did not seem distressed by the mosquitoes that swarmed around us.

Standing on the brick-floored porch, Mr. and Mrs. Woodruff showed me where soldiers of a guard placed on the Maurice River during the War of 1812 rested after crossing the ferry. "The marshes weren't here then," Mr. Woodruff insisted. "In fact, they haven't been here so very long. We used to be able to walk out on firm ground to the river. That's where the ferry used to be, making regular crossings from Bricksboro to Port Elizabeth. Even now you have to go all the way up to Millville to get across. Down the other way, of course, there's Mauricetown."

222

The road that led up from the ferry wharf was all but gone on the Woodruff side. On the other side, use for other purposes had kept it in evidence. But even then it was difficult to conceive that here was a river requiring the protection of enemy ships, that here men in uniform were ferried across under orders, and that the countryside ever boasted greater prominence than I could see.

Mrs. Woodruff opened the door of a back kitchen, often piled high with wood, she said, where the huge fireplace with a rusted side oven was still intact, unused and little changed in more than a century. It was around this fire and in this oven, Leslie Woodruff told me, that the soldiers prepared their meals so long ago. He showed me a kettle, too, which once had hung over the fire. With all this and more as preparation I finally put the question that I have asked of many others, whenever I could, ever since.

"Where on earth did Buckshutem get its name?"

Leslie Woodruff looked at me steadily for a moment before he answered. "I remember a schoolteacher up to the schoolhouse here once asked us all that question. I ain't sayin' I believed the answer any more then than I do now. But all we could do was repeat the story as we had always heard it. They always told us that when the first houses in town were bein' built, a large buck deer appeared from nowhere and ran across the road.

" 'There goes a buck!' someone yelled. 'Shoot him!' And so the town became Buckshutem, just like that!"

Others say the name has an Indian origin but, if it has, none too convincing has ever been mentioned to me. Perhaps one of these days, when there is time to go up and down Maurice River like a census taker, before it is too late, piecing together the river's own story, I will come upon a variant which will hold water.

As for Haddonfield, Elizabeth Haddon's town, now mushrooming to the proportions of a small city, there are few landmarks and only a few persons who will tell you the old tales without the stuffiness that belongs in dusty corners of a museum.

There are some, however, who will recall that Elizabeth Haddon, surely more than an ordinary patron and adviser of the younger Elizabeth Bodly, had as much to do with impersonal proposals regarding streets and shops in Port Elizabeth as she did with the far more personal proposal to John Estaugh, as the legends recall it.

But who will point to Sam Wood's old house of Georgian brick with a stillhouse out back that Elizabeth supervised in what, as long as I can remember, has been a dry town? Who will point to the ancient yews on the lawn and a 1713 knocker on the door, relic of the great lady's earlier house lost in a fire? Who will see in Tanner Street a lane leading to Elizabeth's door from the King's Highway and pausing as it passed the tanner's? Who will remember that there was a potter on Potter Street, that the cobbles of a public swimming retreat wall came from the first street crossings, and that the Revolution swirled and eddied around the Indian King, the tavern that now is a shrine up the highway from the trees under which the Hessians and their pursuers marched?

My own personal and precious recollection was of a day, much further along, when there was time for string music by candlelight for those who would sit on the floor, the steep staircase, and the marble steps of the Pennypacker house, with no interruption from the noise of traffic and with gingerbread and lemonade for all who would linger till ten. All this, too, with memories of the two Elizabeths, has gone.

21 ∽

To the Sea

On the second Saturday in August, when much of the inland world moves seaward, intent upon baring its flesh to the sun, New Jersey celebrates its oldest native festival without knowing it. And although a reasonable facsimile has been introduced at one of the resorts not too far from where it all began, commercial aspects of the sequel are curiously like those which brought ruin to the original.

The girl whose beach gear is tucked away in an over-sized compact, her escort who tags along with bottled lotions and a portable radio, and older companions little concerned with the outmoded role of chaperon—all these and others are part of an exodus begun many hundreds of years ago by the Lenni-Lenape.

What the Indians called the occasion is as uncertain now as the method by which, without formalities, they gathered on the beaches at the same time every year. Later, when the first sun-tan devotees appeared, Big Sea Day was its counterpart, although such names as Salt Water Day, Beach Day, and even Farmer's Wash Day seem to have been used as frequently. At some time between, if not on the Saturday following, there was a secondary "fete" called Little Sea Day but that seems to have been devised, in a homespun and friendly fashion, for participants who never were and seldom can be on time.

My first clue to the routine came, I think, from a paragraph in Gustav Kobbé's *Jersey Coast and Pines:*

"It was the custom among the Indians to flock for one day of the summer to the seashore, where they bathed and feasted on baked clams. The custom survives, and on Beach Day, the second Saturday in August, a point of beach near Wrack Pond is crowded with wagons, in which the farmers, from as far back as twenty miles in the country, have driven their families. Families coming from such a distance usually array themselves in their bathing suits at home and start on Friday afternoon, sleeping in their wagons. It is said that before the advent of the summer visitor put a restraint upon the proceedings on Beach Day, they were decidedly unconventional. While the Indian clambake is no longer a feature of Beach Day, the Indian method of baking clams yields more succulent results than any other. A hole is dug in the sand, in which faggots are burned until it is thoroughly heated. The clams are then dumped into it and covered with wet seaweed. When they open, it is found that the seaweed has imparted a most delicate flavor to them. On clams the Indian was a Lucullus."

This, I can assure you, was the only reference to the matter. The red-covered Baedeker then hurries on to Sea Girt and Manasquan. Sea Girt's residents, Kobbé found, were fishermen and farmers along the shore of Wrack Pond, also known as Sea Girt Inlet, where the summer's influx from Philadelphia in yesteryear "was so considerable that if you shake the genealogical tree of the Sea Girt summer visitor, a Binney or a Biddle is sure to drop off." Manasquan, put down as "more a farming town than a summer resort," was pronounced the chief producer of New York's soft-shell crabs, William Brown's boatworks, established in 1808, and oyster beds "less fertile at present."

My next clue to Big Sea Day was found in yellowing pages clipped from *Frank Leslie's Illustrated Newspaper* for August 29, 1868, predating Gustav Kobbe's wanderings by more than twenty years. The event was given the added name of Salt Water Day and called a Harvest Home Festival, and the sketch showed the fiesta in progress at, of all places, South Amboy. There, if the artist was true to his subject, contact with water had its unhappy moments. Two women, emerging from the shallows in what appear to have been their street clothes, have the forbidding mien of hook-nosed witches who had escaped drowning by inches. One male intruder, perhaps an early life-guard, seems to have carried out his duties on horseback. Against a background of men and women "disporting" themselves in heavy skirts, sunbonnets, overalls, and hats of felt and straw, the obvious gloom is lightened by a beach emporium and tented "ladies' dressing rooms" where the frolickers are making the most of cakes, pies, lemonade, and root beer.

With the sketch and Gustav Kobbé's book in hand I journeyed to Wells' Mills, since then all but cut off from the road through to Waretown and far from either Wrack Pond or South Amboy. I had heard that one of the last unofficial officials of some of the last Big Sea Days was a certain McClelland Estlow. Uncle Till Estlow, then the guardian of Wells' Mills Pond, had mentioned him in a stray fragment of his recollections of the Brookville that had been Tattletown, the Giberson's Mills that now is Keswick, and the "challenge jigs" that once were the high point of dances held on Saturday nights at Whiting. There was a question about Big Sea Day and Uncle Till replied, looking reflectively out on the pond that is still sought out by the favored few who are permitted to fish there, "Oh, you mean Farmer's Wash Day. Yup, my cousin Clell had a lot to do with that."

So together we hurried off to talk with McClelland Estlow at Whitesville, just above the little white church. Clell, with a smile that wrinkled his leathery face, said that there had been no Big Sea Day for more than twenty years. "Used to be held about where Spring Lake is," he said, "but it was all up and down the shore, I guess, not just in any one place."

"Did the Indians begin it?" I asked.

"Maybe, but I never saw no Indians around in my time."

"Were you one of the officials who made the arrangements?"

"There were no officials," Clell told me. "Everybody just made a date for next year, the second Saturday in August, and trusted God to be there."

"That's the way the Indians did it," I assured him, "although they may have invoked the Great Spirit. But I still can't figure out how the Indians knew August from July, or one Saturday from another, for that matter."

"They counted up on moons," Clell said, and exchanged a look with Uncle Till which all but said that there was much that I could not remember and did not know. We sat down in the shade on his front porch.

"It was a day for farmers," Clell said. "Till can tell you that. You could see them coming for miles across the Plains, over the road from Bamber and Dover Forge and Whiting and even the trails through the Forked River Mountains. They got together, somehow, for from forty or fifty miles away, riding down to the beaches in anything that had wheels onto it. Oh, there were all kinds of rigs, everything from a mended-up wagon to a buggy that wasn't very shiny once it took to the dirt and dusty roads on the way. You could always tell it was Beach Day when you saw the clouds of dust start up from different directions all at once."

McClelland Estlow paused and then said, as if defiantly: "They didn't wear no bathin' suits neither!" Then he smiled suddenly. "Thought I'd get you with that one!" he chuckled. "There *were* no bathing suits, boy. Folks going to Beach Day just wore overalls and big straw hats. Most of 'em that got wet in the water was hardy enough to come out and dry off afterwards. For years it was all like one great big family. Sometimes I thought it was like everybody comin' out for Judgment Day." He paused and then added, "All of a sudden-like it was over."

"But what," I wanted to know, "made them give it up? As far as I can find out, it was New Jersey's oldest festival."

Clell weighed his words. "Different kind of people came in. People from the cities that wanted to build shacks, anything at all, so they could splash around and have a Big Sea Day every day. It got too commercial, too. They'd hire a colored man to stick his head through a hole in a blanket and watch him dodge when they threw baseballs at him. Fancy fellows came in and sold souvenirs. There was a game of crack the whip and the whips looked so good that you bought one. Then, with the first crack when you showed it off at home, it broke. And, Till, remember Charlie Anderson and his rattlesnakes? Charlie used to spend a month back in the woods catching rattlers that he'd

228

bring down in a box. He'd charge you ten cents for a look—yep, it got too commercial. And then, in the end, you know what they called it? Wasn't Beach Day any more at all. Farmer's Wash Day is what they said it was and what they were trying to put over was that the second Saturday in August was the only time the farmers took a bath!"

I persisted with questions concerning some kind of organization. Further, with Clell Estlow's being such a good church member, or so Uncle Till said, I thought that maybe there was an association with a religious or revivalist aspect. Were there hymns, or even songs, on the beach? Did everybody sit down in the dunes and listen to a preacher before going home? What was the food of Big Sea Day like? Did anybody bake clams? These and other questions brought no amplification at all. McClelland Estlow had had his say and Uncle Till was ready for the ride home.

All that was before I made a trip to Sea Girt at a time when there was neither basking in the sun nor cavorting in the surf, a time when even in neighboring resorts the boardwalk enterprises developed from the sideshows McClelland Estlow blamed for the collapse of Beach Day had rolled up their canvas and boarded up their windows. I had been making pleas for the revival of the festival when Mrs. R. F. Bucknam introduced herself and lent me a small, fading brochure touching on the past of Sea Girt. In its pages the occasion was described briefly but in all its glory. Big Sea Day was "the time when people for miles about came in sheet top wagons and all sorts of conveyances to meet their friends and bathe. During these early days the upland near the beach was covered with stunted growths of cedars, among which the farmers camped with their families, using the shelter of the trees and their wagons as bathing rooms, from which they emerged in grotesque and primitive costumes for bathing. Many left their homes on Friday afternoon before, sleeping in their wagons Friday night. Hundreds of wagons might be seen passing a given point on their way to and from the sea shore.

"After having spent the day in bathing and hilarity and the greeting of friends and acquaintances, many of the bathers departed to the old taverns, then to be found at intervals along the highways of travel, and there passed the remainder of the day and evening in dancing, drinking and boisterous sports.

"The gathering of these people with caravans upon the beach formed a picture that was unique and full of interest to the curious summer visitor, but his coming and the conventionalities of the present day have drawn a curtain upon the scene which passed into history."

There the reference to Big Sea Day ends as F. Cecil Butler, who wrote the brochure, launches into a more formal history of Sea Girt. Just as I was reflecting on what may have been meant by "conventionalities" and wondering where, even in this present time, they may be hiding, Mrs. Bucknam inquired gently if I had ever heard of Little Sea Day.

It seems that before Big Sea Day vanished to the gallery of half-remembered things, outlawed by an age that frowned on such immodest departures as changing from farm attire to ankle- and wrist-length bathing dress under trees and in wagons, there was an extra "inning."

Through all the records of Big Sea Day, Salt Water Day, and Beach Day there flows the persistent note of friendliness—this and nothing else, I am persuaded, gave rise to an additional session scheduled, by understanding perhaps and surely with no more formality, for the third Saturday in August. Gustav Kobbé gave the festival that lingered in his day a warm, intimate, family aspect. McClelland Estlow recalled it that way, too. Then Cecil Butler echoed the same sentiment in his account, mingling his references to hilarity and grotesque costumes with something like emphasis on "the greeting of friends and acquaintances." Thus it was that *Little* Sea Day was quite simply provided for all those who had to stay at home on *Big* Sea Day.

Changes in the means and purposes of travel that have come through the years have altered the habits of the traveler who, gaining with greater ease even the most remote areas of the coast in spite of traffic and other deterrents, has blundered in on almost every hideaway. New Jersey has postponed the invasion of Island Beach, at least temporarily, by making it a State Park;

and down along the Delaware Bay side of Cape May County such timeless and pleasant retreats as Dennisville, Goshen, and the Dias Creek that should be Dyer's Creek retain much that gave them the charm I found there twenty years ago. I think it was the late Alex Garwood, who went with me on some of my first journeys along the byways, who said that with the completion of the Garden State Parkway we had "seen the last of old Cape May as it used to be." I spoke of all this to Sam Bullock, who planned many of New Jersey's highways, and he was inclined to agree, with reservations.

"If he meant Cape May, the resort, down at the tip of New Jersey," Sam said, "I would say that he was right. But some people won't travel that far, no matter how good the highways are, and the people who will go that distance will be going because they want Cape May the way it is and the way it has been." But down around Dennisville and Goshen—Dennisville used to be just plain Dennis and Goshen won out over another Goshen that became Cassville to avoid the confusion—things will be, we decided, for a long time to come, pretty much the way they have been. "Changes in the older state highways long before the Parkway was dreamed of had taken some of the load from those villages on the west side. You'll remember how Dennisville was cut off the main road long ago," Sam said. I *did* remember but, for the moment, the changes had evaded me. And that is why we are going back.

Although the Garden State Parkway parallels the coast in a general way, not until below Somers Point can the traveler see as well as sense that he is moving along the salt sedges of the bays and little coves. At first he might assume that villages like Bayville, Lanoka Harbor, Waretown, Good Luck, Port Republic, and even New Gretna will be overrun in only a little while. But no one can leave and return to the Parkway at will, so it well may be that the older and more familiar roads and villages down from Barnegat or from Beesley's Point and Cold Spring have been safeguarded for the present.

If the hour is right we pause at an old hotel on the corner in New Gretna, and inquire about the shuddersome painting that used to hang in the bar, with a quotation from *Jersey Genesis* neatly attached to its frame. The subject of the canvas was "The Jersey Devil," native of Leeds Point which isn't far away. The phantom, depicted with a horse's head, was shown in sulphuric emergence from the ooze of a cedar swamp deep inshore, and during the regime of the successor of the proprietor I first knew, someone insisted that the portrait brought bad luck. Thus it was quickly relegated to a cupboard and never brought out, even on request. This time we are told that someone in Bound Brook at last has taken it away.

What the traveler may not appreciate, especially if he has come down the Parkway by means of the troughs and gorges cut through or beside the cities in the north, is that this road of gradual curves and graceful climbs and descents, which identify it all the way to the yellows and grays of the flatlands, takes him through vistas of New Jersey only occasionally seen until now. Until the Parkway came plunging through, and down, and around, these fabled faraways were in many neighborhoods the property of the deer, the birds, seasonal and out-of-season hunters, and, of course, the woodjins, the charcoal burners, the woodcutters, and the forge operators of old. This was country little known even to those hardy inland families that dressed on Fridays for bathing on Saturday. Until these stretches of highway were at last connected, link by link, how many others knew the tang of pungent cedar water, the color of spring in maples near the swamps, and the full symphony of contrast that blooms from the darkly obscure of April and finds its equally glorious way home in late October? Here is an unmatched wonder that keeps pace with names of first families left behind at Lake's Bay, Peck's Beach, Parker's Cove, and the Hatchelder Islands. But who named them? And who named Horse Point or Ham's Island or Poverty Beach?

The wise wanderer will pause as he looks upon the rebirth of the gum trees, the maples in bud in the spongs, with the new greens coming like a downy cloud on the cedar and pine behind them. And we slow down for at least a moment at Double Trouble, surprisingly near now instead of on a trail of rutted sand the way it used to be, remembering not only the beaver that provided the name but also elections held with simplicity, those "for" standing on one side of the road and those "against" glaring from the other. Cedar Creek was Williamsburg and Lanoka was not named, as the real estate men used to say, for an Indian princess, but rather by a whimsical old man named Lane who liked to plant oaks. From here down we come upon the unmarked crossings of the men and women who may have looked upon the sedges but rarely, if ever, saw the sea beyond the inlets.

Swinging inland above some of the more familiar paths and making blind alleys of as many more, the Parkway's double strands of smooth macadam move far inland from Atlantic City and Pleasantville but, even so, keep in touch with the little villages that predate them both. "So many people won't remember," Charlie Leek once told me at Lower Bank, "that not so long ago no more'n a dozen people lived out there." And with his usual sweeping gesture he took in all the area that has become Atlantic City, in those days no more than a wind-swept, dune-rimmed sand spit, still awaiting transformation by a railroad that pushed its way across the marshes with a track-laying car from which the British developed the first military tank. The men who demanded a railroad, among them at least one of the sons of Jesse Richards, had no thought of sea baths or even of the health resort as it was promoted by an Absecon doctor. The promoters kept such ideas in the small print, taking advantage of those who, in a moment of desperation, sought to save a tottering backwoods industrial empire, survivor of bog ore forges and furnaces, with rail connections for shipping between Jackson, Waterford, Winslow, Weymouth, and Philadelphia.

John F. Hall wrote of Atlantic City in 1900 that "to the charm and fascination of the ocean chiefly must be attributed the remarkable growth and prosperity of Atlantic City." Others will argue that Atlantic City is a triumph over the ocean's lingering dangers and that magazines of the 1870's and 1880's carry ample illustrative proof that only the most ardent of the world's politicos and investors would have persisted in making good on their gamble. Up until then bathing in the sea was fashionable up north, where there was money from New York, few offshore islands, and a pleasant journey by boat into Sandy Hook Bay; in the south there was Cape Island, attainable by steamer down the Delaware—there was little between. There certainly was no guarantee that the ordinary man or woman, once having indulged in a bath in the sea, would come back for more. Once a year was evidently enough, even for those who delighted in the festivities of Big Sea Day.

Such developments as boardwalks and bathing suits would have been unthinkable to the sea captains, shipbuilders, woodchoppers, charcoal burners, and glass blowers who had no part in the clamor for railroads. For the most part they were content to move from place to place like gypsies, large straggling families and all, when the wood gave out and the glass sand was reported to be better somewhere else.

Kobbé, quoting an 1840 account by Senator Stockton, included something on bathing at Long Branch which has no counterpart anywhere: "People came here for their health, and after supper everyone went to the beach and there stayed until after ten or eleven o'clock, unless a couple of fiddlers enticed the young people to a dance in the parlors. Every one bathed in the sea; a white flag gave notice that it was ladies' hour, and no man except a husband then ventured on the beach. When the red flag was up the men crowded the surf, and there was no pretense of bathing suits. The hotels were then so far back that the bluffs concealed the bathers. . . . The flag-hoisting was in vogue as early as 1819, for it is mentioned in *Niles's Register* of that date, the writer adding: 'A wag lately hoisted both flags together, which created some awful squinting and no little confusion.' "

On the road over into Avalon or Stone Harbor or Wildwood the woods are thick with birds and holly and weather-bent trees. Especially in winter or early spring, here is one of New Jersey's last worlds apart. Here are the coves of the wild swans, the beaches once crowded with wild geese, the yellowlegs, and the gulls that laugh. For we are just in from the waters of the Great Sound, then Jenkins Sound, then Richardson's, with remembrances of birds that seldom wing their way off course and fish that have become merely names in a book.

I would like to come upon Dennisville almost as if unawares, through South Dennis, then to Goshen, and finally to Dias Creek and Green Creek. From the "inside" road it is necessary to move deliberately out to Delaware Bay if you want to see the water, out to Reed's Beach, or Pierce's Point, or Norbury's Landing. There are newer names as well, especially farther down, like Sun Ray Beach and Sunset Beach and Wildwood Heights. Here where once there was a wild tangle of growth along the bay, with occasional piers and tie-ups for boats known best by fishermen, I always remember John Watson's saying that journeys to Cape May were in the beginning for men and that for women the going for a long time was far too rough. Now, little summer retreats are everywhere.

At Town Bank there was a whaling settlement as early as the 1630's. At Villas the oldest house, or at least one of the last when the jawbones of whales were as frequently dug up in the dunes as they were on Cape Cod, is plainly marked with the name William J. Bate and the date 1846. Now it is empty and in every direction beyond there are stores and gas stations and houses, perhaps the modern variant of the wagons and tents and sheet-topped carryalls of Big Sea Day. The historic marker along the road, almost engulfed in the ever-expanding tangle of streets and cottages, reads, in letters made almost illegible by wind and rain: "New England and Long Island whalemen first settled Cape May on the Delaware Bay shore about 1685. To the sandy bluff called Town Bank came Joseph Whilldin and his wife, Hannah Gorham, grandchild of John Howard of the Mayflower pilgrims."

There was a difference at Dennisville. Leaving the concrete for the old road was like going through a doorway into another world. One house, bearing the name Nathaniel Holmes and the date 1822 would be occupied again in the summer; its furniture was draped in ghostly white. Another house, not far away, was

235

that of James Diverty, who lived there in 1825. Almost at once I knew that everything was pretty much as I recalled it from twenty years before. I remembered going to the post office then to inquire for Captain Ogden Gandy who, someone had told me, had built and sailed the ships from Dennis Creek; the post office had been closed at noon. From there I had gone to one of the two village stores; it was open but several patrons were waiting and a kindly old gentleman with white hair informed me that I would have to wait my turn. "They are home for lunch," he said. "Maybe they'll be back in an hour—or two." This time the post office was closed, just as before, and the door of the store was locked.

For all the time that had gone by, I remembered Cap'n Gandy well—a small, wiry man with a straggly white mustache, with wrinkles in his face that became deep creases in the sunlight. Diverty—that was the name on the old house and that was the name used by so many of the ships whose history the captain knew, ships that were launched in the creek and then winched to the bay, day after day, on every high tide. The *Harry Diverty*, the *James Diverty*, the *Eva Diverty*, the *Deborah Diverty*, the *Emma Jean Diverty*, and the *Jennie R. Diverty*, all named for members of the family.

Then it was that I saw a man coming down the street—friendly, unhurried, walking as if he knew that no traffic in Dennisville could be very dangerous. "I used to know a Captain Gandy here," I told him. "I guess it's too much to expect, but I wonder if—"

"Died ten years ago," I was told, so quietly that the words were all but blown away. "Ninety-two, he was. Had a sister died last year. Over a hundred and three."

"The captain had a sawmill. Is it still here?"

"Just at the end of the street. Still going. Bigger than ever."

"Captain Gandy used to say he was cutting Bible lumber. Cedar from the bottom offshore somewhere or maybe out of a swamp at Port Norris. Said it was where it was since the original Flood. He called it cedar mining."

236

"That's what it was." The stranger smiled and pulled up his collar with a sudden gesture. The wind over the pond was cold. Then, standing by as if in expectation of another question, he cupped his hands and efficiently lit his pipe. "Lumber here comes in from everywhere now," he went on. "The Skinners have the mill. But Cap'n Gandy's gone—and so are a lot more, I guess."

I confess to having had the strangest feeling most of the way home that day. On the Parkway with the sedges on one side and the dark shadows of the wall of trees on the other, the air was charged as if filled with sounds that I knew no one could truly hear—the wheels of patched-up wagons on their way to Big Sea Day, the laughter of men and women at the edge of the surf, more gulls than I have heard since Nantucket, and something like the whine of the saws in the mills at the edge of the swamps.

On the road out of Allamuchy to Johnsonburg there is an ancient milestone, perhaps one of the oldest anywhere. Darkly cut is the legend "3 Mi. to L.G.," but chances are that five out of six persons will disclaim knowledge of its meaning. Then someone, perhaps in the rolling country at Marksboro or among the skull-topped tombstones at Yellow Frame, will reveal that Log Gaol is the old name of Johnsonburg, once the seat of justice for Sussex County. Johnsonburg's tannery, coach-building shop, and Episcopal church have disappeared, but the old Christian church remains and behind it the graveyard in which the small obelisk erected in memory of Joseph Thomas, the "White Pilgrim," is a kind of centerpiece. Joseph's first grave was exclusive and farther away. In spite of clothing of "protective" white, he died of smallpox.

Toms River Genius

I should remember Toms River for Fred Bunnell, who used to write historic pieces for his weekly newspaper, revise them in a nearby daily, and then revamp them so that they became creditable little brochures. It was Fred, I remember, who took me first to Loveladies and Good Luck, and even down to Waretown, forgotten stronghold of the Quaker Baptists.

And I ought to remember Toms River for stories of the first Indian mounds I ever had heard about, for the Revolutionary blockhouse of which Fred had written, for the hanging of Captain Huddy, with its repercussions far up the coast and across the sea, or for the man who built birdhouses and a concrete chapel, calling the place Birdville and hoping for a priest who would say Mass.

And maybe I should quietly remember Tony Then, personable, persuasive, and somehow caught in the cloud that descended on Pinewald, where a few of the first houses and a hospital which first was a mammoth hotel recall a town that grew and failed beside an artificial lagoon where boys, hired for the purpose, caught the same fish all day.

Instead, I remember best an unsung New Jersey painter and a retired librarian of baffling age, who joined forces one day to make the occasion in Toms River far more memorable than many others have been. To the late Edward P. Knox, then, I am appreciably indebted for a countless number of kindnesses, among them colorful sketches of Ong's Hat and Daniel's Bridge, which he insisted on presenting to me because my books led him to places he wanted to paint and people he wanted to know. Another of his favors was the arranging of a strange excursion along the Toms River with an acquaintance, Henry Evelyn Bliss.

Ned Knox, whose Toms River house was filled with the most surprising if uncelebrated of paintings of backwoods New Jersey, had begun sketching unspoiled Cape May County with a headquarters at South Seaville when his last illness came. From the day of Henry Bliss's last visit with me, quite as startling as the last pilgrimage we made together trying to break through Toms River's bustling present to see the patriotic past, I lost track of him. For a while there were annual Christmas cards from California or from an even more beloved Mexico; then, after an interval, there was an ominous silence. All I know is that Henry Evelyn Bliss was long revered among librarians as the man who devised a celebrated system of cataloguing books, just as he is honored now, by me, for his stressing of the importance of Joseph Francis, boat genius of Toms River.

Joseph, whose "pleasant country place" became the Riverview Hotel, was the angular and energetic little man who devised the lifeboat. He invented the "corrugated metallic lifecar" and revolutionized lifesaving methods in the United States and much of the world, but his origination of the lifeboat stands out from an array of astounding achievements, medals, awards, and even titles.

"And he did most of it all," Henry Bliss assured me, "with boats either designed or constructed or tested right out here in the Toms River."

Of special significance more recently, however, would seem to be the fact that Joseph Francis built what Ned and Henry called "flying saucers"—saucer boats or saucers of the sea—circular yachts defying every known rule of nautical science, the first and only ships of their kind fashioned in this country.

"The idea of building this little craft was conceived by Mr. Francis after he had read a European journal telling of an experimental round boat built in Russia," read Henry from lines he had copied, it turned out later, from a big book to which he introduced me, the *Atlas of the New Jersey Coast*, as notable a collector's item as ever graced a Jerseyana shelf.

But before I become too involved with Joseph Francis and his amazing inventions—among them the first Venetian gondola built in America, a double-banked sixteen-oar barge which brought at least one title to this country, and such contrasting items as the Nautilus life-preserver, and a corrugated-iron steam yacht for the Nawab Nazim of Bengal—I must tell you something of the processes by which I stumbled on the remembrances of another unsung Jersey giant and of the Toms River that used to be and never can be again.

I am not at all certain when and where I heard first of Henry Evelyn Bliss. My notes indicate that Ned Knox proposed the meeting. However, I have a feeling that Henry wrote to me in comment on one of my books, making a point of seeking certain family information. Knowing that Ned was on the scene in the area with which Henry seemed to be concerned and that this traveler should see Ned's pictures of the Barrens, the ruined forges, and the broken mills, I sent along Ned's name and address. There followed two occasions, both memorable. One came on the heels of Henry's writing to me to say that he would spend the night at our house. The other was the day in Toms River that followed.

Henry Evelyn Bliss, who wrote letters in a spidery hand—from places ranging anywhere from Dobbs Ferry, New York, to hideaways on the West Coast—was evidently bent on finding the solution of a private mystery which, I concluded, had involved members of his family. The case clearly reached back to a time when fashionable New Yorkers were going farther and farther down the New Jersey coast for their summer recreation, days when settlements along the shore were described as small and straggling.

"Toms River," wrote Gustav Kobbé in 1889, "is beautifully situated on high ground on the north bank of the river which gives it its name. The river is broad and deep from shore to shore, thus giving excellent facilities for boating. The yachting

240

fleet numbers about 150 sail, and during the summer there are two yacht races."

Henry Bliss had written in amusing detail as to what he looked like and how he would be dressed when he arrived at the railroad station where I was to meet him—but he inexplicably omitted two items of his gear that would have identified him anywhere. He described the color of his suit, the hue of his tie, the type of his hat. He said he would be the man I would find carrying a briefcase in one hand and a small overnight bag, plus umbrella, in the other. When he arrived, the color of his suit was not as predicted, nor was the shade of his tie. There was neither briefcase nor umbrella. However, the old gentleman *was* toting two extracurricular items guaranteed to mark him anywhere—two old-fashioned ear trumpets. One, quite large, was for far-across-the-table conversation, as he explained later. The other was for tuning in small talk at his elbow.

All that evening at the house and during the next day, in and out of the car, Henry artfully manipulated those somewhat antiquated and battered instruments with the greatest of ease and with no show of embarrassment whatsoever, even when we were visiting old houses in which neighbors of the Blisses had lived, I feel sure, long ago. Ned Knox, whose hair had been a great crest of white for many years, made an unusual guide, taking the man with the unmusical trumpets to places he had all but forgotten, showing him the made-over houses, the ancient inn at the corner, and other landmarks with the loving familiarity of one whose life had been sea air and misty remembrances longer than he knew.

Ned had warned me that this would be one of my days for listening—and I had no difficulty in hearing everything that was said. Now and then, when I was sure the action would not be too disconcerting, I pulled out my notebook and jotted down a few words which, late that night, I extended from memories of the whole experience. There was mention of the Free Church at Bayville in days when "free" meant "open to any preacher with a message" and when the right to preach, often won by physical superiority, was chiefly important because it was re-

241

warded with the whole collection. There was talk of Cedar Grove, too, on Indian Hill up the north bank of Mosquito Cove.

The old inn became the Parker House which, Henry said, could give its namesake in Boston an argument as to which evolved the famous Parker House rolls. Ned remembered Malcolm Dunn and the other Scotsmen who were gamekeepers at the State Game Preserve in Forked River, unaware until I told them, they informed me graciously, that the Lochiel Brook was named by earlier generations of the Campbells on whose estate they had worked in the old country.

Lanoka peeled off the spurious legend of an Indian princess and became merely an earlier real estate development of a man named Lane who planted a lot of oaks. Laurelton became Burrsville once again and in the transition the shipping point from which water pipes, fashioned at Ferrago Forge, now Bamber, were sent to New York City. Pershing, an interim settlement halfway to Island Heights, had been German, they said, until World War I brought with it that sudden, misguided name-changing fever.

But with it all—assertions that there had been an Army post at Barnegat Park, that Bayville was losing its identity in Holly Park, and that in 1901 there were no houses at all on the south shore of the Toms River, then still spelled Tom's River in honor of either Captain William Tom, an early settler, or Indian Tom —there was an undercurrent. I can assure you that its source was by no means that story of Indian Tom and the reason why many good Toms River people will not eat crabs.

I wanted to ask questions about Joshua Huddy and the blockhouse, about Mormonism in the area, with Elder Benjamin Winchester preaching the first Mormon sermon in the schoolhouse in New Egypt, and with Mormons building a small church, perhaps in the earliest 1840's, on the south side of the river, and about the privateers and the shipping and the actual burning of the village in 1782. But whenever I tried, Ned silenced me with a look. Henry Bliss was trying to rescue a reputation, to correct the verdict that had been found years before against

242

somebody suspected of poisoning somebody else, all deftly accomplished in a cozy family circle. It came out so far and then it retreated in strange silences—I concluded that Henry had been reading old records, scanning old newspapers, and making subtle inquiries here and there. I was sure of that for, suddenly remembering, I knew that there had been something odd in one of his letters before we met. As for names, he never was too clear about them. Afterwards, when I tried to piece together what I had, I concluded that a woman had been involved, hopelessly tangled in what Henry or somebody thought was circumstantial evidence, and that my quest for the lore of Toms River presented Henry with an excellent opportunity to probe further in a not too obvious way.

Somehow, years after, with many of the principals forgotten or in their graves, Henry Bliss was trying through a weird association with places and things to reconstruct the case, in which there was a generous share of romance. We visited one old house in particular, one with something of a widow's walk, far across the river from the present Riverview Hotel and almost opposite another of similar Victorian design. This was where there had been an exchange of signals, Henry said, messages sent from one rooftop to another—and my impression is that it was a Montague-Capulet affair. Someone else in the cast had been a famous actor—the name Tom Placide leaps up at me from a scrawled line. Henry took us with peculiar certainty to the very room in which Placide ended his life.

But the walls told Ned and me even less than the new occupants disclosed to Henry Bliss, at least in anything I heard in this strange eavesdropping. Whenever I pressed for a fact or a name, a gesture reminded me that the celebrated ear trumpets had not been brought along. Henry recognized grown-over lanes, familiar trees, coves that once had colorful names, and roads which, when the old gentleman knew them best, were rutted by carriage wheels. Then, suddenly, Henry Bliss seemed to change. Either he had given up his secret quest or he had found out all he wanted to know or all that could be found out. Suggesting lunch, he switched his conversation to Joseph Francis and old Toms River, saying that it would be nice to see Joseph's home on the way. Ned had a better idea.

"Joseph's house is a hotel now," he said, "and it hasn't changed much." He had made inquiries. "We will eat there," he decided, and so I abandoned the idea of digging up buried murder clues, the kind that Edmund Pearson would have handled very well. Out came the story of an inventor, told by a man who spoke as if he had been the inventor's friend or at least had been steeped in the years of his life—this disarming, birdlike old gentleman had emerged from retirement to undertake a special kind of investigation in a special way. The two ear trumpets suddenly reappeared, this time placed for convenience on a far more modern tablecloth.

Ned Knox persisted in trying to sketch in the background of a Toms River the county seat has forgotten—the village described as having few more than a dozen houses, defended by a blockhouse that fell on March 20, 1782, the thrilling capture of many a prize ship in earlier years of the Revolution, and the selling of captive vessels at sessions of the Admiralty Court held as far away as Allentown. "You can get all this," Ned told me, inasmuch as Henry had not tuned in, "in Edwin Salter's *History of Monmouth and Ocean Counties*. Toms River was a thriving place during the Revolution. Listen to this: 'For a small village, it was evidently quite busy, between the militia, the Refugees, and the arrival and departure of privateers and their prizes; the arrival of boats and teams with salt from the several works along the bay; the departure of teams for West Jersey with salt, oysters, fish—and their return with merchandise—' " Ned could get no further; Henry Bliss was speaking again.

Prior to the departure of Joseph Francis, he was saying, and the records bear him out, the means of saving life were of little worth. "Joseph had to do something about it. After a lot of brain-tearing he emerged with two inventions of lasting importance, the corrugated metallic lifeboat and the corrugated metallic lifecar."

"To these inventions alone thousands of persons owe their safety from an awful death," says the *Atlas* to which Henry introduced me. With lifeboats and lifecars out of the way, Mr.

244

Francis "produced successively other valuable improvements and inventions such as corrugated pontoon wagons, steamers, floating docks, stop-corrugations, harbor and channel buoys, etc. In previous years he made many improvements in wooden boats and other means of saving life, among which were the life and anchor boats, reversed-bottom lifeboats, screw boats, moulded boats, the Nautilus life-preserver, and army hoods."

"Joseph Francis built his first boats in 1811," Henry Bliss said, speaking like a cataloguing librarian whose mind is filled with precise dates and information.

"I thought you said that you had been a friend of Joe Francis!" I exclaimed, in spite of one of Ned Knox's best frowns.

Henry merely smiled and said, "I was and I am!" and then went on with his story. "In 1819 he built a light and fast rowboat which he exhibited at the first fair of the Massachusetts Mechanics' Institute, held in Boston—and he won the first prize." These, I later discovered, were virtually the words of the *Atlas* itself. But at this point the records blandly state that the birth of aquatic sports in America came in 1830, by which time the name of Joseph Francis was familiar to all who were building racing craft for regional or international competition.

Although the Knickerbocker Club of New York was organized in 1811, along came the War of 1812 to eliminate water sports or any thought of them. When the war ended, several attempts at revival were made but none succeeded until 1830, when "one hundred gentlemen of New York," among them Robert L. Stevens, Ogden Hoffman, Samuel Verplank, Charles L. Livingston, Robert Emmett, and John Stevens, established the New York Boat Club, "and here, as I've told you, Toms River came into the situation again," said Henry Bliss. "Their first craft was built by Mr. Francis and, before it was presented to no less than the Emperor of Russia, as the *Atlas* calls him, was pronounced by famous yachtsmen of England the handsomest craft seen in British waters. It was dropped off at Cowes by the United States frigate *Kensington*."

Handsome as the first craft of the new and fashionable club may have been, she was quickly displaced, I learned, by the double-planked barge of sixteen oars called *Seadrift*. Charles F. Hoffman, a writer on the New York *Mirror*, said that "while every nautical man will acknowledge that the model and finish of Mr. Francis's *chef d'oeuvre*, the *Seadrift*, has never been excelled, to him and the club is the merit due for first bringing the noble sport of aquatics into public favor."

"How many of those who hurry along the Toms River now realize that this is where Joe Francis built the models of these ships?" demanded Henry Bliss, without bothering to raise his trumpets to bring in a reply. "A lot of headwork and a lot of handwork went into them. That *Seadrift* was thirty feet long and, if I remember correctly, she was constructed of chestnut oak. She was polished outside and inside and given no paint at all."

"Above the thwarts, fore and aft," says a more expert description, "she was paneled with ebony, rosewood, and mahogany, with knees and rowlocks of brass."

So successful was the *Seadrift* that Joseph Francis was immediately commissioned to build a thirty-foot, four-oared racing boat to compete with English-built boats in a regatta at Quebec. This was the first American-built racing craft to vie with foreign boats. "To the credit of her builder," a contemporary account discloses, "she came off victorious. Her success was attributed to her superiority in model more than to the skill of her oarsmen. She was built of Spanish cedar, one-fourth of an inch in thickness and highly polished. Her weight was sixty pounds, making her the lightest boat of her type built up to that time."

"Joe Francis had all sorts of ideas," Ned Knox broke in. "Didn't he build the first Venetian gondola in this country?" At once I thought of the carriage manufacturer down in Burlington who built rickshas for the Chinese market.

"He certainly did," Henry Bliss replied. "Twenty-seven feet long, she was, and five feet wide—in every possible way a counterpart of the craft most familiar in Venice."

"What on earth was a gondola used for here?" I inquired. "And what ever became of her?"

For once Henry didn't know, but he hazarded a guess. For some years, he said, a gondola was in use in the North River, at Strykers Bay, Bloomingdale, and later was said to have been transferred to Greenwood Cemetery.

Joseph Francis' portable screw boats, built in sections and fastened together in much the same way as are today's prefabricated houses, came later. Still later came molded boats, craft built over a frame; wooden lifeboats with cork in bow and stern and with air chambers under the thwarts and along the sides; the anchor launch, designed to take out anchors in rough and stormy weather sometimes disastrous for longboats, and the reversed, or double-bottom, lifeboats in which the bilge on each side was laid below the line of the keel for the first time.

"When Lord John Hay, commanding the British frigate *Warspite*, was waiting in New York for the completion of the Ashburton Treaty," said Henry, "he heard that Joe Francis was up to something and when he found out what it was he immediately ordered one of those molded lifeboats to take home with him. As for the first wooden lifeboats, these were taken down to the foot of Wall Street and thrown endways into the dock where they quickly righted and freed themselves of water."

"Was all the work on these boats done here in Toms River?" I asked. The view of the river in which Joseph Francis had worked was perfect from the window of the Riverview, even as it should have been. Beyond was a contrasting lawn and in its midst a pergola, recalling an earlier day, if not that of Mr. Francis then surely the era of Henry Evelyn's mystery.

"Much of it was," said Henry. "Joe was down here much of the time, although there was a boat factory in New York. You see, Joseph Francis became a celebrity and he had to be in all parts of the world, receiving honors, supervising construction of boats according to his many designs, and proving generally that ship designing was much more than it had been. When Joe wasn't being consulted by the Imperial and Royal International Shipwreck Society of France, or being commended for the success of his life-preservers by the Shipwreck Society of the American Institute, he was working on a military hood for the War Department—these were waterproof helmets, tested out at Fortress Monroe in 1863.

"The Francis corrugated boats go back to 1843, when Joe augmented his wooden patents with one that called for craft twenty feet long with a gunwale filled with paving stone in the first tryout. I think I remember reading somewhere that in the Woolwich Dock Yard, in England, one of these boats was subjected to tests that no vessel was expected to withstand. To the surprise of everybody she did not suffer the least injury."

Joe Francis had designed and constructed ships for the Dead Sea Expedition of 1848. His boats were used by Professor Maillefert at Hurlgate and received a decoration from the Emperor of France in 1856. "Look up the records," Henry Bliss suggested. "You will note that Joseph Francis, the boatbuilder of Toms River, must have found the going a little rough amid gifts from the Grand Duke Constantine, medals from Emperor Franz Joseph upon the successful use of pontoon wagons, and presentations of knighthood from almost every direction."

As far as I have been able to discover, the saucer boat was one of Joseph Francis' last designs, coming at the end of a distinguished career. It was not until 1877 that his ingenious mind turned out what he called a circular yacht, promptly called the *Sarah Francis*.

Joseph Francis "saw in this round form a new principle was evolved. It always has been conceded," says the *Atlas*, indicating that the inventor was by no means revealing all that was in his mind at the time, "that to obtain speed a vessel must necessarily be built sharp and narrow in order to lessen the friction and resistance in passing through the water. By the advocates of this newly discovered theory an entirely different hypothesis is taken: that to obtain speed, a vessel must be broad and flat, and instead of penetrating the water must ride upon its surface, assuming that the extreme width will give her sufficient buoyant bearing to effect it.

"Apart from the matter of speed, Mr. Francis was assured that in this round form he would obtain the most essential qualities of a pleasure yacht, those of safety and comfort. At first he was at a loss to fix upon a pattern for his guide. Finally, a teasaucer was suggested, which he adopted as his model, and after four months of leisure work, he completed his innovation."

There is evidence to show that this strange contradictory craft was tried out successfully in the Toms River in full view of a gallery of skeptics who had joked in the streets about Joe and his "flying saucers" fifty years before the term was to be applied to strange unidentified objects hurtling through the air.

I tried to tie down a few of the details on the way home, and quoted this passage from Gustav Kobbé:

"Tom's River probably derives its name from Captain William Tom, a sturdy settler on the Delaware some 200 years ago, who, on an exploring expedition to the seashore, discovered, after penetrating the wilderness of pines, the river which now bears his name. On a map published in 1740 there is marked on the point north of Mosquito Cove 'Barnegat Tom's Wigwam,' and some think the stream was named after this noted Indian." I lifted my eyes from the book to ask, "Where does that put us, on the side of William or the Indian?"

Henry had decided to go to sleep, just like that, I thought. But he hadn't. "You mean the Indian and the crabs? You were going to tell me about that."

I told him. The story is that many people in Toms River, apparently descendants of those who knew the tale firsthand, refuse to eat crabs. It seems that the most celebrated catcher of crabs in the Toms River area in earliest days was this Indian called Tom, perhaps the one who had the wigwam with a view. There came a time, after Tom's reputation for good crabs had been justly established, that those he sold were bigger and better than those to be procured anywhere else. Then, all of a sudden, the bottom dropped out of Tom's market. He made despairing gestures with his arms and said merely that he had no more crabs. In comparison to the earlier quantity and quality, this was incredible to the pioneer clientele, and Tom was pressed for an explanation.

What he said went something like this: "Crabs good. Tom and squaw catch 'em. Squaw die. Tom tie squaw down in stream, in big river near point. Crabs come bigger, better than ever. Then come storm. Squaw she disappear. Crabs disappear, too."

23 ∞

Borderline Case:
The Two Tappans

The old gentleman was positive. There was but one Tappan and it was on New Jersey's side of the line. New York had taken much, he said, which once had been New Jersey's, including Staten Island, but surely a whole town could not be smuggled from one state to another.

My reply was as insistent. There are two towns, now, no matter what there used to be—Tappan on the New York side and Old Tappan on New Jersey's. I suggested that the name Old Tappan might very well indicate the greater age of the village that remained on New Jersey's side of the border. It seemed plausible that when a village is labeled "old," then old is precisely what is meant. In this conclusion I was obviously wrong, however, as was proved by a deluge of contradictions that came almost as soon as the statement had been made.

Tappan was Tappan Town to begin with, and Old Tappan, on the New Jersey side and young by comparison, would avoid confusion as River Vale. There is a post office there in what I found to be one of the most characteristic of country stores. J. H. Lachmund, Jr., told me he was the borough clerk and that he could procure for anybody, as he did for me, papers bearing the Old Tappan seal showing that the village was the first borough in Harrington Township, in 1894.

Barber and Howe state that Harrington Township "was reduced, in 1840, about one half, by the formation of Washington

250

from the first portion. It approaches in form to a square and measures across it, each way, about five miles. It is bounded north by Rockland county (New York), east by the Hudson river, south by Hackensack, and west by Washington. The Palisades skirt it on its eastern boundary."

After some statistics, *circa* 1840 or thereabouts, on the soil, the production "of large quantities of orchard fruit," sawmills, gristmills, and a population in excess of eleven hundred, the records declare that "the village of Tappan is just over the boundary line, in the state of New York." There is no mention of a New Jersey neighbor called Old Tappan.

Edward A. Daube, custodian of the old DeWint house in Tappan, now the Washington Masonic Shrine, provided a key to the mystery. He said that when the New Jersey-New York line was finally decided, with a sorting out of the property lines that had been set in the old Dutch land grants, Tappan, where Major André was court-martialed and hanged, actually remained on the New York side.

"A lot of people in New Jersey wanted the honor, if that is what it was, of keeping the place where André was executed," Edward told me. "You see, Old Tappan isn't Tappan at all. And even though it has a few very old houses it has no great age as a town."

Charles DeWolf, whose father was John Herring DeWolf and who lives in the family farmhouse which was surely on the New Jersey side before the border controversy was ironed out, is inclined to agree with Ed Daube. The DeWolf house was first the Herring house and, as such, came to the family by grant of Queen Anne in 1704. "But if you want any real records around here," Charles assured me, "you have to go all the way up to Goshen, New York. That ought to show where we were in the beginning, I'd think."

Beyond all this there is an argument that crops out every now and then in such stores as Lachmund's, involving more than the letters that passed between Major André and Benedict Arnold or the legends of the DeWint and DeClark houses where Washington most assuredly slept. This surrounds the reclamation of

Tappan itself from such ruins as were dramatically etched in no less public a place than *Harper's Weekly* for April 26, 1884. There appeared an unsigned article illustrated with three sketches made by an artist who caught the ghostly decadence that had begun to settle on the village where so much had happened. There is no reference to the DeWint house, or to the tree, now dead, from whose top numerous tar barrels were burned to announce officially the end of the Revolutionary War.

"Of the many localities along the west bank of the Hudson made famous by the war of the Revolution," wrote this traveler of the 1880's, "none is today possessed of greater historic interest than the quaint little village of Tappan, the scene of Major André's imprisonment, trial, and execution. The Tappan of the present is almost identical with the Tappan, or 'Orangetown,' as it was more frequently called, of a century ago." When I re-read these words in an establishment calling itself "the oldest historic tavern" and with the room in which André had been confined directly behind me, I wondered first about the name Orangetown and then whether New Jersey's Old Tappan would not emerge from the description. There still is an Orangeburg up the road from Tappan, after all. I read on:

"Lying in a pleasant valley, a few miles inland from the Hudson, at the extreme northern point of the Palisades, it was, prior to its white occupation, the chosen home of a band of the great Delaware tribe of Indians, who named it Tuphaune, or Cold Stream, from the clear waters of the Sparkill Creek that still ripples as merrily as then among the low meadow-lands and thrifty orchards of the valley. Long before the country passed into the hands of the English, Dutch settlers had founded here the village of Orangetown, to which has been restored its original Indian name slightly anglicized. Its houses still show unmistakably Dutch architecture, and the solid stone walls of many of them bid fair to attest the stolid character of their builders for a century to come.

"Of all the houses of old Tappan, none equaled in size and general air of thrift and comfort that erected in 1753 on the principal street, and not far from the meeting house, by Casparus Mabie, on land that he purchased from Cornelius Myers, who held it by direct grant from the Indians. The Mabie house was built of heavy blocks of red sandstone, with red brick trimmings at doors and windows. As was the custom, the upper story, roof, and broad front stoop, with its low overhanging porch, were built of wood, but of wood so carefully selected and well seasoned that it still retains its position, though the clutch of decay has fastened upon it, and, unless protected, the disappearance of all except the stone walls will be the work of but a few years."

The clutch of decay was indeed unfastened and protection came long ago. The last time I was there, although there was a hole in the floor of the room that served Major André for a cell, "the house which was the principal tavern of the village" was continuing with business as usual. Here Major André, awaiting death, occupied two rooms on the ground floor in the north end of the house, using "the front room as his reception room, and one in the rear as his bedroom. Years ago the partition between this and the adjoining rear room was torn away, and the two combined to make a ball-room for more happy occupants of the house. From this rear room it is said the prisoner could see the gallows erected for his execution, on the top of the hill rising directly behind the village.

"Today this famous house, now known as the 'Old Seventy Six House,' stands empty and deserted, its doors and windows boarded up, its once cheerful stoop so broken and decayed as no longer to afford a safe footing, the roof of its hospitable porch falling in, and hedged from the street by a rank growth of briers and weeds and a row of young locust trees."

It is reassuring to know that the house is again in excellent condition, that thoughtful repairs and replacements were effected long ago, and that while a comparison made where the artist for *Harper's* stood is startling in that outlines all along the street have changed so little, Tappan Town obviously has made a commendable comeback. There is even a marker, one of many in the village, to inform the traveler of all that happened here.

There was no such marker in the 1880's and the intruder,

253

seeking information from the owner, Dr. J. J. Stephens, reported that the gentleman found "this dilapidated piece of property a veritable white elephant on his hands. As the good-natured owner showed the writer over the interior of the Seventy-Six House, he remarked, 'You have no idea of the trial that the ownership of this building is to me. Why, if I were to accede to the request of every visitor, as I have to yours, and undertake to show them this house, I should have my time fully occupied. . . . I cannot afford to do this, and must refuse to allow visitors to enter the house alone and when I do this I am accused of being a churlish, unaccommodating fellow. I have tried in vain to sell the house to the Government, the State, the County, and to individuals; but none of them will buy it. I had tenants for it, but in their hands it was in danger of being carried away piecemeal by unscrupulous visitors.' "

Presumably a change came quickly, inasmuch as the tavern was rescued.

The reporter for *Harper's* spoke of many Dutch fireplaces in the village, each adorned with ancient tiles; the red-brick church built in 1835 on the site of its two predecessors, in one of which André had been brought to trial; and a graveyard out back. There of all places I "met" once again the stonecutter who advertised his work from far-off Middletown. I made a note that I must find out much more about John Zuricher, of New York, who signed all his funereal craftsmanship and proved how deeply he believed in enduring advertising.

The DeWint house itself, around a bend of the road above which a traffic light seemed out of place, is another story. It was rescued by the Washington Masonic Shrine Committee of the Grand Lodge of New York; and when I was there, Ed Daube seemed just the right kind of curator. The house was built in 1700 by Daniel DeClark, who worked the numerals into the bricks between the four downstairs windows. Daniel is supposed to have been a man of means since the bricks were imported from Holland.

Inside, miraculously preserved, some seventy purple tiles, similarly imported, adorn a mantelpiece, each presenting some

254

episode of a Bible narrative. How long Daniel lived there and what became of him, no one knows. It is known, however, that in 1746 the property was in the hands of Rem Remson, of Brooklyn, who sold it to Johannis DeWint and his wife Antje, who had moved up from New York. It was in August, 1780, that Washington was a guest of the DeWints, during a time which was the gloomiest of the period.

The American army had been reduced to a skeleton force. British strategy had shifted its field of operations to the South, capturing Savannah in 1778 and setting up a royal government in Georgia. In May, 1780, Sir Henry Clinton, who had brought his fleet down from New York, captured Charleston, South Carolina, and, with the city, General Lincoln and five thousand men. In the same year General Gates was defeated at Camden, South Carolina, a blow all but fatal to the cause. This was the news that probably came to Washington at the DeWint house, where Johannis and Antje had by this time been joined by their daughter and her husband, Major and Mrs. Frederickus Blauvelt.

It is known that Washington familiarized himself with the whole neighborhood, riding almost daily across into what is now the Saddle River country and returning in the evening to hear the news and as many diverting stories as the Blauvelts could tell in the midst of gracious Dutch hospitality. The bricks outside resounded to the tread of orderlies, and there was always a sentry on duty at a peephole in the north wall. Beyond this, and the consideration that he was on New Jersey ground almost as often as he was anywhere else, details of General Washington's first lingering in Tappan Town are lacking.

Of his next stay much more is known. Nearly all of it concerns "the most melancholy tale of the Revolutionary period." Benedict Arnold had been a darling of the country early in the war but success went to his head. He became jealous of other officers, ignored orders, was officially rebuked on more than one occasion, and accused the Congress of holding up his promotion. He made friends with British officers when it appeared that the American cause was lost. He married a Tory belle of Philadelphia, but soon discovered that he couldn't support the girl in the manner to which she had been accustomed.

By the summer of 1780 he was ripe for treason. Washington, however, continued to believe in Arnold and gave him the command of West Point. As Arnold well knew, West Point controlled the Hudson and was the military key to the whole East.

Every schoolboy knows the story. Except for treachery, the British could not gain the stronghold. There were two big chains, hand-forged, across the Hudson River, each link weighing one hundred fifty pounds. The flower of the American army was at West Point. The British knew, apparently, how Arnold could be trapped, and sent one whom they considered eminently qualified—John André, adjutant general under Clinton with the rank of major. Arnold met André at Stony Point in mid-September, 1780, when Washington was in Hartford conferring with Rochambeau. Arnold then returned to his post and André set out, disguised as a civilian, to regain the British lines. He was stopped by three American marauders, who found his papers and took him to Washington's headquarters at Tappan. Even so, in some mysterious way John André managed to get word to Arnold, who deserted immediately.

What happened to Benedict Arnold after that is sometimes forgotten, even as many forget that André's remains were later disinterred and reburied in Westminster Abbey. Arnold received more than thirty thousand dollars from the British to compensate him for the property he forfeited by his treachery and, in addition, he was given the rank of brigadier general. He commanded the British forces at Richmond and later participated in the attack on New London. However, even his new associates disliked a traitor, and Arnold moved to London where he was used at least temporarily as a source of information by the British ministry. Trying his hand in business in the West Indies, attempting to recoup military glory in the later British-French conflict, he died in 1801, a victim of melancholia, disillusionment, and the curse of Judas.

John André, who even in the words of Washington was "more unfortunate than criminal," was carried off to Tappan where he was ordered tried by a board of officers, Lafayette and von Steuben among them. His defense was spirited but blundering, and he was sentenced to die. He asked to be shot, soldier fashion, but Washington refused the request, declaring that in so doing there might be some implication of doubt as to the prisoner's guilt. He was imprisoned in the old tavern and, on Washington's personal order, was treated with the utmost civility. Meanwhile, Washington remained at the DeWint house in something like seclusion. He did not see John André personally but, according to stories told on both sides of the line, he augmented the food sent to the tavern by the DeWints by adding delicacies from his own table.

An eyewitness tells of what happened on October 2, 1780, amid the bright coloring of the autumn leaves of the Bergen hills and the Ramapos that knew no dividing line:

"I was at that time an officer in Colonel Jeduthun Baldwin's regiment, a part of which was stationed within a short distance of the spot where André suffered. One of our men, being one of the oldest and best workmen at his trade in the regiment, was selected to make his coffin, which he performed, and painted black, agreeable to the custom of those times.

"When the hour appointed for André's execution arrived, which I believe was two o'clock P.M., a guard of three hundred men were paraded at the place of his confinement. A kind of procession was formed by placing the guard in single file on each side of the road. In front were a large number of American officers, of high rank, on horseback. These were followed by the wagon containing André's coffin; then a large number of officers on foot with André in their midst. The procession moved slowly up a moderately-rising hill, I should think about a fourth of a mile to the west. On top was a field without any enclosure. . . .

"In this was a very high gallows, made by setting two poles or crotches, laying a pole on top. The wagon that contained the coffin was drawn directly under the gallows. In a short time André stepped into the hind end of the wagon; then on his coffin—took off his hat and laid it down—then placed his hands upon his hips, and walked very uprightly back and forth, as far as the length of his coffin would permit; at the same time casting his eyes upon the pole over his head, and the whole scenery by which he was surrounded.

"He was dressed in what I would call a complete British uniform; his coat was of brightest scarlet, faced or trimmed with the most beautiful green. His under-clothes, or vest and breeches, were bright buff, very similar to those worn by military officers in Connecticut. He had a long and beautiful head of hair, which, agreeably to the fashion, was wound with a black riband, and hung down his back. All eyes were upon him; and it is not believed that any officer in the British army, placed in his situation, would have appeared better than this unfortunate man.

"Not many minutes after he took his stand upon the coffin, the executioner stepped into the wagon, with a halter in his hand, on one end of which was what the soldiers called a hangman's knot. . . ."

What happened in the ceremonious demise of John André will be the more real if you go up through Old Tappan to the DeWint house, where George Washington ordered his shutters closed upon the sight, to the tavern where André was given a room with a macabre view, and to a hill outside the village where a large stone encircled by a fence with a sagging gate marks the place where the crude gallows stood. You will remember, I am sure, how John André objected to the hangman's nervous fussing with the noose and how he adjusted it himself with studied calm and steady hands.

There was a stillness on the hill that day which, somehow, has ever remained, dipping down across the New Jersey border where a town named River Vale masquerades. Sometimes there is more than that, they tell me, when the wind is right—perhaps the ghostly sound of muffled drums, a sharp order in the dark, and a sigh among the trees to denote that a life has ended. Lately Old Tappan on the New Jersey side has made the most of the Baylor Massacre, which, unless someone is very careful, may be forgotten now that the old millstone has been removed from where the bones of the dead Hessians must remain.

But that is quite another story.

24

Tom Quick and the Ninety-nine Indians

Up in the mountains along the lush and craggy forehead of New Jersey and across the river in Pennsylvania's Pike County, Tom Quick has become a name on a monument, on a fashionable country hotel, and on the lips of insiders who tell the story and outsiders who sometimes twist it out of all resemblance to the truth.

On the monument in the middle of Sarah Street, off Broad, in Milford, Tom is proclaimed as both "the Indian Slayer" and "the Avenger of the Delaware," the latter the distinction he himself liked best. In the many lines that follow on four sides of the obelisk there is no suggestion that the bones that lie beneath, under a fragment of the original tombstone but in their second grave, were those of a man who died grieving because the score of his legendary rifle was ninety-nine and not an even hundred.

I was told at the hotel that a few travelers have inquired if Tom Quick is the proprietor and as many others have shown sufficient curiosity to be given additional information and directions to the monument on which visiting Quicks add their names or initials in pencil. The Quicks of three states—New Jersey, Pennsylvania, and New York—divide themselves into two camps, and perhaps three. There are those determined that Tom Quick never was, and others who suggest that the less one probes beyond the leaflets and inscriptions the better. A third group, outlining reasons for the bloody acts of both Tom and the Indians

259

he had vowed to eliminate, states its case for the most part in hard-to-find imprints, by now collector's items.

I first heard Tom Quick's name from my friend, Alden T. Cottrell, New Jersey State Forester, who said at the outset what I believe to be perfectly true—that there never was, nor can there ever be, a hero-villain anywhere in the annals of New Jersey to match the blood-avenging madness of the man they called "the Indian Slayer." From the moment Tom's father was shot down and scalped by the very natives whose friends the Quicks had been, Tom declared a personal war that continued through the remainder of his life, a vendetta that carried him stealthily back and forth across the Delaware through more than forty years.

I always have had the feeling that there may have been Tom Quick songs as well as tales, sung here and there in the taverns or even to guitar accompaniment in some of the country stores. Someday, perhaps, they will come to light. Meanwhile James E. Quinlan seems to have used the fragment of what may have been one of these at the beginning of his *Life and Adventures of Tom Quick:*

> Hero of many a wondrous tale,
> Full of his devilish cunning!
>   Tom never flunked nor turned pale,
>   Following on the Indian's trail,
> Shooting as he was running.

Then the story begins in earnest:

"Not far from the year 1733, a Hollander, named Thomas Quick, emigrated from the Fatherland to the colony of New York, and not long afterwards located himself in Milford, then known as Upper Smithfield, in Pennsylvania. His circumstances and position were nearly, if not quite, equal to those of a large majority of the affluent and respectable Dutch emigrants of that period. Actuated by a spirit of indomitable enterprise, he 'pitched his tent' considerably in advance of those who had come to this country before him; and according to his descendants, he was the pioneer of Milford or Upper Smithfield."

The monument in Milford makes a more definite statement:

"Thomas Quick, Sr., father of Tom Quick, his oldest child, emigrated from Holland to America and settled on this spot in 1733. He was the first white settler in this part of the Upper Delaware; and his log cabin, saw and grist mill, built on this bank of the Van de Mark, were the first structures ever erected by white men in the settlement of the region."

Dr. Abraham S. Gardiner tells the story in *Tom Quick: Or the Era of Frontier Settlement:*

"Quick thus met with no unfriendly reception. He had come considerably in advance of the other settlers, and on an independent line. He no doubt based his claim to the privilege of settlement upon the right of discovery assumed by the Dutch, French and English alike. By this assumption the rights of the Indians to their ancient grounds were virtually extinguished. The country had not been reduced by conquest. This alleged right by discovery seemed, however, sometimes to be compromised by such dealings with the natives as those which were had by William Penn. The rights of the natives of the valley of the Upper Delaware were especially recognized in what was called, 'The Walking Purchase.' It was the occasional acknowledgement of these rights, and the frequent, special, and flagrant violation of them, which awakened in the minds of the Indians apprehension and hostility. In this part of the valley these feelings were further greatly intensified by the deception practiced upon them by the whites, in the purchase of their furs and game, and especially of their lands. The Indians claimed that under the temptations of the settlers they became stupefied with drink, and when in that condition were led to sell their furs, game, and lands, at half their value. Especially was this true as to the sale and occupation, in 1736, of the territory known as 'The Walking Purchase.' According to the best historical testimony which has yet appeared, this transaction, on the part of the whites, was 'overreaching' to the last degree. Instead of giving their agents directions to walk at the usual gait over the territory—for the land to be conveyed by the Indians was to be as much as a man could walk through in a day—the whites selected their swiftest runners, men of great endurance, and told them to stop for neither food nor rest, and to run from dawn to dark. Thus eighty-six miles were traversed in a straight line on a single day. . . .

"The tract thereby taken from the Indians, and appropriated by the whites, embraced a vast territory" within which "lay what are now known as Wayne and Pike counties, and of course all the natives within these boundaries became subject to the conditions of the alleged treaty. Lands herein were no longer the property of the Lenapes. The Six Nations, their rival and more powerful neighbors, had sold them out to the whites; and now, in the exercise of unlawful but resistless power, these tribes commanded them to withdraw instantly, entirely, and forever from the lands which had been thus, without their consent, conveyed to strangers. The emotions of the Lenapes at this juncture were a mixture of humiliation, pathos, resistance, and revenge."

In contrast to all this, and perhaps unaware of most of it, young Tom Quick, born in 1734, became almost as much of an Indian as the natives who visited his father's house. "As young Tom grew up," James Quinlan wrote, "he became an associate and playfellow" of the Indian boys "and learned to speak the Indian tongue with as much ease and fluency as the aborigines themselves. He was taught by the Indians how to take the otter, the beaver, the muskrat, the mink, etc., and by the time he had become of suitable age, he was a skillful and expert hunter." Young Tom fell in love with the woods and, once smitten, he never again could be induced to do more than roam the forests and swamps and live the life of a trapper. His brothers and sisters were much more domestic in their modes of living. The brothers' names are known—they were Cornelius and James. The sisters married—one becoming Mrs. Solomon Decker, a pioneer of old Deckertown, now Sussex, I once was told, and the other sharing the frontier life of one Francis Magee.

Tom's father prospered, inducing a number of other white settlers to build cabins near his mills at the mouth of a little creek not far from a retreat of thousands of bank swallows when

262

I used to go there. A Dutch school was established and there is a record somewhere that Tom's brothers and sisters were among its first pupils. Young Tom had no taste for that kind of learning, however. If ever he joined the classroom ranks, which is doubtful, he soon hurried back to lessons of the woodlands. "While the younger children were poring over the alphabet, Tom was engaged in the athletic amusements of the Indians. In trapping, wrestling, jumping, shooting, etc., he excelled a majority of the lads his own age, and thus excited the envy of not a few embryo braves."

Long before the French and Indian War, Tom had traced to their sources most of the streams which still empty into the Delaware, by now among the resorts and retreats of those who flee the cities in steaming summer heat. He knew all the Indian paths around Minisink, Mamakating, the Shawangunk, the Wawasink, and even Paupack. He knew the ancient secrets of the Wallpack Bend, the fastnesses of what now is the Stokes State Forest, and the heights near Mount Salem where, as it once was said, "most of the world can be seen." Cornelius and James worked their father's farm. Tom brought home the venison.

Many of the Indians "almost lived in the family of the Quicks" by whom they were clothed when naked and fed when hungry. "The most pacific relations existed between them, apparently, and the red man had received so much kindness at the hands of their friends," said Quinlan, "that the latter imagined that they could rely upon their good will under almost any circumstances. Subsequent events, however, proved that they were mistaken. The increasing numbers of the whites and the encroachments made upon what the natives regarded as their own territory alarmed the Indians." But there was, of course, more to it than that. Token purchases here and there were not enough to overcome the feeling that the white settler regarded the Lenape with an insufferable air of superiority and disdain. Now was the time to take a decisive step.

Admittedly the Quicks had been kind, but also they were the ones who had begun the white man's invasion. Thus they were a symbol of people and acts looked upon with increasing enmity. Dr. Gardiner gives a very sensible estimate of the situation:

"The authorities are conflicting; we follow that which seems to have been generally received. During these peaceful years Quick had gathered around him the comforts of a home. He had taken up what land he needed, and it had yielded promptly to his cultivation. His children had grown to maturity. One of his daughters had married. But his wife had died, as also the little boy (James) of whom we have spoken. The scattered and quiet homes of the settlers now extended up the Valley as far as Cochecton. But this peaceful scene is soon to change. While Quick and his family did not suspect immediate danger from the Indians, yet during the years 1756-7 they spent at least a part of their time in the stone house or fort nearly opposite but some distance north of the mouth of the Van de Mark, on the Jersey shore. That stone house is still standing. It was at that time manned by about fifteen or twenty of the Jersey militia, made up from settlers of the immediate neighborhood."

Tom's father, refusing with Tom to believe ill of those to whom they had been brothers, took no precautions. He found most things he needed for his mills on the Pennsylvania side but, according to all the evidence, he and his two sons crossed the Delaware on the fateful journey, and what followed occurred as the three left the New Jersey shore for home.

They proceeded around a point or ridge not far from the water where, the story goes, the Indian outposts watched them approach "with eager eyes. Two of the men whom they most desired to kill were unwittingly delivering themselves into their power. The opportunity to slay them was not to be lost, even if the main object of the expedition, the destruction of the settlement, was defeated by a premature alarm, which would enable the inhabitants to defend themselves successfully." Dr. Gardiner's version states: "Quick and his sons, with their grist, were out a little distance on the ice, when the Indians, once their neighbors and personal friends, now their foes, and the foes of all who they believed had robbed them of their lands, lying in ambush in the

264

woods which crowned the banks of the river, suddenly opened fire. Quick fell, mortally wounded." The young men, who had not been hit, instantly took hold of Tom's father and "endeavored in hot haste to bear their wounded father away. . . .

" 'I am a dead man!' he exclaimed, 'I can go no further, leave me and run for your lives!' This they did with unspeakable reluctance. The Indians fired upon them as they fled. But the fugitives running a zig-zag course, baffled the aims of their foes, and speeding their way over the frozen Delaware, found safety on the opposite shore. Pausing presently in their course, they listened. The war-whoop and exultant shouts of the Indians resounded in the distance, indicating too plainly that they were engaged in bloody orgies over their helpless and expiring victim. It appears from accounts given at a later period that the unfortunate Quick was scalped, and that by the hand of Muskwink or Modeline, who acted as chief, and who as a boy had been partly raised in Quick's hospitable home, that he was subjected to terrible torture, and then watched with savage delight by his infuriated tormentors, until death came to his relief. . . .

"The noise of the Indian rifles alarmed the occupants of the stone fort. They came rushing out, and hastened down the river only in time to see the tragedy enacted on the other side, and to see Tom and his brothers"—this version suggests that Tom, James (who had died at the age of three in a prior paragraph), Cornelius, and Tom's brother-in-law, Daniel, all were in the party—"running with great speed towards them. The sad tale was quickly told. Not knowing the number of the Indians that might be in the neighborhood, the settlers did not venture to rescue their unfortunate friend. Mrs. John T. Quick, who is still living at the age of eighty-nine, and who resides with her son on the road from Milford to Port Jervis, remembers distinctly hearing, when a little girl of nine years, her grandfather, Daniel Van Gorden, say that he was one of the militia present, and that when Tom Quick reached the Jersey shore he cried, and hollowed, and screamed, and tore his hair by handfuls out of his head, and threw it on the ground. In his frenzy he swore that he would never make peace with the Indians while God let him live. Mr. Van Gorden said there was not a soldier there but shed tears."

So it was that Tom's relentless vendetta began, and, according to the stories that have come to me along the New Jersey byways, mostly in Sussex but often in Warren, Tom Quick regretted on his deathbed that his tally of dead Indians was one short of the hundred he had promised himself. "But, as we said before," wrote Dr. Gardiner, "Tom Quick was now transformed. He took to himself the title of the 'Avenger of the Delaware.' He who had hitherto been a friend of both white and Indian, now carried within him a double spirit. Having no sentiment but that of friendship for the settlers and love for his kindred, he had intense hatred and loathing toward the Indians. The deadly rifle of Tom Quick robbed many an Indian wigwam of its husband, father, and head, and the tribe of many a brave. Long after what the Indians called 'peace times' had come, one and another of their number continued to fall."

Two years after the outburst between the Indians and whites had subsided, Tom went to the house of a man named Decker, perhaps a tavern. Muskwink, ringleader in the scalping and torture of Tom's father was already there, tipsy and talkative. Surely Muskwink and Tom must have recognized each other but there is no record of that. Muskwink "at once claimed Tom as an acquaintance and wished to drink with him," the narrative elusively declares. Tom refused and, moreover, called Muskwink a name. This infuriated the Indian, who at once began to boast of his exploits on the warpath, adding for good measure a description of the murder of Tom's father. "He asserted that he had scalped the old man with his own hand—mimicked the grimaces of the dying man—showed how he appeared while in the agony of death, and to corroborate his assertions, exhibited silver buttons." A variant refers to the buttons as buckles. Whatever they were, Tom stood up. These were buttons taken from his father's coat, the coat he had been wearing when he was shot down on the river ice.

Tom grabbed a musket from the rafters, and ordered the Indian to leave at gunpoint. Muskwink rose slowly and sullenly and went to the door, Tom close behind him. "No one who was present seemed to think that murder would grow out of the affair; for no one appeared to have curiosity sufficient to make him attempt to witness its termination, which would have been the case, if it had been supposed that Tom intended to do more than compel the Indian to leave the neighborhood." Gardiner goes on:

"Tom drove the savage into the main road leading from Wurtsboro to Carpenter's Point. After proceeding about a mile toward the latter place, he exclaimed: 'Indian dog, you'll kill no more white men!' and, aiming the musket, which was loaded with a heavy charge of slugs, shot the savage in the back between the shoulders. Muskwink jumped two or three feet from the ground, and fell upon his face dead. Tom took from him the buttons which had belonged to his father, drew the dead body to a tree that the wind had torn up by the roots, and, kicking some leaves and dirt over it, left it there. . . . After killing the Indian, Tom returned to Decker's, put his musket in its proper place, drank a glass of rum, and left the neighborhood. Several years subsequent, the land upon which Muskwink was killed was cleared and ploughed by a man named Philip Decker, when the bones of the Indian were 'turned up.' "

The indication here would seem to be that the killing of Muskwink launched the long and gruesome trail of murder. However, Abraham Gardiner, who had had time to read all the books that had been issued, supplementing their accounts with what he could learn from those who could recall their grandparents' stories, suggests that Muskwink's death was only the semicolon in a long and tedious sentence. At one point he recorded the calling of a council in which an Indian prophet was consulted as to the whereabouts of braves who were disappearing, one by one. "He declared," wrote Dr. Gardiner, "that 'the missing braves had fallen victims of the rifle of Tom Quick, who yet haunted the forests of the Delaware like an evil spirit.' " Three Indians volunteered to track Tom down, used up a year in learning his whereabouts—and then it happened. Only one Indian came back.

Tom is said to have disregarded both age and sex in his ruthless campaign. One incident involves a defenseless brave, his squaw, and their three children, who were ordered from their canoe and put to death one by one. Others recall Tom's seeming enjoyment of murder in the killing of unsuspecting Indians, intent upon the skinning of a deer or a bear or paddling peacefully with the current on a faraway stream, unaware of death at the water's edge. Still others do their best to mix death and a kind of macabre humor, as in the tale of the seven Indians who surrounded Tom and were asked if they would help him split the log on which he was working—he caught them all by their fingers by knocking out the wedge. In spite of Dr. Gardiner's superlatives in behalf of the author's diligence in ferreting out and putting down the Tom Quick legends of the 1850's, he failed to note that many were obviously apocryphal and many others had added so much cold blood as to render Tom Quick an incredible character. Be all that as it may, the slaughter of the seven Indians seriatim was the subject of a scene painted boldly on the door of the Tom Quick Inn in Milford when I was there.

Even I as a comparative stranger have talked with men and women—in Hainesville, in Layton, in Libertyville, and over on the Pennsylvania side—who have spoken of Tom Quick even as their grandmothers and grandfathers may have spoken to the author of the *Life and Adventures*. Some have shown as much enthusiasm as soldiers of the French Empire exhibited in their recollections of Napoleon. Some have said merely that they have heard the name. A host of others have pictured Tom as being six or seven feet tall, raw-boned, fire-eyed, long-haired, barefooted, and with a voice that either bellowed or was as quiet as it was little used. Except for the business that was Muskwink's last on earth, nearly all have described Tom as being more than temperate and with a remarkable liking for sweet cider. Toward the end, they say, he seemed to have trafficked with ghosts, wandering off to all the places where he had tracked down first owners of the land, one by one, until the count, officially, was ninety-nine.

Many have asked why no effort was made to capture Tom, why there was no show of law and order, and why the self-styled "Avenger of the Delaware" was not locked away somewhere as a menace to the peace. Dr. Gardiner has answered this question:

"Tom Quick was not destined to fall by the hand of Indian foes, nor to be successfully captured by white men. The authorities of the general government had, however, often resolved to arrest Tom, and on the death of Muskwink, they made the attempt. They feared that his deeds might bring on another Indian war. During, or about, the holidays that followed Muskwink's death, which took place in the autumn, the arrest was made. Tom was at the time near Carpenter's Point, New York. The officers were to take him to Newton, New Jersey, and there bring him to trial. On their way to Newton, it became known through the country round that Tom had been arrested, and that his life might be forfeit for the death of Muskwink.

"A rescue was immediately resolved on. The course of the officers would lead them past Christopher Decker's tavern. Daniel Van Gorden, who, as we have seen, witnessed the tragic death of Tom's father at the hands of Muskwink and his companions, planned a ruse in the shape of a frolic at the inn. He went through the neighborhood and raised all the neighbors he could, men and women, young and old, and before night set in there was a large and lively company assembled. Shortly after dark the officers who had Tom in charge drove up. Tom was in the back part of the sled, bound with cords. Just as they were driving up, the doors of the tavern were thrown open, and all went out to the stoop to greet them. Van Gorden fiddled, and everybody pretended to be glad at Tom's capture. The sled stopped, and all must have something to drink. The bottles and glasses were taken out to the company in the sled. Tom was not only tied, but guarded by men set to watch him. But before he goes off, the neighbors must treat Tom, as well as the rest. While all were drinking, and Van Gorden, to use his own words, stood and sawed his fiddle as hard as he could, to draw off the officers' attention, the neighbors cut the ropes which bound Tom.

Tom jumped out of the sled and made for the river. He ran its eastern shore until he was abreast of the lower end of 'Punkey's Island,' where he plunged in amid ice and snow, and struggled on until he reached the Pennsylvania side. The officers did not attempt to follow him. The darkness was such they could not see him. Besides, they discovered that the frolic was a ruse, and that they were among Tom Quick's determined friends."

Tom still was not entirely out of danger. The government offered a reward for his capture. More than one hundred men undertook to find him. But Tom, after drying out at the home of Cornelius DeWitt, hid away among the hills. "His friend, Jacobus Rosekranz, was as usual true to him. Once a week he visited Punkey's Island. He went there in the silence and darkness of midnight. His friend Rosekranz was in waiting to meet him, to discuss affairs, and to furnish him necessary supplies. . . . After a while the public excitement subsided; the current feelings, always cordial towards Tom, grew deeper and stronger among the settlers; and the 'Avenger' returned to the peace and society of his friends." In recording the death of Tom Quick about five miles from where he was born, Dr. Gardiner, honoring tradition but not fact, says that Tom died "of that virulent disease, small-pox." He adds that "His savage foes, when they heard of his death, resolved to secure his dead body and burn it to ashes. In the accomplishment of their purpose, they brought forth from the grave a veritable Samson. The disease of which he had died, it is asserted, inoculated the whole tribe; 'so that the dead which he slew in his death were more than they which he slew in his life.' "

Bibliography

BARBER, JOHN W., and HOWE, HENRY. *Historical Collections of the State of New Jersey.* New York: S. Tuttle, 1844.

BISBEE, HENRY H. *Place Names in Burlington County, New Jersey.* Riverside, N. J.: The Burlington County Publishing Co., 1955.

BOYER, CHARLES S. *Early Forges and Furnaces in New Jersey.* Philadelphia: University of Pennsylvania Press, 1931.

BRODHEAD, L. W. *The Delaware Water Gap: Its Scenery, Its Legends and Early History.* Philadelphia: Sherman & Co., 1870.

GARDINER, REV. ABRAHAM S. *Tom Quick: or, The Era of Frontier Settlement.* Notes and Supplementary Facts Suggested by the *Legend of the Delaware* by the Hon. William Bross. Chicago: Knight & Leonard, 1888.

GORDON, THOMAS F. *A Gazetteer of the State of New Jersey.* Trenton: D. Fenton, 1834.

KOBBÉ, GUSTAV. *The Central Railroad of New Jersey.* New York: G. Kobbé, 1890.

————. *The New Jersey Coast and Pines.* Short Hills, N. J.: G. Kobbé, 1889.

LARISON, C. W., *Geografy: A Text Buk in Fonic Orthografy.* Ringos, N. J.: Fonic Publishin Hous, 1885.

————. *The Tenting School: A Description of the Tours Taken and of the Field Work Done by the Class in Geography in the Academy of Science and Art at Ringos, N. J.* Ringos, N. J.: C. W. Larison, 1883.

New Jersey Archives. Newark, N. J.: New Jersey Historical So-
  ciety, 1880–. First and Second Series.
PICKARD, MRS. KATE E. R. *The Kidnapped and the Ransomed. Being
  the Personal Recollections of Peter Still and His Wife "Vina,"
  after Forty Years of Slavery*. Syracuse, N. Y.: W. T. Hamilton,
  1856.
SALTER, EDWIN. *A History of Monmouth and Ocean Counties*. Bay-
  onne, N. J.: E. Gardner & Son, 1890.
STILL, DR. JAMES. *Early Recollections and Life of Dr. James Still*.
  Philadelphia: Printed for the author by J. B. Lippincott &
  Co., 1877.
VAN SICKLE, EMOGENE. *The Old York Road and its Stage Coach
  Days*. From Articles which Originally Appeared in the Hun-
  terdon County *Democrat*, Flemington, N. J. [Somerville,
  N. J.]: Published by the author, 1937.
WATSON, JOHN F. *Annals of Philadelphia and Pennsylvania in the
  Olden Time*. Philadelphia: Published by the author, 1850.
  Reprinted by Leary-Stewart & Co., 1909. 3 vols.
WOODWARD, CARL RAYMOND. *Ploughs and Politicks. Charles Read
  of New Jersey and His Notes on Agriculture, 1715–1774*. New
  Brunswick, N. J.: Rutgers University Press, 1941.

A Note on the Author

by John Cunningham

He was a concert violinist, an author, an Episcopal priest. He taught in a one-room school, labored as a young Camden newspaperman, won state-wide fame as a folklorist. He led tours in the Pine Barrens and lectured everywhere. He was the first to write extensively about the state, and he wrote with such warmth and enthusiasm that at least two generations of people who believe in New Jersey fell under his spell and owe an enduring debt to him. Despite his accomplishments, he never became pompously serious. He was Henry Charlton Beck.

Two careers beckoned to him after graduation from Haddonfield High School: the ministry and music. He enrolled at Virginia Theological Seminary after high school but never attended because of lack of money. He played in concert orchestras for fifteen years, but he never made it to the big time of music. Extremely bright, but without formal qualifications, he taught in a one-room school immediately after leaving high school.

When Henry Beck was twenty, he joined the Camden *Courier-Post* as a cub reporter. He saw his typewriter as an instrument of expression; shortly before his death he defined his career: "I just sit down and tap it out like any rewriteman." The "tapping" turned out six detective novels, all published but none distinguished. Assigned to write about South Jersey in the early 1930s, the young newspaperman found himself enthralled by tales spun to him in Penny Pot, Apple Pie Hill, and Ong's Hat, in Batsto, Calico, and Crowleytown. He had found his life. He listened, he tapped out his stories, and he became known to a limited *Courier-*

273

Post readership. Then, in 1936, E. P. Dutton gathered together his early newspaper stories and published them as *Forgotten Towns of Southern New Jersey*.

It was a smash hit. Other books followed on New Jersey, six in all. His knowledge of the state made him the logical choice to be editor of Rutgers University Press for a brief tenure (1945–1947). His emphasis on folklore led to the founding of the New Jersey Folklore Society, with Henry C. Beck the only possible choice for president.

His desire to be a minister never waned. He studied for the Episcopal priesthood while at Rutgers Press and received ordination in 1949. He preached and he ministered, and did so very well, yet he continued writing a weekly full-page article for the Newark *Star-Ledger*.

A listing of his accomplishments, however distinguished, does Henry Beck only slight credit. It tells little of this gentle, witty man except that he worked far beyond the capacity of most of us. It tells nothing of his charm as a guide through the Pine Barrens, nothing of his kindnesses to the few of us who were just beginning as writers when he was at his peak.

He was often called a historian but he insisted that he was "only a folklorist." His goal was to seek out those who have lived history, have them tell it in their own terms. He was, in fact, an oral historian long before the National Endowment for the Humanities poured out funds to make oral history academically respectable. Because of his books, Father Beck may be regarded by some as a historian. But his leg often was pulled by those whom he interviewed, and he, in turn, could put entertainment above scholarship. Above all, be sure of this: he never wittingly gave less than his best.

Henry C. Beck died in 1965. Those of us who knew his varied, parallel careers and who encountered his name from High Point to Cape May were surprised to learn that he was only sixty-two years old when he died. Few persons accomplish so much in so short a time.

Index of People and Places

West, Amy, 117
West, George Sr., 117
West, George Jr., 117
West, James, 117
West, Thomas Biddle, 117
Westbrook Fort, 5
Westfield, 79, 82, 91, 95
West Millstone, 121
West Point, N. Y., 256
Weygandt, Cornelius, 183
Weymouth, 173, 233
Wharton, Joseph, 165, 172, 175
Whilldin, Hannah Gorham, 235
Whilldin, Joseph, 235
White family, 140
White House, 87, 88
White House Station, 88
Whitesville, 227
Whiting, 227, 228
Whitman, Walt, 95
Wildwood, 234
Wildwood Heights, 235
Wilkins, Amos, 144
Wilkins, Nathan, 145
Wilkinson, Nathaniel, 161
Willets, Colonel John, 220
Willets, Mrs. John, 221
Willets, Reuben, 219
Willets, Stephen, 217, 218
Williams, Douglas, 40–46
Williamsburg (see Cedar Creek)
Williamstown, 184–87
Willing, Mrs. Edward S., 158
Willow, Angelina, 144
Willow Grove and Park, 78, 82
Winchester, Benjamin, 87, 242
Winslow, 186, 187, 192, 198, 233

Winter, Dan, 39
Wistar, Caspar, 178, 182, 188
Wistar, Johannes Caspar, 178, 179
Wistar, Richard, 178, 181, 188, 189
Wistarburgh, 177–92, 201
Wolfe, General James, 98
Wolfrum, Joe, 137
Wood, Dr. George B., 166
Wood, Sam, 224
Woodbury, 190, 209
Woodglen, 26, 69
Woodland Township, 140, 141
Woodruff, Leslie, 222, 223
Woodruff, Mrs. Leslie, 222, 223
Woodstock, Vt., 133
Woodward Trial, 77
Woolsey Station, 119, 122, 124
Woolston, Robert, 145
Worlidge, John, 203
Worthless City, 165
Wrack Pond, 226, 227
Wright, Brigadier General Elias, 175
Wright, Benjamin, 34
Wright, Ned, 220
Wright, William, 63
Wurtsboro, 267
Wyckoff, George, 126
Wyckoff, Uncle Billy, 126, 127

Yardley, Pa., 121

Zelley, S. Stockton, 162
Ziegler, Theodewald (see Sickler, David)
Zuricher, John, 254

291